The Essence

By the Same Author

Shifting the Paradigms of The Normal Christian Church (1994)

Baptism in Water & The Spirit (1995, 2008, 2019)

Lord of All (2002)

A New Kind of Baptist Church—Reframing Congregational Government for the 21st Century (2010)

They Want Me to Be an Elder—What Do They Do? (2018)

Boundaries—Rediscovering the Ten Commandments for the Twenty-First Century (2018)

The Essence

Unpacking Jesus' Sermon on the Mount

BRIAN N. WINSLADE

Foreword by **Brian C. Stiller**

RESOURCE *Publications* • Eugene, Oregon

THE ESSENCE
Unpacking Jesus' Sermon on the Mount

Copyright © 2020 Brian N. Winslade. All rights reserved. Except for brief quotations in critical publications or reviews, no part of this book may be reproduced in any manner without prior written permission from the publisher. Write: Permissions, Wipf and Stock Publishers, 199 W. 8th Ave., Suite 3, Eugene, OR 97401.

Resource Publications
An Imprint of Wipf and Stock Publishers
199 W. 8th Ave., Suite 3
Eugene, OR 97401

www.wipfandstock.com

PAPERBACK ISBN: 978-1-5326-9534-6
HARDCOVER ISBN: 978-1-5326-9535-3
EBOOK ISBN: 978-1-5326-9536-0

Manufactured in the U.S.A.   03/05/20

All Scripture quotations, unless otherwise indicated, are taken from the Holy Bible, New International Version®, NIV®. Copyright ©1973, 1978, 1984, 2011 by Biblica, Inc.™ Used by permission of Zondervan. All rights reserved worldwide. www.zondervan.com

The "NIV" and "New International Version" are trademarks registered in the United States Patent and Trademark Office by Biblica, Inc.™

To Elizabeth . . .

My best friend, wife and
life-long companion

Contents

Foreword by Brian C. Stiller — xi

Preface — xiii

Acknowledgments — xix

1. Salt and Light — 1
  - *The contemporary reputation of the Church* • *The metaphor of salt* • *Purity* • *Preservative* • *Flavour and Seasoning* • *The metaphor of light* • *Illumination of truth* • *Visibility* • *Post-Christian or Pre-Christian*

2. Laws Are to Be Broken — 12
  - *Love-hate relationship with rules* • *Oral and Scribal Law* • *Devolution into pedantic legalism* • *Don't throw the baby out with the bathwater* • *Don't neglect the Old Testament* • *Connect with God through love, not legalism*

3. Murder by Intent — 24
  - *Killing by anger* • *Acts of discrimination* • *Character assassination* • *Reconciliation before worship* • *Love for God requires love for others*

4. Sexual Purity — 35
  - *God's sexual ethic* • *Lust = adultery* • *Taking radical action* • *Removing the 'bait stick'* • *Grace in our weakness* • *No room for judgmentalism*

5. The Ugliness of Divorce — 46
  - *Clarity on God's hatred of divorce* • *The cultures of Jesus day* • *Shammai vs Hillel* • *Marriages are complex* • *Repentance for our failure* • *God's grace toward those who fail*

6. Honest Talk   57
• The whole truth • The sacredness of an oath • Frivolous swearing • Evasive swearing • Always keep our promises • Don't compartmentalize your life • Sacred oaths are unnecessary

7. Living in a World Full of Nasty People   67
• Lex Talionis—law of retribution • Let the punishment fit the crime • Turning the other cheek—coping with insults • Giving up our legal rights • Going the second mile—serving willingly • Disempowering the bully

8. Rising above Offense   77
• Nowhere in the Bible are we told to hate our enemies • We will have enemies • Treat enemies the way God does • Pray for those who persecute us • Show the family likeness • Be perfect—grow up!

9. How to Be Generous   88
• Performing for an audience of One • The principle of generosity • The principal of anonymity • The principle of reward • God sees what we do

10. Learning to Pray   100
• Do it for God's eyes and ears • Babbling like pagans • The prayer agenda • Hallowed be your name • Your kingdom come • Your will done on earth • Our daily bread • Forgive as we have forgiven • Lead us not into temptation • Deliver us from evil

11. Going Without   113
• For an audience of one • Why do it all? • Different examples of fasting • Is it a command or an option? • What has it cost us to follow Jesus

12. Treasure Hunter   124
• What do we value? • A different world • Treasure that moth can destroy • Treasure that rust can destroy • Treasure that thieves break in and steal • We can't serve two master

13. Antidote to Worry   136
• Trusting in money • God cares for and provides for his creation • The foolishness of trusting in our own resourcefulness • Worry is an expression of distrust in God • God's money-back guarantee

14. The Unqualified Critic   146
• Forming conclusions • We never know all the facts or the whole person • Impossible to be totally impartial • None of us are good enough to judge another • Did Jesus and Paul contradict each other? • Are we entitled to our opinion?

15. How Approachable Is God?   157
• Designer deities • God is always approachable • God is always faithful and dependable • God is our Father in heaven

16. Pay It Forward   169
• The golden rule • The positive law of reciprocity • Our place of work • Our business transactions • Random acts of kindness • Our response toward our enemies

17. Choice   180
• Life is full of choices • Law of cause and effect • The point of entry is narrow • The road to life is a narrow road • Only a few find it • Choosing to be holy

18. Telling the True from the False   191
• Don't be gullible • Investigate—check the validity of what is communicated • Test the message against the counsel of Scripture • Consider the fruit of the prophet's life and ministry

19. Religion or Relationship   203
• There will be a day of reckoning • Some surprises when we get to heaven! • Religion is not the same thing as relationship • Charismatic is not necessarily Christian • How can we know for sure?

20. Building on the Right Foundation   214
• Storms are a fact of life • Stability is directly proportional to foundation • Follow the manufacturer's instructions • Do what he said!

Bibliography   225

Foreword

What more can one write about Jesus? A question not surprisingly noted by book editors. While there exist standard references, which layout linguistic and cultural details surrounding the life and times of Jesus, each generation is challenged to find fresh and creative ways of connecting Jesus to their world. Multiply that by the tens of thousands of groupings, divided by layers of generations, and it won't surprise those same editors that each generation needs to hear the Gospel in ways they uniquely listen to and read.

Watch adults in a church service or meeting when the speaker says, "I have a story." Body language gives it away. Heads come up, bodies shift in their seats, and eyes focus on the speaker. Nothing, it seems, gets our attention as does a story.

Stories and metaphors take hold of my mind. Ideas find themselves framed by the richness of story, linking into my learning, experiences, and cultural connections. They give resonance of color and depth of field into my processing as the layers of meaning and understanding are peeled back, all by word pictures.

Listening via a storyline instinctively translates in ways that allow me to connect to the essential truth. Caught up in the storyline, I can imagine. And imagination is what Jesus brings into what he wants us to learn. The beauty and simplicity of the language Jesus uses does not beg for explanation. For anyone, of any culture or language, the effect is instant.

You will discover that this writer, Brian Winslade, in *The Essence — Unpacking Jesus' Sermon on the Mount*, leads us into seeing and feeling storylines and word pictures. They help make sense in any language; they fit into any cultural context and rise with clarity as idioms and symbols pointing us to his essential message.

Winslade's helpful and valuable guide to Jesus' "sermons" will be of value to you in three distinct ways.

His "unpacking" Jesus' Sermon on the Mount helps us in framing the entire message of Christ's Kingdom. Ironically, people flub around in trying to make sense of that term. Confused by religious nationalism and claims some make about God being for their country or party, we need reminding that his kingdom rests in the womb of his wisdom, vision, and love. My sense is that if you can get your mind and heart around the meaning of his kingdom, you'll be startled into a new understanding of the entire workings of the Gospel.

Secondly, as Winslade introduces us to the rich analogies and word pictures in Jesus' "sermon," it creates melody, lifting your study group or church to read from a new score of Christian living. Jesus took the visual, the tactile, the felt, and parlayed that into his majestic tunes. Preachers who get bogged down into doctrinal formations triggering glassy stares and fatigued ears, desperately need to learn from Jesus.

Thirdly, Brian Winslade equips us to use material that helps us break past two huge factors we face—especially where western secularism rules: fatigue and reaction to the use of religious terms and the many who have no clue as to what they refer. The fast pace of generational change brings into play new minds, ears, and hearts. Somewhat defensive, more and more generations are impoverished by their own parents who make little to no effort in introducing them to the Gospel, be they Roman Catholic or Protestant. Jesus provides a way back into those minds.

Be you a preaching pastor or Bible study leader, in your hands is a powerful heart-opener from Jesus. My friend Brian Winslade has carefully taken this central and pivotal teaching of Jesus and opened it in new ways that will help you in refreshing peoples' hearts for the life-lifting power of his message.

As its sounds reverberate, trust this message to be recreated in others, a heart message accentuated by the Spirit whose presence and power brings life to those who are attracted to listen.

You have in your hands a game-changer for those willing to hear the heart and soul of Jesus, his Kingdom, and his Gospel.

Brian C. Stiller
Global Ambassador
World Evangelical Alliance

Preface

The teaching of Jesus of Nazareth is unparalleled in the history of our world. Countless wise words have been spoken and recorded by great leaders, but none come close to the depth and insight of the words of Jesus. Their impact on people all around the world, over twenty centuries, is nothing short of extraordinary. Amongst Christians and non-Christians alike, Jesus of Nazareth is universally revered as a phenomenal teacher.

As world-influencers go, Jesus was an enigmatic figure. He wasn't born into wealth and little is known of his formal education. He didn't come from a prominent family. Indeed, judging from the offering made by his parents sixty days after his birth, the family was not wealthy—at least at that time.[1] Apart from a brief sojourn in Egypt as a baby, he never traveled beyond his home country, imbibing and inculcating worldly wisdom. While his mother is honoured throughout history, we know little of his father; assuming he died during Jesus' young adult years—having trained his son in the arts of carpentry. Jesus was not a writer, leaving no extant legacy of wisdom as a reference. Yet one of his closest followers would later claim that if written records of all he said and did were made the world would not have room enough for the books that would be written.[2] And where he actually lived, for the three short years of his formal ministry, was not renowned for its international prominence. Palestine, to the Romans, as an annoying and troublesome backwater within its empire.

Yet, the words and teachings and activities of Jesus are acclaimed the world over. Few would dare suggest they are unimportant or irrelevant; rather singularly and immensely influential in shaping the histories of

1. Luke 22-24; Leviticus 12:6-8
2. John 21:25

our world. From obscurity and poverty, no one has impacted the world to the same extent as Jesus.

Some assume that Jesus lived a nomadic lifestyle during his three years as a prophet-teacher and that he did not have an actual home. While it is true his ministry was extensively itinerant, and he did liken himself to foxes and birds that has "no place to lay his head,"[3] he did have an actual hometown—at least for some time. His family roots were in the Galilean town of Nazareth, where he grew up and most likely took over his father's carpentry business before his ministry began. We refer to him as "Jesus of Nazareth." But a great deal of his teaching and miracles actually occurred in a region about fifty kilometers northeast of Nazareth, in small towns and villages that surrounded the Sea of Galilee. In one of these towns in particular, on the northern end of Lake Tiberias, Jesus made his home-base—in a place called Capernaum.[4] It was a strategic relocation for Jesus following the arrest of John the Baptist. From there, several of the locations mentioned in the Gospels, where Jesus' taught and healed, were easily accessible.

The geography surrounding Capernaum and the Sea of Galilee is hilly. These hills were favorite places for Jesus. He would retreat to them often to pray and to catch some alone time. They were also locations where he liked to teach. As his reputation and notoriety increased, large crowds—sometimes numbering several thousand—would gather to hear him. On such occasions it would have been impracticable for him to teach inside the town where he lived, as gathering crowds would have been a civil nuisance and could have brought local commerce to a standstill. So, he stepped outside the city boundaries and invited people to come and hear him on surrounding hillsides.

One such place, about two kilometers in a straight line, is a particular hillside where Jesus is said to have given some of his most remarkable teachings. It is commemorated today as the *Mount of Beatitudes*, with a Catholic Chapel atop—constructed in 1939 by Franciscan Sisters (interestingly, with financial support from Italian ruler, Mussolini). Whether this is the exact spot, no one knows for sure; it could have been at a range of other locations. But it was at a place like this, just outside his hometown of Capernaum, and with a natural amphitheatre making it possible for large crowds to hear his words, where Jesus delivered what has come

---

3. Matthew 8:20
4. Matthew 4:13

to be known as his famous *Sermon on the Mount*, recorded in Matthew's Gospel, chapters five, six, and seven.

The *Sermon on the Mount* has been revered over the years as the *essence* of all that Jesus taught about God, and how we relate with him. Several descriptive metaphors have been employed to describe its foundational importance. It has been called the *"Core of the Christian Apple,"* the *"Compendium of Christ's Doctrine,"* the *"Magna Charta of the Kingdom,"* and the *"Manifesto of the King."* In short, were a person to grasp nothing else of the teaching of Jesus apart from that contained in the *Sermon on the Mount*, he or she probably acquires the gist of all he was on about. As one commentator suggests: ". . . in the *Sermon on the Mount* we have the essence of the teaching of Jesus to the inner circle of his chosen men."[5]

Over the years, Bible scholars have debated the structure of the *Sermon on the Mount*. Was it a singular discourse—given all at once—or was it a collection of sayings or teaching given over a period of time, some of which having been given on a hillside overlooking the Sea of Galilee? Perhaps the contemporary association of a word like "sermon" is confusing, as if it is to be taken as a singular discourse it is rather complex and not structured in ways taught by contemporary teachers of homiletics. By contrast, those arguing for the *Sermon on the Mount* as a singular discourse are quite disparaging and dismissive of those who see it as a compilation of various teachings, referring to: "a collection of 'sayings' that unknown 'editors' had thrown together as one might throw marbles into a sack."[6] Some have even suggested that when we take the sermon as separate sections, Jesus' words can be misinterpreted as a series of laws dictating unachievable conduct—perhaps even more relentless and meaner than Moses![7]

Maybe an argument for questioning the "singular discourse" nature of the *Sermon on the Mount* is that parts of it appear to have been given at different times and places. This book follows the record of the disciple Matthew, where the teaching was said to occur on a Galilean hillside. However, Luke records very similar sections of teaching by Jesus, given on a "level place," sometimes referred to as the *Sermon on the Plains*.[8] Is

---

5. Barclay, *The Gospel of Matthew, Volume 1*, 84
6. Willard, *The Divine Conspiracy*, 148
7. Willard, *The Divine Conspiracy*, 149
8. Luke 6:17

it too far-fetched to imagine that Jesus, as an itinerant preacher, preached the same message in different locations?

Whether or not the *Sermon on the Mount* was spoken, and therefore intended to be read, as one singular discourse is not the subject of this book. However, the charge that Jesus was introducing stricter and more invasive laws than Moses is strongly contested. It is more plausible that Jesus was helping the people of his day understand the intent of the *Law of Moses* at a time when its' purity and essence was being corrupted by the oral teaching of religious leaders. This theme is taken up in more detail in Chapter 2; suffice it to say that the ordinary people of Jesus' day primarily understood the *Law of Moses* through oral tradition, rather than having personal access or possession of written Scriptures for themselves. Add to this the development of pedantic legalism and ridiculous definitions of the *Law of Moses*, that evolved in the period between the Old and New Testaments, the popular understanding of all that Moses laid down was seriously maligned and distorted. Ordinary people "heard" an interpretation of the *Law* that often missed the original point or intent. Indeed, far from laying down a sterner view than Moses had recorded, Jesus sought to bring clarity and life to that which had become rigid religion.

This is not to suggest that the ancient culture of Israel in Jesus' day was intellectually simple and unintelligent. That would be a grave misunderstanding. As Dallas Willard alludes to: "In Jesus' day Jerusalem was a glorious city, routinely flooded by hundreds of visitors, including multitudes of brilliant people from all over the known world."[9] However, from reading the words and actions of Jesus in the Gospels, it is clear that Jewish religious systems and infrastructure was seriously missing the original point of God's relationship with his chosen race. The richness of the *Law of Moses* had been over-exegeted by zealous scholars a few hundred years before the time of Jesus. The rise of the scribal law (adding definition to what Moses had given), and the emergence of the cult of the Pharisees in preceding centuries, meant much of Jewish faith had lost its way. Religious teachers gave overly rigid definition to core principles, with the motive of either proving one's own righteousness, or condemning those who could not attain the high standards of the *Law of Moses*.

Simply put, by the time of Jesus, there was serious need for a corrective understanding, both of what God is really like, and how we behave before him. At the beginning of his ministry, Jesus sought to clarify a

---

9. Willard, *The Divine Conspiracy*, 152

range of misunderstandings about life and faith and all that it means to follow God's ways. This is an essential interpretive key for understanding much of the *Sermon on the Mount*.

As the very essence of Jesus' teaching, the *Sermon on the Mount* has been appreciated not only by Christ-followers. "The Jesus of dogma I do not understand," a Hindu professor once said to E. Stanley Jones, "but the Jesus of the *Sermon on the Mount* and the cross I love and am drawn to." Similarly, a Muslim Sufi teacher spoke of how "when he read the *Sermon on the Mount*, he could not keep back the tears." [10]

The book you are holding seeks to explore this essential and timeless teaching of Jesus, and in particular, where it intersects with life in the twenty-first century. Beginning with a careful exegesis of why he said what he did, and to whom he said it, the emphasis is placed upon application of Jesus' teaching for a contemporary world. His audience may well have been exclusively Jewish, but the import and application of Jesus' teaching apply to all cultures.

A careful student of the Bible will quickly note that the sections of this book begin after the passage often referred to as the *Beatitudes* (Matthew 5:1-12). In the opening section of Jesus' *Sermon on the Mount*, he beautifully describes eight pathways to real and profound happiness in life. There is no particular purpose in starting this study after the *Beatitudes*, except to note that each statement in Matthew 5:1-12 warrants a chapter of their own . . . and this work is possibly long enough as it is. Each chapter in this book began as a talk given in a church service, and perhaps, if my publisher will indulge me, a "prequel" book may yet emerge that illuminates the richness of each of the *Beatitudes* in their own right.

One closing comment to make in this introduction: who is the intended audience of this book? The short answer is anyone who will read it! The particular audience in mind is the ordinary, average follower of Jesus who seeks to understand and follow the teaching of Jesus. This book does not pretend to be a scholarly work that competes for the attention of academics. There are plenty of those available already, although notably most of their authors have passed on. While hopefully accurate to robust Bible scholarship, this work is intended to offer an "accessible" exploration of Jesus' essential teaching, easily understood and applied without possession of a degree in theology. That is not to cast aspersions upon

---

10. Stanley Jones, *Christ at the Round Table*, 38,60

other scholar works; merely to suggest that for most ordinary Christ-followers, academic writing often sacrifices readability on the altar of academic complexity.

In this work, each chapter concludes with discussion questions that might be considered personally by the reader, or perhaps taken up by small-groups of believers who wrestle together with the implications of Jesus' words for twenty-first-century living.

A third intended audience are pastors and preachers who may find useful ideas for teaching the essence of Jesus' words. The richness and application of the *Sermon on the Mount* is vitally needed in the twenty-first century, and something every preacher needs to tackle at some stage in their ministry.

May the essence of Jesus teaching continue to transform us all!

Brian Winslade
2020

Acknowledgments

The impetus for this book began as a sermon series in the church I lead in my home country of New Zealand. Over the forty years that I have been a pastor, I have found Jesus' words in his "sermon" on a Galilean hillside, absolutely compelling and essential preaching material on which to focus. Hence the title!

In addition to preaching through the *Sermon on the Mount* in 2019, my church leaders offered me a short sabbatical where I could refine preaching notes into written-prose, including an opportunity to visit Israel. Walking in the footsteps of Jesus, especially around the shores of the Sea of Galilee (Lake Tiberias), added color and depth to Jesus' timeless wisdom.

I warmly acknowledge the help of Jennifer Holland, a member of my church, in helping revise my initial drafts into a more readable format. In addition to her work as a schoolteacher, Jennifer is a skilled and experienced editor of technical textbooks and has a theological degree in her own right. Not only was she able to guide my transition from spoken-word to written-prose, she was also able to offer some invaluable theological reflection on some ideas I was proposing.

Authors are seldom able to copy-edit their own work. So my gratitude also goes to Chris Gardner (former newspaper editor) and Dick Somers (experienced columnist), who both have a skilled eye for detail, and further checked the manuscript for grammar and spelling.

Finally, I acknowledge the help and guidance of Matthew Wimer and the editors at Resource Publications of Wipf and Stock for helping this book come into being. May its pages bring glory to God and deeper maturity amongst those who, like me, follow Jesus Christ.

1

Salt and Light

Consider the reputation we as followers of Jesus have in our world. How do people view us? What can we do to influence the perception they hold?

There was a season in the history and culture of western countries when the social norms and values that most people lived by were relatively close to those described in the Bible. There has never been an absolute alignment, but there was a time when the clergy and members of their churches were well respected. They were like an unofficial or honorary moral conscience for society. That is not to suggest, of course, that Christians and churches have not had their critics. While espoused Christian values over the 1600 years since Constantine (who claimed to have converted to Christianity and declared it the favored religion of the Roman Empire) might have been valued, our reputation has not always been stellar. Being held in honor does not necessarily equate with an enthusiastic reception. Take, for instance, this infamous diary entry Robert Louis Stevenson once recorded as if it were a remarkable event: "I have been to church today and am not depressed."[1] Or this from the nineteenth-century poet, Oliver Wendell Holmes, who once confessed: "I might have entered the ministry if certain clergymen I knew had not looked and acted so much like undertakers."[2]

To be brutally honest, the popular perception of Christians has often been someone with a boring colorless lifestyle, devoid of fun and

---

1. Barclay, *The Gospel of Matthew, Volume 1*, 121
2. Coffin, *The Collected Sermons of William Sloane Coffin, The Riverside Years*, 298

lacking in excitement. Yet, those who have chosen to follow Jesus Christ, and who live within his kingdom, claim their resolution to do this was the most excellent decision they have ever made.

If it is any comfort, this is nothing new. The earliest Christians sometimes experienced similar critiques. Exactly as Jesus had predicted it would be, living according to God's values often brought them into conflict with the popular culture of the day, and at times led to nefarious suspicion. For two tumultuous years in the middle of the fourth century, Flavius Claudius Julianus (often referred to as Julian the Apostate) reigned as Emperor of Rome and unsuccessfully tried to turn back the religious tide toward paganism. Although part of the extended family of Constantine, Julianus opposed Christianity; he simply did not like the look of Christians: "Have you looked at these Christians closely? Hollow-eyed, pale-cheeked, flat-breasted all; they brood their lives away, unspurred by ambition: the sun shines on them, but they do not see it: the earth offers them its fulness, but they desire it not; all their desire is to renounce and to suffer that they may come to die."[3]

Charming!

Perhaps it was for reasons like this that Jesus gave his first followers some wise advice on how to live in a hostile world. Advice that would not only help them survive and flourish but also gradually influence the people they lived amongst and transform them.

> [13] You are the salt of the earth. But if the salt loses its saltiness, how can it be made salty again? It is no longer good for anything, except to be thrown out and trampled underfoot. [14] You are the light of the world. A city on a hill cannot be hidden. [15] Neither do people light a lamp and put it under a bowl. Instead, they put it on its stand, and it gives light to everyone in the house. [16] In the same way, let your light shine before others, that they may see your good deeds and glorify your Father in heaven.
>
> Matthew 5:13–16

When Jesus referred to his followers as *salt* and *light*, he was offering them a profound compliment in terms of their status and potential to influence the world. He also bestowed a compelling challenge—the responsibility of being his agents of change. Regardless of how we might feel about ourselves, according to Jesus, the Christ-follower is more than

---

3. MacArthur, *The MacArthur New Testament Commentary, Matthew 1–7*, 242

a bottom on a pew or an insignificant cog in the big machinery of society. They are God's agents of transformation and hope in a broken world.

When Jesus' original audience heard him use the metaphors of salt and light what mental pictures would have come to mind?

In the world of Jesus' day, salt was a highly valued commodity. Greek culture regarded it as a divine substance, and the Romans had a saying: "There is nothing more useful than sun and salt." The English word "salary derives" from the Latin *salarium*—literally "salt money." Jesus' use of the salt metaphor, as a descriptor of what it means to be one of his followers, conveyed a powerful momentum and message to his listeners. Ordinary people at that time did not tend to think of themselves as being particularly significant.

Salt was renowned for three valuable properties:

1. PURITY

No doubt the glistening whiteness of salt contributed to this connotation. In the ancient world, salt was regarded as the purest of all things, since it came from the purest of all things—the sun and the sea. Perhaps because of this association with the idea of purity, salt was the most primitive of offerings made to pagan gods. Even the Jews added salt to some of their sacrifices.[4] So, to Jesus' original audience, referring to his followers as the "salt of the earth" would have been understood, at least in part, as a descriptor of their purity. Not only were they purified or made clean by all that God had done for them, they were also called to a high standard of purity in their conduct and relationships. Christ-followers were to seek to be men and women of unmixed moral standards and integrity; pure and honest, credible examples of purity amidst a compromised and polluted world.

Reading on into the New Testament, this was a theme other Biblical authors picked up. For instance, the apostle Paul's challenge to the Ephesian Christians:

> [3] . . . among you there must not be even a hint of sexual immorality, or of any kind of impurity, or of greed, because these are improper for the LORD's people. [4]Nor should there be obscenity, foolish talk or coarse joking, which are out of place, but rather thanksgiving.
>
> Ephesians 5:3–4

---

4. Exodus 30:35; Leviticus 2:13

2. PRESERVATIVE

Before the days of refrigeration, salt was used to keep food from going rancid or decaying. It was like an antiseptic warding off infection and preserving food from bacterial corruption. Jesus' original hearers might have gleaned from this metaphor that his followers would have a role to play, protecting society from moral and spiritual corruption. Christ-followers, by their presence and participation in a community, were to be like an antiseptic or preservative, preventing the spread of spiritual perversion

Imagine a scenario at work or a social function where an idea is proposed that is dishonest, lewd or immoral. The Christ follower's presence, and their voice, might be a moral preservative that prevents truth decay or moral corruption. By contrast, staying silent or not speaking out might indicate complicity in something that devolves into a collective evil.

3. FLAVOR AND SEASONING

Certain foods without the additive of salt, taste bland. However, with a pinch of salt, they become pleasant and palatable. Salt adds flavor and body to food. No doubt, Jesus had this in mind when he called his followers to be salt within their community, neighborhood, family, or workplace. Sadly, that is not always our experience. Some followers of Jesus give an altogether different impression. As noted, rather than bringing a positive flavor to a group of people, the resulting taste is sour and unpleasant. Christians are perceived as "wet blankets" or the "fun police."

When Jesus employed the term "salt of the earth," he implied a positive contribution. As representatives of the Kingdom of God here on Earth, his followers were to model purity and integrity. By their presence and participation, they would preserve society from the spread of moral corruption, perversion, and decay. God intends that they bring the flavor, joy, and spice of life in God's kingdom to the communities in which they live.

What, then, did Jesus mean by salt that loses its saltiness? He describes it in stark terms: ". . . it is no longer good for anything, except to the thrown out and trampled underfoot."

Some have found this a puzzling statement because salt does not ever lose its taste. One explanation suggests Jesus had in mind the cooking ovens of his day, typically constructed outside a house. Built of stone on a base of tiles, to retain heat, a thick bed of salt was laid under the tiled floor. Over time the salt base would perish, the tiles would be taken up, and the salt removed and throne on the road outside the door of the house. It had lost its power to heat the tiles and was now worthless.[5] Jesus' point was clear: His followers are supposed to make a difference in their world; if they fail to add flavor or act as a preservative, they are of little purpose or value and lose their credibility.

Jesus employs a second metaphor, describing his followers as the "light of the world." Once again, Jesus used a word picture rich in meaning for his original audience. The Jews would speak of Jerusalem as being a "light to the Gentiles;" a "beacon of truth" about God. A famous Jewish rabbi was often called a "lamp of Israel." In the Hebrew mind, light and truth were synonyms. Truth brings illumination, in the same way people speak of throwing light on a subject or illuminating truth that is hidden or guarded. Jesus was suggesting that by their presence and participation in the world, his followers would bring light and illumination of truth into the darkness. Perhaps more correctly, they are reflectors of light from its source, rather than being the source of light themselves. They act as mirrors displaying the character of God and the difference he makes in a person's life.

One of the salient features about light, even the tiniest little flicker, is that it dispels darkness. Light and dark are mutually exclusive; you cannot extinguish light by darkness. Darkness is always defeated by light.

To cite another example from Robert Louis Stevenson—a record in his diary of an incident from his childhood. He was seated by a window at nightfall (before the days of electricity) watching a lamplighter walking up a street lighting the gas street lamps. As each lamp was lit pockets of roadway were immediately illuminated in the darkness. His nurse came into the room and asked him what he was doing, to which he replied: "I am watching a man make holes in the darkness." That is an excellent description of the responsibility entrusted to a follower of Jesus. By their presence, in whatever circumstance they find themselves, they are making holes in the spiritual darkness of this world. By presence, by words spoken, by good deeds, or by lifestyle and behavior, they enlighten others to the truth about Jesus.

Jesus developed his analogy of light with two specific examples. He talked firstly about a "city on a hill" and "which cannot be hidden." Villages,

---

5. Barclay, *The Gospel of Matthew, Volume 1*, 121

whenever possible, were built on the top of hills and in the evenings when homes were lit up, night travelers could see the location of a town from miles away. The lit-up town helped the traveler find their bearings.

The second example Jesus gave possibly needs more explanation. He said you do not "light a lamp and then put it under a bowl." Instead, you put it on a lampstand so that it can illuminate the whole room. In those days, particularly amongst the poor, the most common source of light in a house was a saucer-like bowl that held a pool of oil and a floating wick. It sat on a lampstand, which was often a protruding stone built into the wall of the house. In those days there were no such things as matches, and it was not easy to re-ignite a lamp that had gone out. So, when people went out for the evening or went to bed at night, the lamp would be placed under a basket-like bowl that would allow it to burn low, but not extinguish it. The lamp would continue to burn, but the house would be in darkness. When light was needed, the "bowl" would simply be removed. The principle behind Jesus' metaphor was simple: when you light a lamp, its purpose is to provide light. You do not light a lamp intending to place it under a bowl; you light a lamp because you want to see. Light is by definition, visible.

Having sought to grasp an understanding of Jesus' metaphors of salt and light in the minds of his original hearers, how are we to understand their implications for the twenty-first century? Where and how do these words challenge the lives of Christ-followers today?

Perhaps the first application might be that it is impossible that a true follower of Jesus can be kept hidden. The flavor of one's connection with God, or the illumination of truth, leaks out and affects those around them. As it has been said: "There can be no such thing as secret discipleship, for either the secrecy destroys the discipleship, or the discipleship destroys the secrecy." A lot of people mistakenly think the essence of being Christian is merely a matter of belief or philosophy. In other words, believe the right things, and you are in! Actually, it is not enough to just believe in God or to accept that Jesus is God's son. Even the devil believes that, and such belief certainly does not make him a disciple! No, if the light of God is truly and genuinely ignited in a person's life, then that will inevitably show. Light always overcomes darkness; its nature is to illuminate.

There is a humorous story of a rather pompous minister who was "filling in" as a Sunday School teacher in a class of ten-year-old boys. He began by asking them the question: "Why do people call me a Christian?"

To which none of the boys responded. He asked them again; still no response. So, he asked them a third time: "Why do people call me a Christian?" Finally, one boy tentatively put up his hand: "Because they don't know you?" In other words, the fabric of a person's life is inevitably visible to others. When Jesus truly is LORD, the impact of that fact on character and personality is noticeable. If it is not, there is a need to revisit the source of the light and to be reignited.

Another application might be the challenge to deliberately engage in the social structures of our society. There is a call here to visible preemptive action. Salt that stays in a saltshaker is not useful or helpful, nor is light hidden under a bowl. To employ a different and more graphic analogy, it has been suggested that: "Christians are like manure. All piled up in a heap they tend to stink; spread over a wide area, they make things grow!" Being a follower of Jesus does not take us out of society; it embeds us within it where we are able to bring a godly flavor. Consequently, there is a need for more followers of Jesus to leave the isolation of their Christian enclaves and engage in areas of civic influence—at a national or local level. Imagine the impact of many more followers of Jesus deliberately serving on bodies such as school boards, sporting administration bodies, and neighborhood-watch groups. Those who choose the career of teaching are worthy of special honor recognition for the strategic opportunity they have to be salt and light, shaping the minds of the next generation. Likewise, those who work in a range of other industries, such as media or trade unions or the health industry or the legal system—add to the spheres of their influence the flavor and light of kingdom thinking.

Could another application of Jesus' salt and light metaphor be as simple as deliberately getting to know our neighbors, our colleagues at work, the people we exercise with at the gym or commute with each day on the bus or train? A tragic reality across too many churches in the twenty-first century is the fact that Christians rarely ever (meaningfully) socialize with non-Christians. Most people who become followers of Christ identify a friend or a relative who was salt and light in their midst, pointing them to Jesus. If Christ-followers only socialize or hang out with fellow-followers of Jesus, welcome to the last generation of the church! By contrast, what might happen if we invited a family next door or a colleague from work for a meal—taking the opportunity to get to know one another, and allowing them to taste our salt and see our light?

Another opportunity for becoming salt and light to those around us might be something as innocuous as performing a random act of kindness for people in a difficult situation—perhaps a neighbor, a work colleague or a relative who is in need. Jesus clearly linked the broadcasting or shining of light to doing good deeds:

> ¹⁶In the same way, let your light shine before others, that they may see your good deeds and glorify your Father in heaven.
>
> Matthew 5:16

Doing something practical to help a person in need is a great way to reflect the God of love and truth. It may be an act as simple as baking a cake, preparing a meal or helping them build a fence or clear their yard.

Perhaps a further application might be as simple as being conscious of our demeanor. What kind of flavor, or what colored light, do we display in our casual interactions? Are we diffusers of joy or dispensers of relational caustic-soda or sour vinegar? Do we portray an image of Christian faith that is warm, friendly and fun or something which looks more exclusive, boring and dull? Christ-followers might sprinkle salt or display light by the warmth of their smile to a stranger, or by kind words exchanged with a shopkeeper. Salt spills from them in how they treat the person who serves them in a restaurant, or the driver who wants to change lanes in front of them on a busy road. Likewise, in places of employment, the way employees treat their bosses and the way the bosses treat their employees is an opportunity to diffuse light into the darkness. Does a Christ-follower effectively steal from his or her employer through a lack of punctuality and diligence at work, or are they known for being hardworking and honest? What kind of language do colleagues hear coming out of their mouths and what jokes do they laugh at or tell?

This is a far from an exhaustive list of ways we can apply Jesus' advice about being salt and light. However, let me close this chapter with an interesting question a friend put to me about the spiritual climate of my home country, New Zealand. At the time, we were meeting in Washington DC and part of a special task force that had as its brief the reshaping of an international Christian organization. My friend did not know much about my home country, but he did know a lot about mission and evangelism. He asked the question: "Is your country *post-Christian* or *pre-Christian*?"

I fumbled for an answer at the time, and the way I responded probably was not that profound. However, it is a question I have given a lot of thought to since and I have concluded that how we answer this question has an undeniable influence on how we as Christ-followers view the responsibility we have to be salt and light. It has profound missiological implications affecting the way we approach our society and our attitude toward our culture.

In a *post-Christian* society, the attitude and activity of many Christians involves inviting people to "come back." They look at their increasingly un-Christian culture and lament at how different it is today from what it once was. They throw their moralistic hands in the air at what they perceive to be godless changes in their national culture and rail against its encroaching evil. They sometimes romanticize what it was like a generation or so ago. People today might not currently be in church, but they once were. And if/when people do come back to church, they will know what to expect and how to behave. In a *post-Christian* society, the language of the church is often grumpy at government or shaking a lobbying fist about lapses in moral legislation, and the way the state is not caring adequately for the marginalized. Christian leaders are apt to quote the famous line attributed to Edmund Burke:[6] "The only thing necessary for the triumph of evil is for good men to do nothing," and with it they demand the right to be heard as they speak to a sinful culture—that really should know better. The church assumes a posture of power and tends to see itself as a political prophet provoking the moral conscience of a nation with its need to "come back" to God. Words like "renewal", "revival" and "restoration" all make sense in a *post-Christian* world as people pray and work to regain or clawback what they perceive they once had.

In a *pre-Christian* society, the approach is very different. It reminds me of my experience as a missionary in a country like Bangladesh, where Christians are a minuscule percentage of the population. There is less talk about "gaining back" that which we "never really had." There are no assumptions about former godly values. There is no rear vision mirror in a *pre-Christian* society—only a forward-facing windscreen. The starting point for mission is very different. Christians are less angry and disappointed at the lack of righteous behavior seen around them because they realize that the masses they live amongst do not know any better and are yet to encounter God for themselves. Instead, Christians focus more energy on showing the better way to live—less stick and grizzle; more role-modeling and demonstration of the difference God makes in people's lives. When something corrupt or immoral or unhealthy pops up on the

---

6. Edmund Burke: an Anglo-Irish statesman and philosopher, member of British parliament 1766–1794.

society's political radar, they do not necessarily shy away from speaking to it as God's representatives. However, the premise or soapbox on which they stand is predicated upon their character, good relationships, sound reasoning, and caring actions, rather than an appeal to spiritual values that they presume everyone understands.

Maybe, the best way to be salt and light is to live in such a way that the reputation, character, and behavior of Christ-followers raises a heap of positive questions. The apostle Peter put it like this for the Christians of his day:

> [12]Live such good lives among the pagans that, though they accuse you of doing wrong, they may see your good deeds and glorify God on the day he visits us.
>
> 1 Peter 2:12

SMALL GROUP DISCUSSION QUESTIONS

Matthew 5:13–16

1. When Jesus used the metaphors of salt and light, they had specific significance to the people of his day. What contemporary metaphors might he use to get the same message across in our day?

2. What are some examples of sprinkling "salt" or "shining light" in your workplace/neighborhood?

3. What is a twenty-first-century Christian response to sinful behavior in the workplace or social network or one's extended family? How do we stand up for kingdom values?

4. A pizza delivery company (in New Zealand) distributed condoms to local home letterboxes as part of its advertising campaign of their "meat lover" pizzas. What would a "salt" or "light" response be to such a campaign?

5. What examples do we have (or know of) where Christian "salt" or "light" has helped change a situation?

6. Why do you think Christians, who seek to live by biblical values, are increasingly regarded is narrow and intolerant?

2

Laws Are to Be Broken

On the foreshore of Galveston, Texas, stood the Flagship Hotel. It has since been demolished, due to severe damage that occurred during a devastating hurricane that battered the coast in 2008. It was originally built in 1965, on top of a pier jutting three hundred yards out into the Gulf of Mexico, with seven floors and 250 rooms. Among other marketing strategies, hotel management encouraged patrons to bring their fishing gear and fish off the pier during an incoming tide. However, some enterprising guests also thought it was possible to fish directly from the balconies of their hotel rooms. In response, hotel management erected signs in the hotel rooms that stated, "No fishing from the balcony," but the practice continued. The signs prohibiting the activity had little effect.

The issue for the hotel had to do with the heavy sinkers on the fishing lines that patrons cast into the sea. Either for lack of leverage in casting, or simply because their fishing lines were too short, the lines sometimes failed to reach the water. On the ground floor of the hotel was a restaurant with large plate glass windows. The heavy sinkers on the short fishing lines would now and then swing back and smack into these windows. The cost of replacing the windows was high. And even if the glass did not break, it was understandably disconcerting for patrons, who were gazing out to the Gulf of Mexico as they ate their meals, to have a lead sinker crash into the window beside them! The hotel management tried all sorts of strategies to prevent people from fishing from their balconies. In the end, they stumbled onto a simple solution. They removed the signs from the hotel rooms that stated, "No fishing from the balcony." And the practice stopped![1]

In a postmodern and civil-libertarian world, there can be a love-hate relationship with rules and regulations. While the need for rules is understood, prescriptive boundaries, regulations and laws are often resented. Sometimes, publishing laws to prohibit a particular activity instead plants the idea into the mind of people who had not previously considered that behavior. If you doubt the truth of this, try telling a nine or ten-year-old child that they cannot do something, and then watch them try!

The people of Jesus day also had a hard time with rules and laws and religious regulations. They felt as if a heavy weight had been laid across their necks. Living in the twenty-first century, it is hard to imagine the effect of legalism in the times and culture of Jesus: suffice it to say, it was pretty tough. At one point, Jesus made a fascinating statement about laws and legalism that many over the years have found quite confusing. Indeed, what he said seems to represent the antithesis of spiritual freedom for which Jesus is usually renowned:

> [17]Do not think that I have come to abolish the Law or the Prophets; I have not come to abolish them but to fulfill them. [18]I tell you the truth, until heaven and earth disappear, not the smallest letter, not the least stroke of a pen, will by any means disappear from the Law until everything is accomplished. [19]Anyone who breaks one of the least of these commandments and teaches others to do the same will be called least in the kingdom of heaven, but whoever practices and teaches these commands will be called great in the kingdom of heaven. [20]For I tell you that unless your righteousness surpasses that of the Pharisees and the teachers of the law, you will certainly not enter the kingdom of heaven.
>
> Matthew 5:17–20

There are some sections in Jesus' *Sermon on the Mount* that are easy to grasp at first reading. Other parts require a little more homework and cultural understanding to fully grasp the point Jesus was making. This passage falls into that latter category.

We usually associate Jesus' teaching as offering freedom from rules-based or legalistic religion, but here he appears to be promoting

---

1. https://thepeoplegroup.com/2009/04/focus-on-the-positive-to-reduce-negative-behavior/

adherence to the law. Indeed, some have wondered whether these words, attributed to Jesus, may not have been his at all. Perhaps they were added by Matthew in his biography of Jesus since it was directed to a primarily Jewish audience.[2] After all, Jesus himself was a frequent "lawbreaker," and it was ultimately on this charge that he was sentenced to death by the Jewish leaders of his day.

While I can understand the rationale for such a view, I find this argument unconvincing. Jesus' words here are consistent with the rest of his teaching, but they require a fuller understanding of the original context in order to comprehend his point.

To begin with, when Jesus made this statement, he was most likely responding to something people were saying about him. He was correcting misguided or misunderstood opinions about the nature and purpose of his ministry. Some may have been assuming Jesus was starting a brand-new religion and that all the old laws of Israel, which people in his culture had grown up with, were now irrelevant and had been superseded—as if God was ruling a line in the sand and was starting over. Jesus was at pains to point out that this was not the case.

It is important to understand the way the "Law of God" was perceived by Jesus' primarily Jewish audience. In those days, there were four ways that the term "Law" was used. Firstly, there was what we refer to as the *Ten Commandments*,[3] which today provides the basis for common law in most countries. Secondly, the *Pentateuch*, consisting of the first five books of the Old Testament, was often referred to as the *Law of Moses*. These writings gave detailed descriptions of religious ceremonies, family life and business relationships. Thirdly, the *Law and the Prophets*, which essentially equated to the Old Testament in our Bibles. Fourthly, there was the *Oral or Scribal Law*, representing the mode of teaching about God and his ways most often heard by the ordinary people of Jesus' day.

Keep in mind that in those days, books as we know them today, did not exist. A significant proportion of the population was illiterate, and those who could read would have had limited access to copies of the Scriptures to read for themselves. Written copies were only ever kept in the Temple or synagogues, and most people would have learned about the *Law of the* LORD, through the mouths of others.

---

2. Barclay, *The Gospel of Matthew, Volume 1*, 127
3. Exodus 20:1–7; Deuteronomy 5:6–21

It is essential that we understand the history of the *Oral or Scribal Law*. Over a period of several hundred years, before the time of Jesus, religious leaders and teachers within Judaism had sought to define in more specific detail the regulations and stipulations that Moses recorded for God's people. Concern arose that lax or ambiguous interpretation of the Law of God could lead to people breaking the Law inadvertently, thereby becoming guilty of sin and incurring the wrath of God. Such was their perception of God's nature. "Break the law and experience God's displeasure and wrath; obey the law (scrupulously) and God will reward you with salvation and eternal life."

Over the years, a class of men known as the Scribes emerged from within the Jewish religious system. Their task was to elaborate on the broad principles contained within the *Law and the Prophets*, an endeavor which resulted in literally thousands and thousands of specific rules and regulations. By the time of Jesus, the number and pettiness of these religious rules had become ridiculous and burdensome. For example, the *Law of Moses* talked about the principle of the Sabbath Day, which was to be kept holy and free from work. However, enforcing such a law called for clarity around what constituted as "work." The Scribes set to and came up with rigid definitions. First, they said: "to carry a burden (load) on the Sabbath Day is an act of work." But this then required a definition of what was meant by "a burden." They came up with the following: "food equal in weight to a dried fig, enough wine for mixing in a goblet, milk enough for one swallow, honey enough to put upon a wound, water enough to moisten an eye-salve, paper enough to write a customs house notice upon, reed enough to make a pen . . ."[4] Carrying such things on the Sabbath was deemed to be breaking the *Law of the* LORD, and was therefore, a sinful act!

When it came to the "work" of writing something on the Sabbath Day, the Scribes defined it like this: "He who writes two letters of the alphabet with his right or left hand, whether of one kind or two kinds, if they are written with different inks or in different languages, is guilty. Even if he should write two letters from forgetfulness, he is guilty, whether he has written them with ink or with paint, red chalk, vitriol, or anything which makes a permanent mark . . ."[5] The Scribes could spend endless hours arguing over whether it was lawful for a man to lift a lamp from one place to another on the Sabbath, or whether a tailor sinned if he went

---

4. Barclay, *The Gospel of Matthew*, Volume 1, 128
5. Barclay, *The Gospel of Matthew*, Volume 1, 129

out with a needle mistakenly stuck in his robe! Initially, all these petty rules and regulations were not written down; they were passed on from one generation to the next by oral tradition—hence the term *Oral Law*.[6]

All this acts as an interpretive key for understanding many of Jesus' statements in his *Sermon on the Mount*. He spoke into a context significantly influenced (controlled) by oral traditions and pedantic legalism.

If this sounds strange to our enlightened twenty-first-century sensibilities, the Jews are not the only race in human history to get tied up by pedantic laws. In 1657, Oliver Cromwell was alleged to have drafted a law banning the making and eating of Christmas mince pies in England, because of its historical symbolic connection with Roman Catholicism. In the United States, several cities and state ordinances are nothing short of bizarre, and some of them are yet to be formally repealed. For example:

- In Lexington, Kentucky, a law rendered it illegal to carry an ice-cream cone in one's pocket.
- In Waterloo, Nebraska, barbers were forbidden to eat onions between seven a.m. and seven p.m.
- In the state of Massachusetts, it was against the law to eat peanuts in church or to use tomatoes in making clam chowder.
- In Zion, Illinois, it was illegal for anyone to give lighted cigars to dogs, cats, and other domesticated animals kept as pets.
- In Gary, Indiana, persons were prohibited from attending a movie house or theater or riding a public streetcar within four hours of eating garlic.
- In Nicholas County, West Virginia, no member of the clergy was allowed to tell jokes or humorous stories from the pulpit during a church service.
- In Carrizozo, New Mexico, it was forbidden for a female to appear unshaven in public.
- In New Jersey, a person could be arrested for slurping soup in a public restaurant.

Nevertheless, in the time and culture of Jesus's day, the teaching of the original *Law and the Prophets* (the Old Testament) had been

---

6. Later on, in the third century, they were written down in vast volumes known as the *Mishnah*, and later on again, dozens of commentaries were written on the *Mishnah*, known as the *Talmud*.

somewhat distorted and polluted in the popular understanding of the masses because of this commentary. That which started out as a record of God's loving dealings with his chosen people had been reduced, at times beyond recognition, to an endless set of pedantic rules and regulations. Without the facility to read the original Scriptures for themselves, the general understanding of the people was based on the oral teaching of the Scribes as experts of the Law. As a result, people lived in fear of breaking these laws and thereby incurring God's wrath.

In addition, a religious order, called the Pharisees, emerged about a hundred years before the time of Jesus. This group dedicated themselves to observing the Law down to the last detail and acted as religious enforcers. The image of God they presented was distorted and confusing, and on numerous occasions throughout his public ministry, Jesus, by his words or actions, ran afoul of the strict observances imposed by the Pharisees.

Enter one Jesus of Nazareth onto the stage of first-century Israel! He was a puzzling enigma to the religious establishment and a breath of fresh air to the ordinary people who lived in fear of breaking God's law. He claimed to be representing God, but his approach was a lot more relaxed. He lived and behaved as someone unfettered by these pedantic regulations. Indeed, one of the ways he gained notoriety was through standing up to, and challenging, the teaching of the Scribes and Pharisees. He repeatedly broke their petty rules by doing such dastardly deeds as healing people (showing the mercy of God) on the Sabbath Day. He exposed the stupidity of the *Oral and Scribal Law* and how it put an unbearable burden onto the backs of people.

It is not hard to imagine how the people of the day would have seen in Jesus a glimmer of hope. When *they* had broken the law, as taught by the Scribes and the Pharisees, they had been punished and censored. But when Jesus did so, he seemed to get away with it. The cruel yoke of the *Law* was seemingly being broken. To use contemporary parlance, it was if the popular commentary was going viral on "social media" about Jesus, and speculation grew that he was introducing a whole new religious system. "Forget the old law—God is starting over again!" It was this kind of misunderstanding to which Jesus said, "Whoa!"

> [17]Do not think that I have come to abolish the Law or the Prophets; I have not come to abolish them but to fulfill them . . .
>
> Matthew 5:17

What was Jesus saying? Firstly, he was effectively saying: "Don't throw the baby out with the bathwater!" The problem was not with the Old Testament *Law and the Prophets*; the problem was how the law had devolved at the hands of the religious leaders becoming a pedantic and trivial legal code. The way the people were being hounded and beaten up by the law was not what God had in mind when the commandments were given, or the Old Testament was recorded.

Secondly, Jesus wanted those interested in following him to understand the continuity and place he had in the long-term history of God's dealings with humanity. Jesus did not just appear randomly out of the blue; he was not wiping out the past and beginning something from scratch. He was the embodiment and fulfillment of what the Old Testament had foreseen. For thousands of years, the Scriptures predicted the coming of the Messiah. They pointed forward to a day when God would visit his people, and the ideal or intent of the Law would be fulfilled. Jesus was positioning himself as that fulfillment of the Law.

Coming forward two thousand years, if that is the point and context into which Jesus was speaking in his day, what might the application from a passage like this be to our contemporary age? Is this just helpful historical information, or are there principles here that also apply in the twenty-first century? Two immediately come to mind:

1. LET US NOT NEGLECT THE OLD TESTAMENT

Some Christ-followers today have an ambivalent attitude toward the Old Testament. They like the God of the New Testament, but they are not so sure about the God of the Old Testament. Or if they do like him, they perhaps assume he went through an anger management program sometime between the books of Malachi and Matthew! Obviously, Jesus would not approve of such a view. Jesus was quite clear in stating that his teaching and ministry did not abrogate or disqualify the *Law and the Prophets* (the Old Testament). To put that another way: to follow Jesus and to regard him as a mentor, we might want to read the books he liked to read! Or to use Jesus' own words:

> [19] . . . whoever practices and teaches these commands will be called great in the kingdom of heaven.
>
> Matthew 5:19

What can be acknowledged is that there are some passages in the Old Testament that make for difficult reading. Some of the specific laws in its early books pertained to an era in human history that is very different from the twenty-first century, in terms of technology and human relations. However, whenever history is read, it is important not to overlay a contemporary understanding of life onto what was recorded thousands of years before. Contemporary thinking looks at our world through very different lenses to those who lived thousands of years ago. Likewise, reading some of the prophetic books are a bit like looking through someone elses mail, in many cases the message contained relates to specific circumstances and may not be readily generalized.

It is also worth recognizing the theological principle known as "progressive revelation." The picture of God, and what he is like, contained in the Old Testament was expressed in the primitive or limited understanding of the day; Jesus, however, is the ultimate (complete) revelation of what God is really like. People like Moses or David lived thousands of years before the time of Jesus, recording God's activity and his order for the world through the sociological lens of their day. A contemporary view of God is now based more on the historical record or revelation of Jesus, rather than just the Old Testament. Indeed, the Old Testament is now read through the interpretive lens of Jesus. This does not mean we can neglect the ancient stories of God's dealings with humanity and his chosen people. Jesus did not appear out of a vacuum. His coming and his ministry were foretold on hundreds of occasions, and the account of his ministry requires the backdrop of the Old Testament story. Maybe Paul had something along these lines in mind when he said:

> [16]All Scripture is God-breathed and is useful for teaching, rebuking, correcting and training in righteousness . . .
>
> 2 Timothy 3:16

When Paul wrote those words, the concept of Scripture available in his day was limited to the *Law and the Prophets*. Maybe some were wondering if it was still relevant. Paul's response: "The Old Testament still has God's breath on it."

2. WE CONNECT WITH GOD THROUGH LOVE, NOT LEGALISM

Jesus' teaching must have been a breath of fresh air to the people of his day. The dominant religious worldview was all about ethics, the performance of rituals, and obedience to rules; religion essentially defined what you could or could not do. The God of love and grace was hidden and distorted through fear of breaking the law and avoiding or encountering punishment. Jesus brought an altogether different revelation of God.

Rigid legalism is certainly not limited to the time of Jesus. Many reading this book may have come through religious systems where it all felt like rules and regulations. "God loves those who are good and gets angry at those who are naughty." Maybe the concept of God gleaned is essentially that of a mean, angry old judge just waiting to punish those who disobey. We placate him by going to church every so often, or by taking communion, confessing our sins, and giving money to charity. The Pharisees and religious leaders of Jesus' day taught that the way to be righteous—in right standing before God—was to obey endless rules and rituals. Jesus taught another way. Acceptability before God is not a matter of doing good religious works, as much as the forging of a friendship or relationship with God based on his mercy and love toward us. This was no doubt what Jesus had in mind when he said:

> [20] . . . unless your righteousness surpasses that of the Pharisees and the teachers of the law, you will certainly not enter the kingdom of heaven.
>
> Matthew 5:20

If there were Pharisees in the crowd when Jesus said these words, one could only imagine how uncomfortable and angry they must have become. He was pulling the rug out from under the feet of the religious leaders; this was not a Dale Carnegie "how-to-win-friends-and-influence-people" moment. There was nothing inherently wrong with the Old Testament *Law of the* LORD, except that trying to become right with God through, or by, keeping them to the letter was impossible to achieve. Under that line of reasoning, those who disobeyed any of the *Law of the* LORD were deemed unrighteous and, therefore, outside the favor of God. However, the broad picture of the Old Testament story that Jesus painted pointed to a day in the future when the Son of God would come and purchase our righteousness. He would personally atone for our sins and reconcile us to his Father. This would be Jesus' ultimate mission. His death on the cross was like the sacrificial lamb in a Jewish atonement ritual. His resurrection from the grave defeated the power of sin and death. He came to be the fulfillment of what the *Law and the Prophets* all pointed toward. Righteousness is now achieved, not by complying with a whole list of religious "works," but by inviting Jesus Christ to assume the leadership role over our lives—submitting ourselves to his control and LORDship. All of this was what the Old Testament *Law and the Prophets* foretold would happen.

Eugene Petterson's *"The Message"* paraphrase captures the words of the apostle Paul in his letter to the Roman Christians:

> Saving is all his idea, and all his work. All we do is trust him enough to let him do it. It's God's gift from start to finish! We don't play a major role. If we did, we'd probably go around bragging that we'd done the whole thing! No, we neither make nor save ourselves. God does both the making and saving . . .[7]
>
> Ephesians 2:8,9 (The Message)

The people of Jesus' day had been told that the way one earns access to God's favor is by doing more good things than bad things. Jesus said it is not possible to do enough good or righteous things to earn or merit God's favor. Relationship with God is something he has purchased for us all out of his own suffering from the resources of his love and mercy.

Does that mean then that there are no rules or laws of the LORD by which we now need to abide? If people are made righteous by personal relationship and trust in Jesus, does that mean freedom to do whatever we want? No, that would be an equal and opposite error—into which some Christians have drifted. Some have assumed that because everything now is "grace," all the old definitions of sin are discarded—a God of love and mercy merely accepts everyone regardless of how we behave. Paul addressed this issue repeatedly in his letter to the Romans.[8] That was not what Jesus had in mind at all. The laws or the values of God are still in place. God's grace doesn't remove them. It is just that connection with God is not achieved through trying to keep the rules. It is the other way around. Christ-followers keep the rules *because* they now have a relationship with God.

---

7. Peterson, *The Message*.
8. Romans 6:1–2; 6:15; 7:13

St Augustine had a great way of explaining this. He said: "Love God and do what you will."[9] In other words, when a person loves the LORD, living by his values and standards is not a harsh obligation, but a liberating joy. Love for God draws the follower of Jesus toward his standards and values. Obedience does not come from fear; but in response to God's love, that he pours into the hearts of those who follow him.

---

9. Augustine of Hippo, *Homilies on the First Epistle of John*, Homily 7.

SMALL GROUP DISCUSSION QUESTIONS

Matthew 5:17-20

1. How do you respond to the person who says that Christianity (religion) is just a list of rules and regulations—no freedom?
2. Jesus said that he didn't come to abolish the law and the prophets, but to fulfill them. How would you explain "fulfilling the law" to someone new to the Christian faith?
3. In what ways can twenty-first-century Christianity come across as too legalistic?
4. What is the meaning of "righteousness" as Jesus used it in v.20?
5. How does a person "enter the kingdom of heaven" (v.20)?
6. What was Jesus driving at in Matthew 7:21-23?

3

Murder by Intent

Few breaches of the law stir the emotions more than the crime of murder. The premature ending of a human life is a heinous act. However, one of the more morbid and twisted aspects of western culture is its fascination with TV and movie dramas that depict and then solve crimes involving murder. Murder mysteries are prime-time television viewing and best sellers in bookstores. By the time an average child in the United States completes High School, he or she will have witnessed 16,000 murders (or their aftermath), and over 200,000 acts of violence.[1]

Our legal systems delineate categories or gradations of murder based upon the degree of premeditation. For instance, in my home country, the New Zealand Crimes Act (1961) defines murder as an act where an offender means to cause, or is likely to cause, the death of another. While there are other ways people are killed (like manslaughter), the definition of murder implies intent and forethought as to the consequences of an action.[2]

In that regard, most readers of this book would be comfortable with this definition of murder, and probably even more so on the fact that they have not committed this particular crime. The people of Jesus day thought they knew a lot about murder too. It was a serious crime with a

---

1. Senate Committee on the Judiciary. Children, violence, and the media: a report for parents and policymakers. September 14, 1999. Accessed 14 June 2006. http://judiciary.senate.gov/oldsite/mediavio.htm.

2. For a defendant to be found guilty of murder, the prosecution must prove both the *actus rae* (the act itself) and the *mens rae* (and the mental state of intending to kill another).

severe penalty, and the sixth of the Ten Commandments clearly forbade it. However, when Jesus spoke to a crowd of followers gathered on the side of a hill, he added a rather radical and expanded definition:

> ²¹ "You have heard that it was said to the people long ago, 'You shall not murder, and anyone who murders will be subject to judgment.' ²² But I tell you that anyone who is angry with a brother or sister will be subject to judgment. Again, anyone who says to a brother or sister, 'Raca,' is answerable to the court. And anyone who says, 'You fool!' will be in danger of the fire of hell. ²³ "Therefore, if you are offering your gift at the altar and there remember that your brother or sister has something against you, ²⁴ leave your gift there in front of the altar. First go and be reconciled to them; then come and offer your gift. ²⁵ Settle matters quickly with your adversary who is taking you to court. Do it while you are still together on the way, or your adversary may hand you over to the judge, and the judge may hand you over to the officer, and you may be thrown into prison. ²⁶ Truly I tell you, you will not get out until you have paid the last penny.
>
> Matthew 5:21–26

There is a crucial interpretive key in these words of Jesus that explains the context into which he was speaking. His discourse begins with the words:

> ²¹ You have heard that it was said to the people long ago . . .

A similar phrase is employed in several subsequent sections of Jesus' *Sermon on the Mount*. As noted in Chapter 2, ordinary people of Jesus' day, unlike today, did not have personal copies of the Scriptures to read and study for themselves. Many were illiterate and written copies of the *Law and the Prophets* resided in the Temple and synagogues. Consequently, teaching about the ways of the LORD, for most people, happened orally—from the mouths of religious leaders and teachers. Therein lay a problem. As over several centuries leading up to the time of Jesus religious teachers and scholars had tried to define, in ridiculous detail, all the laws of the LORD—down to the "nth" degree. The intent may have been laudable, but in the process, it could be said they squeezed the life out of the *Law of Moses*. Pedantic legalism ruled the day, and right standing with God was perceived as achievable, and proven by meticulous keeping of all the rules and regulations developed by the religious leadership. Life could be viewed as one big scorecard where you could check-off all the laws you had not broken or the sins you were not guilty of committing. For many within the religious leadership community, this approach culminated in an immense sense of pride: "I haven't done that . . . therefore I must be righteous before God." No doubt, when it came to the Sixth Commandment, there was little hesitation, "Nope, never done that! Never murdered anyone."

But Jesus' words brought a radical challenge to their sense of righteousness: "Hang on a minute. Maybe there is some misunderstanding here. A person may not have committed the actual crime, within the letter of the law, but what about the spirit of the law?" Jesus prefaces his challenge with a familiar phrase, repeated several times in subsequent sections of his sermon: ". . . but I tell you." While few may have physically committed the act, how many have entertained the thought?

As a humorous aside, Ruth Graham (wife of the evangelist Dr. Billy Graham) was interviewed about her marriage. At times it cannot have been easy being married to a man who traveled extensively and was always in the public spotlight. The interviewer asked whether she had ever entertained the thought of being married to someone else; had she ever contemplated divorce? Her response was: "No, I've never thought of divorce in all these thirty-five years of marriage, but," she said, "I did think of murder a few times!"[3]

There was likely a certain amount of "jaw-dropping" amongst those listening to Jesus when he talked about the subject of murder. For starters, he suggested the crime did not merely occur in the hands of the murderer. The deed is initiated by the head and the heart. To put that another way, in the eyes of God, murder, or the destruction of another person's life includes a range of other thoughts and actions that are equally destructive. According to Jesus, a lot more of us are technically guilty of murder than we might have thought. He offered three specific examples, each of which was probably quite shocking:

1. ANGER TOWARD ANOTHER PERSON

> [22]But I tell you that anyone who is angry with a brother or sister will be subject to judgment . . .
>
> Matthew 5:22

---

3. Gibbs and Duffy, *Ruth Graham, Soulmate to Billy, Dies,* http://content.time.com/time/nation/article/0,8599,1633197,00.html

What did Jesus mean here? His words sound rather harsh. If anger is a definition of murder, is there anyone who is not guilty? Surely everyone becomes angry at someone or something at some stage? Some might claim that according to his definition, Jesus himself was guilty of murder. After all, he got pretty steamed up at moneychangers and merchants in the Jerusalem Temple, overturning tables and driving the merchants out with a whip![4]

The Greek language, in which the New Testament was written, had two words which are translated as anger in English. *"Thumos"*[5] described anger or wrath that flares up quickly, blazes with ferocity, but then calms down just as quickly when all the fuel has been consumed—similar to a hay barn on fire or the flash of road-rage which might be experienced when someone cuts us off on the freeway. It flares up and then dies down; it does not last or linger. Everyone gets angry at some stage and perhaps for a moment loses their cool. While not necessarily warranted or good, it is also relatively commonplace. Indeed, some would advocate venting our anger rather than letting it fester inside.

The other word, *"orgē,"* described the kind of anger that is long-lived and cultivated—frequently with a view to revenge.[6] It expressed the anger of a person who nurses his or her hurt to keep it warm. Anger that simmers with bitterness and resentment, sometimes for years or generations. It was this lingering kind of anger that Jesus referred to as being equivalent to murder. Passive aggression might be another manifestation of this type of anger—bottled-up or subdued resentment that festers.

The kind of anger Jesus was talking about was more serious. Jesus was referring to anger that is cool and calculating; that broods and stews over wrongs that have been done against a person. Anger that refuses to forget and plots revenge—perhaps even to the extent of wishing a person dead or otherwise removed from a situation. We once lived next door to a woman who, after an inconsequential argument, had not spoken to her brother for forty years. Whenever she spoke of her brother, her eyes and body-language seethed with venom and hatred. Jesus suggested that in the eyes of God, this kind of anger toward another constitutes nothing less than murder. They may not have been shot with a gun, but the thought of doing so is just the same.

4. Matthew 21:12; Mark 11:15; John 2:15
5. Vine, *An Expository Dictionary of New Testament Words,* 47
6. Vine, *An Expository Dictionary of New Testament Words,* 47

So, before putting a check on the scorecard indicating never having committed murder, perhaps consider carefully whether there are people against whom there remains a nurtured grudge and anger kept warm? From God's perspective the act of murder is simply the outward manifestation of an internal condition.

2. ACTS OF DISCRIMINATION

> ... Again, anyone who says to a brother or sister, 'Raca,' is answerable to the Sanhedrin.
>
> Matthew 5:22

There is cultural background here that needs to be unpacked for readers of Jesus' words. Being "answerable to the Sanhedrin" was a metaphor for being brought before the highest court in the land. Only those guilty of grievous crimes had to face the Sanhedrin, and Jesus was using this phrase to illustrate the severity of this act. The impact of the word *"raca"* is impossible to translate into English, which is why several translations import the original word into the English text. It referred more to the tone of voice than to an actual description of a person.[7] Dallas Willard suggests it may have originated from the sound one makes to collect spittle from the throat in order to spit.[8] It conveyed an accent of contempt or egregious insult through the way one person accused another of being contemptible or empty-headed. To call someone *"raca"* was deeply insulting, derogatory and demeaning.

A contemporary example might occur through the sin of racial discrimination. Calling someone *"raca"* was like a person of one ethnicity looking down on a person of a different ethnicity—regarding the color of skin as evidence of intellectual and moral inferiority. Another example might be socio-economic discrimination—regarding people of wealth as inherently superior or more sophisticated and intelligent than those at the poorer end of the financial continuum.

So, calling someone *"raca"* was more serious than just name-calling. It infused the insult with an attitude of contempt and discrimination. Perhaps Jesus' regarded this as particularly significant because calling someone "a no-hoper", "useless" or "trash" effectively kills a person's hope

---

7. Barclay, *The Gospel of Matthew, Volume 1*, 121
8. Willard, *The Divine Conspiracy—Rediscovering Our Hidden Life in God*, 169

for change or improvement, it involves the destruction of a person's self-esteem and murders their dream of bettering themselves. The repeated calling of a child "dumb" or "thick" or "clumsy," or constantly comparing them to a sibling ("Why can't you be like . . . ?") is like verbal *in-formation* and is received by the spirit of an individual, potentially becoming a blueprint for his or her development so that they eventually embody that which they were called.

Jesus said that such contemptuous discrimination is nothing less than the crime of murder. Through judgments and prejudice, the future potential of a person, created in the image of God, is killed. And God regards that as seriously as if their physical life was taken.

3. CHARACTER ASSASSINATION

> . . . anyone who says, 'You fool!' will be in danger of the fire of hell.
>
> Matthew 5:22

The word translated as "fool" in our English Bibles was the Greek word *"moros"* (from which we get a word like "moron," historically used to describe someone of low intelligence or a mild intellectual disability). However, in its original Greek context, this word did not so much refer to intellectual limitations as it did to moral foolishness.[9] It described the person who is a scoundrel, or who "plays the fool," or who "fools around" in terms of moral conduct.

Jesus was not merely talking about insulting someone by calling him or her an idiot or stupid, unpalatable as that might be. Rather, he was addressing character assassination—casting a slur on their character by labeling them immoral or corrupt. For Jesus, the crime of destroying a person's reputation was as serious as the crime of ending someone's life. He viewed gossiping about another person behind his or her back or spreading malicious rumors that destroy a person's reputation, to be as serious as killing them. Imagine the damage done to a person's reputation when wrongly accused of something like sexual abuse. Regardless of later proof and substantive evidence against the charge, mud sticks. An individual can lose job, family and friends over an unproven and false accusation.

---

9. Vine, *An Expository Dictionary of New Testament Words*, 444

In other words, what a person says or writes about another can be like a deadly poison. Or as James puts it, the tongue is like a small fire that can set an entire forest ablaze.[10] We might be tempted to think that we would never assassinate the character of another person—we're not guilty of that! However, every time a juicy piece of gossip is listened to, let alone passed on to others, there is complicity in another person's destruction.

> An old Yiddish parable told the story of a man who had a problem with gossip. One day he felt convicted about this and asked his rabbi for advice: *"Tell me how I can make amends."* In response, the rabbi told him to take three pillows, go to the public square, cut the pillows open, wave them in the air, and then come back and report what happened. The man did as was suggested and then hastened back to the rabbi's chambers. "I did just what you said Rabbi and the feathers blew in the wind all over the town."
>
> "Good," the rabbi smiled. "Now, so you can realize how much harm is done by gossip. I want you to go back to the square and collect all the feathers!"

Murder, according to Jesus, is not merely the ending of another person's physical life. In some respects, that might even be the kinder thing to do. It can be far more painful and hurtful to be the object of another person's anger, discrimination, or character assassination. The act of murder does not begin in the hands of the murderer but in his or her heart. Not many have taken the life of another, yet countless others of us are guilty of something similar through the intent of our heart or by words from our mouths.

But then, Jesus went a step further and said something that must have sounded outrageous to his original audience. He linked the attitude of a person's heart toward others with their attempt to have a right relationship with God. For the people of Jesus' day, repairing broken or strained relationships with God required atonement through the sacrifice, of an animal, bird or the first fruits of a crop. The sinner's hands were laid upon the offering, words of repentance were spoken that transferred guilt onto the animal or produce, and then it would be sacrificed or destroyed in the sinner's place. Now, however, Jesus suggested an idea that challenged the efficacy of this system:

---

10. James 3:5–9

> [23]"Therefore, if you are offering your gift at the altar and there remember that your brother or sister has something against you, [24]leave your gift there in front of the altar. First go and be reconciled to that person; then come and offer your gift."
>
> Matthew 5:23–24

The Temple sacrificial system was a means of restoring a broken relationship. Justice would be satisfied, and the person who offered the sacrifice would be declared to be back in right relationship with God. In a crude sense, the sacrificial system might be likened to the paying of a speeding fine or a parking ticket. Having paid the fine, liability for the infringement is canceled, and the "broken" relationship with the State is restored.

The problem with the sacrificial system was that the concept of sacrifice had become rather sterile and mechanical. As if to imply: "It does not really matter about the attitude of the heart, so long as I perform the ritual and offer the sacrifice, everything will be okay. I can do whatever I like so long as I pay the sacrifice afterward." Jesus suggested that the attitude of a person's heart is more important than the act of sacrifice he or she performs.

What Jesus was suggesting was not really anything new. According to Jewish law, if a sacrifice was to be effective in restoring relationship with God, it first had to include confession of sin and genuine repentance. Part of that repentance would include the setting to right of that which was wrong. For instance, if a person was making a sacrificial offering to assuage for a sin of theft, their sacrificial act was not regarded as complete until that which was stolen in the first place had been returned or, if necessary, compensation had been paid to the offended party. Repentance means much more than feeling sorry or apologizing for what has been done. Remorse is not the same thing as repentance. Repentance, by definition, implies restitution.

Jesus applied that principle to other interpersonal relationships. The bottom line was this; restoration of an individual's relationship with God (being made righteous) is not possible until there has been a setting right of broken relationships with other people. God will not declare a person righteous before himself if there are people with whom they know they have a fractured relationship. It is not possible to punch someone in the nose, and then expect God to accept a sacrifice of praise and worship—as if nothing has happened. First, the offending person needs to go back and seek forgiveness from the one they offended, putting their relationship to rights, only then will their worship toward God be acceptable. This was the point behind Jesus' statement in Matthew 5:25–26 where he alludes to something like a disputes tribunal or court that settles property disputes between two parties.

> [25]Settle matters quickly with your adversary who is taking you to court . . .

Do not leave a matter unresolved, he suggests, and wait for someone else to adjudicate because the outcome is likely to be worse.

A genuine relationship with God requires we maintain, to the best of our ability, right relationships with other people. It is not possible to hold a grudge or unresolved grievance against another person and expect to have a close friendship with Jesus. This was a particular theme the apostle John picked up on:

> [11]. . . whoever hates his brother is in the darkness and walks around in the darkness; he does not know where he is going, because the darkness has blinded him.
>
> 1 John 2:11

> [20]If anyone says, 'I love God,' yet hates his brother, he is a liar. For anyone who does not love his brother, whom he has seen, cannot love God, whom he has not seen.
>
> 1 John 4:20

To know harmony with God requires that unresolved conflict with others be addressed. In one sense, that is a very humbling thing to have to do. In another sense, it is one of the most liberating experiences a person can have as a follower of Jesus. There is nothing quite like the sense of relief and joy experienced when a broken friendship is restored. But more than that, it brings a fresh sense of release and fellowship with God who the previously broken friendship with others had kept at a distance.

From time to time, people say of broken relationships: "Time will heal." In other words, "Don't bother to try to resolve the situation with the person you offended (or who has offended you). Simply leave it alone, and in time it will heal". There may well be some situations where that works, but in most cases, it does not. Time seldom heals. Ignoring broken relationships is more akin to putting a band-aid on a cancerous tumor.

When it is covered up, it is not necessarily seen, but it does not make the sickness go away. A tumor needs to be surgically cut out, and then after surgery and removal of infection, time certainly will heal. On the other hand, tumors may sometimes go into remission. They appear as if they are no longer there, but when triggered in some way, they flare into life once again. Broken friendships can be a bit like that. All appears calm and happy for a season, but then another blow is suffered, and all the old pain and hurt come back to the surface. The time to set a broken relationship to rights is always sooner rather than later.

General James Oglethorpe was a British soldier, member of parliament, and a philanthropist in the eighteenth-century. He once said to John Wesley, "I never forgive, and I never forget." To which Wesley replied, "Then, Sir, I hope you never sin."

SMALL GROUP DISCUSSION QUESTIONS
Matthew 5:21–26

1. Why do you think Jesus linked anger with the crime of murder?
2. Ephesians 4:26 says, "in your anger do not sin." When does anger become sinful?
3. What's the best advice you have been given for handling anger?
4. If God takes a dim view of discrimination, how come a system like apartheid claimed a theological basis?
5. What is your experience with the power of a rumor?
6. Tell about an experience of reconciliation with someone that brought renewal in your relationship with God?

4

Sexual Purity

The announcement was made in a way undoubtedly calculated to result in maximum embarrassment. The year was 2005, and the state-run television news and current affairs program had just presented an exposé on a distasteful website in Germany, owned by a New Zealander. The site depicted young women and children in sexually explicit activities, as part of a "kiddie-porn" network. At the end of the presentation, the reporter stated that at least twenty-three New Zealanders were known to subscribe to this website. Identities of nine had been verified, along with the range of professions they represented. Then the bombshell. The reporter stated that one was a Baptist minister . . . and the show abruptly concluded! Whether or not this was the reporter or producer's intent, the way the revelation was left to hang put every Christian minister under an ominous cloud of suspicion.[1]

Given that thousands of people, from a range of different professional backgrounds, access dubious websites, why would a Christian minister rate a mention? No doubt the reason it was newsworthy was because Christians claim to live by different values. On issues like sexual morality, Christians assert a moral high ground. They seek to live by ethics God has laid down for his followers, and those who teach Christian

---

1. At the time, I was the CEO of the Baptist movement in New Zealand. I wrote to the producers of the program asking for further information. They declined to give it to me, however, on the following week's episode they did read out a letter from me stating that the Baptist movement takes this kind of accusation seriously and regards such behavior as abhorrent.

values are supposed to live exemplary lives. Deep shame and embarrassment are felt when high-profile Christian leaders fall morally. The impact of such failures on the name, the credibility of the church, and what it stands for, is devastating.

One of the tragic disappointments regarding the twenty-first century church is that it is increasingly hard to identify distinctive moral values compared to those who are not part of its ranks. Would that such blurring of distinction was due to non-Christians adopting biblical values. Rather, Christians are behaving more and more like those who are not. Ron Sider, in his challenging book, *"The Scandal of the Evangelical Conscience"*[2] suggests that the gap between born-again-Christians and irreligious people is pretty narrow when it comes to issues like pre- or extra-marital sex, divorce, abortion, racist attitudes, financial corruption, and materialism. Christians are just as bad as everyone else. Christ-followers have less and less right to claim the moral high ground.

Perhaps the need for clarity around a subject like sexual ethics is not as contemporary as people think. Two-thousand years ago, Jesus addressed the topic of sexual promiscuity head-on through his sermon on a Galilean hillside:

> [27]"You have heard that it was said, 'You shall not commit adultery.' [28]But I tell you that anyone who looks at a woman lustfully has already committed adultery with her in his heart. [29]If your right eye causes you to stumble, gouge it out and throw it away. It is better for you to lose one part of your body than for your whole body to be thrown into hell. [30]And if your right hand causes you to stumble, cut it off and throw it away. It is better for you to lose one part of your body than for your whole body to go into hell.
>
> Matthew 5:27–30

Religious leaders and teachers tended to treat the *Laws of Moses* with strict and pedantic legalism, believing God was pleased with those who kept or obeyed the law to the letter, and angry or judgmental toward those who broke it. They displayed religious pride about being able to say that they had not broken specific laws. They must, therefore, be righteous (i.e., in a right relationship) before God. On this, and a range of other topics, Jesus seemed to be saying: "Not so fast . . . maybe you haven't

---

2. Sider, *The Scandal of the Evangelical Conscience*.

broken the letter of the law, but what about the spirit behind it?" That was certainly his position with respect to the issue of adultery.

When Jesus talked about the subject of sexuality, it is safe to assume that most of his audience agreed that adultery was, in fact, a sin. Sexual connection with a person to whom you were not married was off-limits. It was prohibited by the seventh of the Ten Commandments that God gave to Moses:

> ¹⁴ You shall not commit adultery.
>
> Exodus 20:14

If Jesus were preaching his sermon on the Mount in our day and age, he might not make that kind of assumption! For a lot of people in western cultures, the topic of human sexuality is a non-issue. "What is the big deal; who is to say that boundaries on sexual activity between consenting adults are anyone else's business, let alone God's, or even relevant to talk about?" Many, even within the church, wonder if historical teaching on human sexuality is anachronistic and obsolete. God and sex do not usually make it into the same sentence. When Jesus talked about adultery being more than the physical act, at the very least the people listening to him had a uniform understanding of God's view on sexuality.

There is an important point to note upfront when beginning to look at this topic. Contrary to what some might think, the God of the Bible is not anti-sex. Some of those purporting to speak on his behalf, over the years, have not always given that impression. The fact is: sex was God's idea. In his creation of humanity, God made us sexual beings with God-given emotions and drives that find fulfilment in sexual expression. In contrast to other created beings, the human race was designed by God to enjoy sexual intimacy for more than just the purpose of procreation. That which might crudely be called "recreational sex," as an expression of intimacy between two people who love each other, was God's idea from the very beginning. Way back in the first book of the Bible, he expressed it like this:

> ²⁴For this reason a man will leave his father and mother and be united to his wife, and they will become one flesh.
>
> Genesis 2:24

Sexual intercourse, the literal meaning of "one flesh," is not carnal or dirty. It is something God designed as a beautiful and meaningful expression of mutual love. Actually, God went further still and suggested an ideal for the human race, whereby the expression of sexual intimacy finds its most profound meaning. Sex was designed by God to be enjoyed or experienced only within the confines of marriage. Sex is a beautiful, intimate expression of love and affection—that carries God's blessing—when it occurs between a couple committed to each other in marriage. Sexual encounters outside of marriage are less than God's ideal or plan and contravene his design. The same teaching carried over into the New Testament. For instance:

> [4]Marriage should be honored by all, and the marriage bed kept pure, for God will judge the adulterer and all the sexually immoral.
>
> Hebrews 13:4

To be clear, if the Bible is our primary resource for determining God's values, sex before marriage, or sex with someone who is not one's husband or wife, conflicts with God's plan for the human race. God is not a restrictive or punitive killjoy; his design for sex is much deeper than the physical connection of genitals. It is so much more than the mechanical act and was designed as a sacred expression of the love-bond between two people who are committed to each other for life. When sex happens before marriage, it cheapens or trivializes the nature of that sacred bond. And when sex happens with someone outside of marriage, it is hugely destructive and hurtful, fracturing the love-bond of trust and intimacy to which a married couple have committed themselves. It is not right. It is a defiant act of disobedience to the plan God had for his creation.

Maybe in Jesus' culture, such statements were unnecessary. In the twenty-first century, with its many competing voices on sexual ethics, there is a need for candor and clarity. Indeed, for some people, the teaching of the Bible on matters of sexual ethics is a stumbling block that causes them to question their resolve to follow Jesus. That kind of thing also happened in his day. There were people interested in following Jesus, who liked what he did, said and stood for . . . until he started saying things that conflicted with some of their lifestyle choices. Although some of them gave up on him at that point, others sought his help to change and align themselves with his values.

But then, Jesus made a statement about sex that was very different from the popular voices the people had heard. He suggested a more radical definition of adultery that would have surprised his original audience:

> ²⁸But I tell you that anyone who looks at a woman lustfully has already committed adultery with her in his heart.
>
> Matthew 5:27

Remember, Jesus is talking to people who probably thought adultery was not an issue for them; they had never done anything like that. After all, it was a capital offense for which one could be stoned to death! Adultery was a righteousness issue most felt comfortable they could put a check beside. Jesus, however, suggested that adultery is not merely the physical act. Outward action is simply the final phase of sin that begins in the heart or mind of a person. Looking lustfully upon another person is the same as taking them to bed and having sex with them.

Now, it is important to clarify something Jesus was *not* saying here. He was not saying that a natural physical attraction toward someone is sin, per se. Nor is he challenging our appreciation of beauty or good looks.[3] Jesus was talking about looking upon someone with lustful thoughts or sexual desire—mentally undressing them or imagining what it would be like to lie with them sexually. Lust describes those thoughts that linger and awaken sexual drives for the other person. It is the feeding of imagination with fantasies of sexual play. Such lustful thoughts and imaginings, Jesus said, are nothing less than actually committing adultery with that person.

One can only speculate about the looks on the faces of Jesus' original audience when he said this. Many had possibly been feeling comfortable and pleased with themselves; they were not guilty of this type of sin. But now Jesus seemed to suggest that if they had red blood in their veins, they were guilty of sin—no room for smug self-righteousness here!

This may have been an issue in the first century, but it would have to be acknowledged that it is becoming harder and harder in our contemporary age to avoid lustful thoughts. We live in a world that is increasingly and unapologetically sensual. Clothing is deliberately designed to draw attention to body shape and sexual desire, rather than to disguise it. Television, movies, commercials, and junk mail frequently feature nudity and people in erotic poses. How many times in an average TV night's viewing are couples observed in sexual poses? Sex on television is no longer under the covers—increasingly there are no covers! Then there is the ease of access to pornographic images on the internet; just a few clicks

---

3. Willard, *The Divine Conspiracy -Rediscovering our Hidden Life in God*, 184

away on a mouse button. At the risk of sounding frivolous, for most men in contemporary western cultures, to be not "turned on" by the amount of sex-plicit material that bombards them may well indicate a need for someone to check they still have a pulse!

How does one cope?

One approach might be to do what some Muslim cultures do. Taking as a principle the need for modesty, the culture places the blame for creating lustful thoughts in men onto the women, therefore the men keep their women covered up! If a man is tempted sexually, it must be because a woman is exposing too much of her flesh, and thereby luring him to lustful thoughts. We learned this living in the Muslim country of Bangladesh. The rationale we heard was, "the fire needs to be kept in the fireplace," so a woman should be covered from head to foot lest she is the cause of temptation to a man.[4] This approach is essentially blame-shifting. It is a bit like the pathetic excuse Adam gave back in the Garden of Eden over the infamous apple: "It is not my fault . . . the woman made me do it!"

Jesus' advice was unequivocally different. He suggested personal responsibility on the part of the person who is tempted. In essence, he counseled a proactive response rather than reactive:

> [29]If your right eye causes you to stumble, gouge it out and throw it away. It is better for you to lose one part of your body than for your whole body to be thrown into hell. [30]And if your right hand causes you to stumble, cut it off and throw it away. It is better for you to lose one part of your body than for your whole body to go into hell.
>
> Matthew 5:29–30

Now, what on earth was Jesus suggesting here? If his broader definition of adultery gave cause for pause, this remediation strategy seemed incredibly severe. Was he really talking about the mutilation of bodies? One young man some years back, who possibly had mental health issues as well, read these words and took Jesus literally. He had a problem with sexual fantasy and took Jesus seriously enough to emasculate himself! Is that really what Jesus was suggesting should be done, or was he talking more figuratively?

---

4. Historically true in European culture (e.g. displaying an ankle) and not unlike the imposition of responsibility for rape being the clothing, unaccompanied state, or unwise behavior of the victim today.

Obviously, Jesus was not talking about literally cutting off a hand or plucking out an eye. He was talking about removing the source of temptation. If certain things in a person's life tend to lead them to disobey God's values, or act as a stumbling block, be ruthless and cut such things out of their lives.

The Greek word translated in our English Bibles as "cause to stumble" (*skandalon*) is interesting. It describes the "bait stick" in a trap for animals.[5] A "bait stick" is the stick or arm on which bait is fixed that lures an animal into a trap. It is the stick that holds the cheese that the mouse stands on and triggers the trap to fall on its neck. Or if capturing a person, it describes the line laid across the pathway that they catch their feet on, tripping them up and causing them to fall into the trap. It became a metaphor for something that caused a person to stumble or to be tripped up. The English word "scandal" comes from the same root, as in when a person is tripped up in moral failure.

What Jesus was saying was quite simple. Get rid of the "bait sticks" in one's life. Destroy or remove those things that act as a lure toward temptation. In the same way as plucking out an eye or cutting off a hand is a ruthless, radical action, so be ruthless and radical in pruning those things that provide a source for temptation or stumbling.

When Jesus talked about the eye and the hand, he was probably alluding to a well-understood analogy. There was a saying amongst the Jewish Rabbis: "The eyes and the hands are the two brokers of sin."[6] The eyes are the medium through which temptation comes, and the hand is the instrument through which the action is committed. Both are crucial elements in the act of sin.

Several practical applications might be considered when taking Jesus' advice as worthy principles to live by. Maybe there are friendships a person has which influences them to the extent that they inevitably end up doing what they know is wrong. Might it be better to cut off that friendship and be lonely than to have lots of friends now but spend eternity in hell? Does a place of employment offer an unreasonable risk of temptation? In the same way that it would be plain stupid for an alcoholic to get a job at a brewery or a liquor store, a person's choice of career or employment might provide an unreasonable lure toward corruption and sin. Might Jesus suggest it is better to be unemployed now than to have

---

5. Vine, *An Expository Dictionary of New Testament Words*, .801
6. Barclay, *The Gospel of Matthew, Volume 1*, 147

full employment in this life but spend eternity in hell? If a man cannot control his thought life every time he goes to the beach and sees women in skimpy bathing suits, maybe he ought to cut out going to the beach. Better to sacrifice a suntan than to spend eternity roasting in hell.

When Jesus taught his disciples how to pray, he encouraged them to include the following request: "LORD, lead us not into temptation."[7] It is an excellent prayer to pray but be careful lest God respond: "I am not the one leading you into temptation . . . you are doing that well enough on your own!" Maybe there are lifestyle choices that need to be made so that the Christ-follower stops putting him or herself in a position where they are likely to be tempted. According to Jesus, sin is not merely the physical action a person takes, but the thoughts entertained in his or her heart. A person does not commit adultery at the point of which bodies touch in intimacy. Adultery begins first with entertained thoughts; if there are areas of weakness you have or situations where temptation is more significant, for goodness sake, take affirmative action. It is far better to avoid or cease actions that bring pleasure now than to let them destroy the life promised to you in the future.

In closing this chapter, a pastoral note is called for, since this was possibly the intent behind Jesus' words. Remember, Jesus was speaking to people who had been taught that righteousness with God was all about keeping rules. And no doubt his broader definition of adultery was intended to knock some people off their self-righteous perch as many more were judged guilty than first thought. What is to be done with that kind of revelation? Given that sin muddies or blurs a relationship with God, what does a person do with the revelation that he or she has been tripped up by cerebral adultery? Some reading this book may have gone even further, perhaps causing the break-up of a marriage? Is God then perpetually angry with them? Have they crossed a line from which there is no return? The answer to such a question must be a resounding: *"No!"* . . . As long as they are admitting they have disobeyed the values God calls us to live by and are honestly seeking God's help. No one, without exception, is beyond the reach of God's grace and mercy. The revelation of God that Jesus portrayed is one of love and compassion toward those who admit they have fallen short of his standards, and who seek his help to stop doing those things they know are wrong.

---

7. Matthew 6:13

That said, some have assumed, incorrectly, that a God of grace merely turns a blind eye toward sinful behavior. As if grace means there now is no such thing as sin. But that is not what the Bible teaches at all. Such a notion is the kind of misunderstanding that Dietrich Bonheoffer referred to as "cheap grace" when he wrote of forgiveness without repentance or communion without confession or baptism without discipline.[8] The Bible teaches that grace and mercy follow confession and repentance. There is endless, limitless, repetitive grace toward those who admit their falling short, but confession and repentance are the keys that unlock that door.

There are strong statements in the New Testament about God's judgment upon those who deviate from God's values—whether sexual sin, financial fraud or even slander and gossip. But that judgment is not for those who merely fall or fail. It is for those who are wilfully defiant—who know better but defy God's advice. There is a difference between weakness and defiance. All people are sinners and susceptible to weakness and failure. That never justifies wrong behavior, but God loves unconditionally and understands the human predicament. He lived in a human body also. It was Jesus who did not condemn the woman caught in adultery but told her to "Go now and leave your life of sin."[9] And when a person turns to him and asks his forgiveness, he forgives their sin and cleanses them from unrighteousness. The judgment passages in the Bible are not for those who admit their weakness or who struggle to live up to God's standards. The judgment passages are for those who stand defiant and who tell God, in effect, that he is wrong! Their actions or behaviors are not what condemns them, but their defiance is an altogether different matter.

On the contrary, the words of hope that the apostle John wrote are what the Christ-follower holds on to:

> [9]If we confess our sins, he is faithful and just and will forgive us our sins and purify us from all unrighteousness.
>
> 1 John 1:9

And for those who think they are still guiltless on a subject like sexual sin, be careful that you do not indulge in the equally heinous sin of self-righteousness. Or as the famous preacher, F. B. Meyer once said: "When we see a brother or sister in sin there are two things we do not

---

8. Bonhoeffer, *The Cost of Discipleship*, 47
9. John 8:11

know. First, we do not know how hard he or she tried not to sin, and second, we do not know the power of the forces that assailed him or her. We also do not know what we would have done in the same circumstances."[10]

---

10. Brown, *Christianity Today*, April 5, 1993, 17.

SMALL GROUP DISCUSSION QUESTIONS

Matthew 5:27–30

1. Why do you think the gap between the (moral) behavior of Christians and non-Christians is not that wide these days?
2. Do the morals portrayed in the media (TV, movies, books) merely reflect societal values on an issue like sexuality, or are they shaping them?
3. Why do you think the Bible makes such a big issue about sexuality?
4. What does a verse like 1 Corinthians 10:13 communicate to you?
5. How would you respond to the person who says that viewing pornographic material is a victimless pastime?
6. What are some specific, concrete steps that we can take to avoid the temptation to lust?

5

The Ugliness of Divorce

It was a Wednesday evening. Our family was seated around the table, enjoying our evening meal. At the time, our children were ten, seven, and two years of age. Our second son nonchalantly looked at us and asked matter-of-factly, "Mum and Dad, when are you going to get *your* divorce?" My wife and I looked at each other, nonplussed, and wondered from where on earth, this question had come. We could not think of any conflicts between us that he might have overheard. Our instant response, of course, was "Never!" We assured him of our love and commitment to each other as his parents, which he took at face value, and then kept on eating his dinner. We think what had prompted the question was news that parents of school friends were separating and divorcing. To his young mind, these were not unusual family dynamics and therefore, were something he could anticipate happening in his family at some stage in the future.

The next verses in Jesus' *Sermon on the Mount* are confronting, particularly for those who have experienced the pain of marriage breakdown.

> [31]"It has been said, 'Anyone who divorces his wife must give her a certificate of divorce.' [32]But I tell you that anyone who divorces his wife, except for sexual immorality, makes her the victim of adultery, and anyone who marries a divorced woman commits adultery.
>
> Matthew 5:31–32

Expositional preachers will understand that one of the great things about systematically preaching a series through a book of the Bible, is that when tricky or contentious subject-matter arises, no one can point the finger and claim the preacher is targeting them in particular. It is merely the next passage in the series. One of the not-so-great things about working systematically through a book of the Bible is that tricky or contentious topics cannot be skipped or avoided! These words of Jesus are important for all Christ-followers to understand, even if they are a little uncomfortable.

Once again, Jesus couches his comments in light of oral teaching people have received about the *Law of Moses*: "It has been said . . ." Ordinary people of that day did not have access to the Old Testament Scriptures for themselves. They relied on what others told them the *Law* said, which was problematic because those doing the oral teaching were prone to take broad Scriptural principles and turn them into pedantic rules and regulations. People had a general idea of what the Scriptures taught, but in many instances, it was skewed and had become heavily legalistic.

Actually, something similar can occur today also, especially with particular moral issues that the Bible addresses—such as the subject of divorce and remarriage. Many assume they know all that the Bible has to say about this, based on what they have heard from others. While the Bible is readily available to all, too many approach it superficially and fail to understand, nor inquire into, the original context or historical backdrop behind the words that the writers of Scripture recorded. To be sure, many commentators lament disturbing biblical illiteracy in the contemporary church, but equally concerning are those churches and Christ-followers who can quote or cite the Bible, but with next to no exegetical understanding of the original life situations that a particular passage was addressing. Evangelical Christianity is apt to defend biblical authority, but on the whole, has alarmingly poor hermeneutical skills in mining biblical truth appropriately for a contemporary world. Verses are quoted out of context, and simplistic answers cited for deep and complex life issues.

All of this is to suggest that in the twenty-first century, Jesus might well say to this generation: "You have heard that it was said . . . ," as he did in his own day.

When it comes to grappling with Jesus' teaching on divorce and remarriage, context needs to be carefully considered. While many Christ-followers are convinced they know the Bible's position on divorce; it is all quite simple or cut and dried. The go-to passage quoted is *Malachi 2:16*, typically from the *Revised Standard Version (RSV)* of the Bible:

> ¹⁶"I hate divorce," says the LORD the God of Israel . . .

In other words, the case is made . . . problem solved . . . divorce is something God hates and, frankly, there is not a lot else to say. However, other Bible translations offer a slightly fuller rendition of that particular statement in Malachi 2. Take the *New International Version*, for instance:

> ¹⁶"The man who hates and divorces his wife," says the LORD, the God of Israel, "does violence to the one he should protect," says the LORD Almighty.

Same verse; slightly different nuance. Now, the point being made here is *not* to suggest that God does not hate or disapprove of divorce. Rather, that care is necessary when quoting a single verse out of context like this, so that heavy condemnation (intentional or otherwise) is not brought to bear on those who have struggled to live up to God's standard. More than a few divorced people have been made to feel that they are hated by God on account of their marriage failure.

To express this another way, there are many other things that God hates as much as divorce. God hates all sin, including the sins of gossip and slander, fraud and deceptive business dealings, oppression of the poor, materialism and greed. Bible-believing evangelicals have sometimes singled out and hurled judgmental rocks in response to certain "moral" sins, while at the same time ignoring other sinful behaviors on display within their spiritual glass houses!

While it may be true that God hates, or severely dislikes, divorce, it must also be acknowledged that God continues to love and care for those people who have been divorced. Those of us who never have had to face the pain of a marriage break-up, should tread carefully and avoid making simplistic judgments regarding the parties involved.

Statistics on marriage breakdown in the twenty-first century do not make for pretty reading, particularly within the developed world. The rate of divorce within the Christian church is also far from flattering. The Christian moral high-ground does not appear all that high. The same was true for the people of Jesus' day. Indeed, the time at which Christianity entered the Roman, Greek, and Hebrew world, has been described as a unique period in history when the marriage bond stood in the greatest peril of destruction.[1] It is essential to understand this particular context which Jesus was addressing.

The Hebrew world of Jesus day was increasingly influenced by Greek and Roman culture. Amongst the pagans, marriage and sexual faithfulness between a married couple, was pretty loosely adhered to. Women had few rights, and men were mostly free—even encouraged—to enjoy sexual liaisons with other women at will. Greek and Roman philosophers went on record suggesting: "We have courtesans for the sake of pleasure; we have concubines for the sake of daily cohabitation; we have wives for the purposes of having children legitimately, and of having a faithful guardian for all our household affairs."[2] In short, sexual fidelity in marriage was not a big issue.

Marriage, amongst the Jewish community at that time, was not hugely different from their Greek and Roman neighbors. However, their eyes were blinded by the belief that there was not a race that honored marriage more seriously than they did. Marriage was deemed a sacred duty for a man and something they were bound to undertake. The only valid reason for a Jewish man to be unmarried was because he was devoting himself to study of the *Law* or had a highly contagious illness. A single man's existence created questions and was generally regarded as a breach of the commandment to be fruitful and multiply.[3] No doubt this was an accusation the bachelor Jesus, and his parents, would have had to answer as well.

At the time of Jesus ministry, there was a substantial gender-power differential within marriage. All the power was essentially in the hands of the husband. If the relationship turned sour, it was only possible for a woman to divorce her husband if he agreed to it. Men seldom did this because that would mean admitting indiscretion on their part. That cloth, however, did not cut both ways. A man could divorce his wife at will, citing a statement such as the one Moses made in Deuteronomy 24:1:

> [1]If a man marries a woman who becomes displeasing to him because he finds something indecent about her, and he writes her a certificate of divorce, gives it to her and sends her from his house . . .

---

1. Barclay, *The Gospel of Matthew, Volume 1*, 150
2. Demosthenes, as quoted by Barclay, *The Gospel of Matthew, Volume 1*, 153
3. Barclay, *The Gospel of Matthew, Volume 2*, 196

Just like that! The marriage was canceled, and the now-former wife had to move out. A translation of an ancient divorce certificate went something like this: "Let this be from me your writ of divorce and letter of dismissal and deed of liberation, that you may now marry whatsoever man you choose..."[4] All a man had to do was hand such a document to his wife, in the presence of two witnesses, and the marriage was terminated.

In reading Jesus' commentary on a subject like divorce it is crucial to do so with first-century middle-eastern eyes. It was a particularly deplorable situation for women. There was no single-parent pension or child support for the divorced woman. There would have been a degree of shame surrounding her divorce and shunning by others in the family or local community. The divorced woman was often impoverished, and the only likely scenario for survival was for her to marry again, and probably to someone down a few rungs on the social ladder.

Around the time of Jesus, the situation was further exacerbated by a theological debate between two schools of Jewish thought amongst religious leaders of the day. One school centered around the teaching of a prominent rabbi, Shammai (50 BC-30 AD), who took a stricter interpretation of the *Law of Moses*. The other school gathered around another influential rabbi, Hillel, who died in 10 AD at the (supposed) ripe old age of 120. Both of these men were profoundly influential in the development of the detailed legal interpretation of the *Law of Moses* that the people were taught orally by the Scribes and the Pharisees.

On the matter of divorce, and what might constitute a wife's crime of being "displeasing" or "indecent" in the eyes of her husband, these two men landed on different interpretations. The Shammai school was strict and austere; the Hillel school more liberal, generous, and broadminded. Shammai said that the definition of indecency was sexual immorality or adultery. That, he said, was the only grounds for legitimate divorce. Hillel, on the other hand, suggested a man could accuse his wife of indecency if she did things like: spoiling his dinner by putting too much salt in it; talking to men in the streets; being troublesome and quarrelsome; going out in public without her head covered, or speaking disrespectfully of her husband's parents.[5] Another famous rabbi (a few years after the time of Shammai and Hillel) suggested a cause of indecency, as grounds for divorce, might be that a man finds another woman whom he considers

---

4. Barclay, *The Gospel of Matthew*, Volume 1, 151
5. Barclay, *The Gospel of Matthew*, Volume 1, 152

to be more attractive. In other words, all the trump cards were all in the hands of the husband. If he developed a "snit" with his wife (or felt attracted to another woman), he could easily engineer a case for indecency. In today's legal parlance, it might be labeled as "irreconcilable differences" or "no-fault" divorce. Around the time of Jesus, the dominant view amongst religious scholars and teachers favored Hillel over Shammai, which resulted in rampant divorce.

It was into this kind of situation that Jesus offers an opinion as to how the *Law of Moses* should be interpreted. The two verses cited above from the *Sermon on the Mount* are one of two occasions where Jesus weighed into this debate. The other is Matthew 19, where religious teachers tried to trap Jesus into saying something they could condemn. How can Jesus' advice be summed up? Firstly, he takes a swipe at the popular understanding of the day:

> [31]"It has been said, 'Anyone who divorces his wife must give her a certificate of divorce'...
>
> Matthew 5:31

As he does in other sections of his famous sermon, it is as if he were saying: "Hold on a minute, there is a whole lot more to the ending of a marriage than a man merely giving his wife a certificate." Perhaps he had just watched a divorce certificate being handed to a wife, or maybe a woman had come to him in this desperate circumstance. In any case, he was challenging the teaching religious leaders were giving as being a little truncated or incomplete. Marriage, said Jesus, is not to be treated lightly or flippantly. It is not something that can be concluded by a legal document produced on the flimsy whim of a selfish husband. Marriage is a sacred bond between a man and a woman that is supposed to last until death separates them. An easy or no-fault divorce may be possible in the warped legal framework of any culture, but that is not what God prescribed in his guidelines for living.

Implicit in Jesus' comments is a defense of women, who were hugely disadvantaged in the culture of his day. It was not right in the eyes of God for women to be mistreated and made vulnerable to the emotions and chauvinistic behavior of their husbands. Dallas Willard describes it more graphically:

> "For the woman ... there were only three realistic possibilities in Jesus' day. She might find a place in the home of a generous

> relative, but usually on grudging terms and as little more than a servant. She might find a man who would marry her, but always as 'damaged goods' and sustained in a degraded relationship. Or she might, finally, make a place in a community as a prostitute. Society would not then, as ours does today, support a divorced woman to any degree or allow her to support herself in a decent fashion."[6]

It might even be said that Jesus was the prototype feminist who stood up for equality and parity between men and women. He honored women, arguing that they were deserving of the same justice and fairness accorded men; he considered them co-equal partners.

The second issue Jesus addressed was the sanctity and permanence of the marriage relationship.

> [32]But I tell you that anyone who divorces his wife, except for sexual immorality, makes her the victim of adultery, and anyone who marries a divorced woman commits adultery.
>
> Matthew 5:32

What was Jesus saying here? Some have wondered whether he was aligning himself with the Shammai school of legal interpretation, suggesting the only legitimate grounds for divorce was sexual immorality. He may have been doing just that. But perhaps he was also imparting his understanding of Jewish law, that suggested divorce was actually unavoidable, some even believed it compulsory, when a case of adultery occurs. It is the act of sexual immorality which effectively severs or destroys the marriage, rather than the issuing of a certificate. The consequence, therefore, of making a divorced woman destitute or cast-out, for reasons other than adultery, effectively forced her to marry again in order to survive—which meant now she and her new husband technically fell into the category of adulterers.

On the other occasion where Jesus talks about divorce (Matthew 19) he lifts the debate above the arguments between the schools of Shammai and Hillel and points people back to the permanence of the marriage bond:

> [4]"Haven't you read," he replied, "that at the beginning the Creator 'made them male and female,' [5]and said, 'For this reason a man will leave his father and mother and be united to his wife,

---

6. Willard, *The Divine Conspiracy -Rediscovering our Hidden Life in God*, 191

and the two will become one flesh'? ⁶So they are no longer two, but one flesh. Therefore what God has joined together, let no one separate."

Matthew 19:4–6

In other words, rather than looking for sufficient reasons to justify the break-up of a marriage, in order to avoid the judgment of God and others, prioritize God's ideal—the permanence of this relationship, until death separates. This was Jesus' counsel and advice. Marriage was never meant to be situationally contingent, nor based on emotion and sentimental feelings.

Despite all of this, the fact remains that some marriages do fail. On the one hand, it is important to uphold the standard of God's word and promote the ideal. On the other hand, it is equally important to acknowledge that living in a sinful, fallen world means that no one attains God's standard all of the time. There must be a pastoral response of love toward the sinner. God is not taken by surprise when people—especially his followers—fail and fall. He knows their hearts and the struggles they embrace. His love and compassion are not reserved for sinless people but perhaps abounds all the more for those who confess and repent of their sin.

Very rarely is the break-up of a marriage caused by only one party. Sometimes in anger or hurt, one party may put all the blame onto the other, but this is almost always unfair. It takes two to forge a marriage, and it usually takes two to tear it apart. What, then, is the future for the Christ-follower who fails in reaching God's ideal for marriage? Surely, the God of the Bible is in the business of restoring repentant sinners and putting broken people back together again. To that end, it is hard to reconcile the notion that a repentant divorcee must be kept at arms-length within the church or relegated to a B-Grade Christianity. Yet that is the experience (literal or perceived) of many divorcees. Is divorce any more black of a sin than others, which every person is guilty of, from time to time? It certainly must not be classified as an unpardonable sin. God may hate divorce, but he unequivocally still loves divorced people—just as much as he does those who are married, single, or widowed.

Perhaps the challenge for those who have been divorced might be undertaking a meaningful act of repentance. Regardless of whose sin initiated, or exacerbated, the breakdown of the marriage, surely there is a case for an unconditional apology and asking of forgiveness—even years after the fact? It won't necessarily restore the relationship. Marriage and divorce are mutually exclusive states in law and the eyes of God. While a couple is still legally married, they are married; and once a couple is divorced, they are no longer husband and wife. Maybe for some, there lingers deep hurt and resentment toward the partner to whom they used to be married. However, before God, might there be room for ending hostility and seek as much restoration of the relationship as is possible? Maybe a phone call, a letter, or a face-to-face visit, that accepts personal responsibility and projects humility from a God-like conscience.

Some may say that it is all very well for someone who has never been through the pain of divorce to suggest this approach. And maybe there are layers or stages of forgiveness and restoration that could take time to accomplish. However, this will inevitably be God's intention (or family characteristic) for his children. To be sure, this chapter has barely scratched the surface of divorce and remarriage. Marriages are complex and dynamic relationships that require commitment and effort. Their foundation is so much deeper than emotions and feelings. The love that binds a marriage together must be seen as more of a *verb* than a *noun*. It is less a subjective feeling, and more a tangible action. It is less reactive and more proactive. The love that God sheds abroad in the hearts of his followers, by the Holy Spirit,[7] gives us the power to love the unlovely, rather than only those who love us back. Is it too trite and condescending, therefore, to suggest that if God can command and enable people to love their enemies, he can surely give them the ability to love those we committed to in marriage?

The issue in most marriage breakdowns surely traces back to unforgiveness. Sometimes the sin that needs to be forgiven is broad and deep and immensely hurtful. Nevertheless, there is the case for suggesting that those who do not forgive others have a short memory given how much they have expected God to forgive them. There might just be a *quid pro quo* when it comes to forgiveness.

George W. Crane was an American psychologist, physician, and a syndicated newspaper columnist who worked extensively in the field of marriage and defining compatible relationships. He told the story of a wife who came to see him full of hatred toward her husband. "I don't only want to get rid of him, I want to get even. Before I divorce him, I want to hurt him as much as he has hurt me."

---

7. Romans 5:5

Dr. Crane suggested she, "Go home and act as if you really loved your husband. Tell him how much he means to you. Praise him for every decent trait. Go out of your way to be as kind, considerate and generous as possible. Spare no efforts to please him, to enjoy him. Make him believe you love him. After you have convinced him of your undying love, and that you cannot live without him, then drop the bomb. Tell him you are getting a divorce. That will really hurt him."

With revenge in her eyes, she smiled and exclaimed, "Beautiful, beautiful. Will he ever be surprised!" And she set about to do it with enthusiasm—acting "as if." For two months, she showed love, kindness, listening, giving, reinforcing, sharing. When she did not return, Dr. Crane called her. "Are you ready now to go through with the divorce?"

"Divorce?" she exclaimed. "Never! I discovered that I really do love him." Her actions had changed her feelings. Motion resulted in emotion. The ability to love is established not so much by fervent promise, as often repeated deeds.[8]

---

8. Petersen, *The Myth of the Greener Grass*.

SMALL GROUP DISCUSSION QUESTIONS

Matthew 5:31–32

1. Why do you think God places such a strong emphasis on the permanence of marriage?
2. In what kinds of situations might the failure of a marriage be okay?
3. What do you consider to be the reason(s) so many marriages today are failing?
4. What advice would you like to offer a newly married couple?
5. What kinds of things work best in keeping a marriage healthy and alive?
6. Why do you think some Christians are harder on the issue of divorce than they are on other moral issues? What experience have you had/seen of this?
7. In your opinion, what is the most helpful thing Christians can say or do to help marriages in our society last and flourish?

6

Honest Talk

At the beginning of the twenty-first century *Wikipedia* defined honesty as: ". . . a facet of moral character and connotes positive and virtuous attributes such as integrity, truthfulness, and straightforwardness along with the absence of lying, cheating or theft. Honesty also involves being trustworthy, loyal, fair, and sincere."[1]

In the late 1980s, in Columbus, Ohio an armed car overturned spilling $2million onto the freeway. Only $400,000 was recovered. The rest disappeared amongst the crowds of people who stopped and scooped up the cash. Some people were honest enough to return what was not theirs: A person by the name of Malvern Kaiser gave back $57,000.[2] Apparently, in situations like this if a person knows the one who loses money, they generally return it; if they do not know them, 75 percent of the time they are more likely to keep the cash.

A similar scenario occurred in 1988. A low paid restaurant waiter found a briefcase containing a large amount of cash in a parking lot—no owner in sight. No one saw the waiter find it and put it in his car in the early hours of the morning. However, for the waiter, there was never any question as to what he should do. He took the briefcase home, opened it, and searched for the owner's identity. The next day he made a few phone calls, located the distressed owner and returned the briefcase, along with the $25,000 cash that it contained! The surprising thing about this episode was the ridicule the waiter experienced at the hands of his friends

1. https://en.wikipedia.org/wiki/Honesty
2. Source unknown . . . but a great story!

and peers. For the next week or so he was called a variety of names and laughed at, all because he possessed a quality the Bible holds in high regard: integrity.[3]

Jesus spoke about honesty and called his followers to raise the bar on integrity with regard to the words people speak and the promises they make:

> [33]"Again, you have heard that it was said to the people long ago, 'Do not break your oath, but fulfill to the LORD the vows you have made.' [34]But I tell you, do not swear an oath at all: either by heaven, for it is God's throne; [35]or by the earth, for it is his footstool; or by Jerusalem, for it is the city of the Great King. [36]And do not swear by your head, for you cannot make even one hair white or black. [37]All you need to say is simply 'Yes,' or 'No'; anything beyond this comes from the evil one.
>
> Matthew 5:33–37

To fully grasp what Jesus was saying here, first-century Middle Eastern context and culture needs to be understood. The concept of honesty, swearing an oath, or making a solemn promise, was serious business in the time of Jesus. It all stemmed from the *Law of Moses* and the Ninth Commandment:

> [16]You shall not give false testimony against your neighbor.
>
> Exodus 20:16

In other words, do not tell lies, exaggerate the truth, or hide the whole truth. This included a prohibition on the telling of a blatant untruth and *also* telling only a half-truth or giving limited information resulting in a false impression.

Around the time of Jesus, there were several sayings amongst Jewish rabbis on the issue of truthfulness and honesty:

"The world stands fast on three things: On justice, on truth, and on peace."

"Four persons are shut out from the presence of God: the scoffer, the hypocrite, the liar, and the slanderer."

"One who has given his word and who changes it is as bad as an idolater.[4]

---

3. *Today In The Word*, July 1989, p.18
4. Barclay, *The Gospel of Matthew, Volume 1*, 158

Another particularly stringent brand of teaching suggested truthfulness even to the point of rudeness or discourtesy. For example, refusing to compliment a young bride for looking charming and beautiful on her wedding day, if in fact, she did not! Or the casual response: "Fine thanks!" when a person is asked how they are although in reality they are having a terrible day! Some of the stricter religious teachers of Jesus' day would call that a lie. (Of course, there are times when not being candidly truthful is the lesser of two evils, like when a wife asks her husband: "Honey, does this dress make me look fat!" The absolutely truthful answer might be: "No, honey, it's your fat that makes you look fat." But it is probably smarter to leave the room or go for a walk than answer a question like that . . .)

One of the mechanisms for guaranteeing the truthfulness of what a person said, in Jesus day, was the formal swearing of an oath. It essentially intensified the consequences of being untruthful. The idea was rooted in the Third Commandment:

> 7"You shall not misuse the name of the LORD your God, for the LORD will not hold anyone guiltless who misuses his name."
>
> Exodus 20:7

Many have misinterpreted the Third Commandment as referring to use of the name of the LORD as a profanity. For example, when uttered on experiencing a fright, hitting one's finger with a hammer, or as an extra emphasis of delight. While such language is inappropriate, and perhaps might be extrapolated from the commandment, the original meaning had more to do with using God's name to verify a statement. A person invoked the name of God as a witness or guarantor that he or she was being truthful and honest. For instance: "In God's name I declare that I am telling the truth about . . ." which in an idiomatic sense meant: "If you do not accept my word go and ask God." If God's name was used within a statement or promise, he became an additional party in the transaction. Or to use a banking metaphor, he became like a guarantor on a loan from the bank.

The other implication of the third commandment was that when a person invoked the name of God in making an oath or a promise, they had better be sure they really were being honest and truthful. It is one thing to hoodwink a fellow human being but messing with God's good name or character is something else! To break such an oath would be misusing the name of the LORD or taking it in vain. Not only is the oath-breaker discredited; so also, is God whom they have made a partner in the promise.

In the world of Jesus' day, swearing an oath, in the name of the LORD, was a serious deal. In all matters, they were supposed to be totally truthful; if they swore an oath, they were to be doubly so. A number of statements in the Old Testament underscore this:

> ¹²Do not swear falsely by my name and so profane the name of your God. I am the LORD.
>
> Leviticus 19:12

> ²When a man makes a vow to the LORD or takes an oath to obligate himself by a pledge, he must not break his word but must do everything he said.
>
> Numbers 30:2

> ²¹If you make a vow to the LORD your God, do not be slow to pay it, for the LORD your God will certainly demand it of you and you will be guilty of sin. ²²But if you refrain from making a vow, you will not be guilty.
>
> Deuteronomy 23:21–22

Perhaps a contemporary situation might be the vows and promises made in a wedding service. A man and woman joining together in marriage will undoubtedly have told each other many times before the day of their wedding that they intend to love and honor each other for the rest of their lives. Yet, there is something more sacred and binding about making those same promises before, or in the presence of, God and witnesses. Likewise, the oath taken by a witness in court, where they swear to tell the truth, the whole truth, and nothing but the truth. Vows made to or before God are regarded as particularly binding.

This was the concept behind oaths or promises that Jesus was discussing. But then he made a statement that seems to cut across the whole idea of swearing an oath:

> ²⁴ . . . But I tell you, do not swear at all.

What was the background to this? It was another occasion where the popular oral teaching about God's values may have been lost in translation. By the time of Jesus, there were two areas where the practice of swearing an oath had become something of a farce. The first is what one commentator calls *frivolous swearing*.[5] People were making oaths or formal vows when no such oath was necessary or proper. They would swear an oath over the pettiest things, with the collateral effect of diluting or watering down a genuinely sacred promise. Perhaps a contemporary example might be: "In God's name, I promise to buy a bottle of milk on my way home from work tonight" or "As God is my judge, I will mow the lawns on Saturday afternoon!" The concept of an oath depicting something significant and important was cheapened through being used frivolously. Language of solemnity and the sacred, used for the wrong purpose, lost its significance.

The second way that people were misrepresenting the concept of an oath is what might be termed *evasive swearing*.[6] Over the years, Jewish thinking had begun to differentiate between different types of oaths and promises. The general principle of endeavoring to be truthful and honest remained, but in the strict and ludicrous legalism leading up to the time of Jesus, a series of escape clauses and a hierarchy of oath-taking had been introduced. Some oaths were deemed absolutely binding, while others might allow for wriggle room. An oath that invoked the name of God was definitely binding. Such a vow or promise had to be honored. However, those oaths that succeeded in evading or avoiding the name of God specifically were supposedly not quite so binding. A person might be able to wriggle out of that obligation. Remember the little saying children say: "Cross my heart, hope to die, stick a needle in my eye . . ." The invitation to a painful punishment vouched for their truthfulness, but later they reveal that when they made that promise, they had their fingers crossed behind their back, which somehow released them from the promise.

A ridiculous situation had developed, which Jesus alludes to in verses 34 and 36, where people were making vows in the name of "heaven," or by the "earth," or by "Jerusalem," or by one's "head." Because the name of God was not explicitly referenced, when the crunch came, people felt they could break their promise. God was not personally named in the transaction; therefore, it was not binding.

---

5. Barclay, *The Gospel of Matthew, Volume 1*, 159
6. Barclay, *The Gospel of Matthew, Volume 1*, 159

Jesus was saying that in the realm of God's kingdom: this is not right. Three specific and timeless applications emerge from what Jesus said on this subject of integrity in our speech:

1. ALWAYS KEEP THE PROMISES WE MAKE

When we say we will do something, we should follow through and do it. When we claim to be telling the truth, we should tell the whole truth. The idea of only having to fulfil a promise that invokes the name of God was rejected by Jesus. That is not the way of his kingdom. To use a legal analogy, it would be a bit like saying verbal promises or statements of intent are not enforceable and only those contracts made in writing are binding. Actually, there is no difference in law between a verbal agreement and a written one; they both carry the same weight. The difficulty with an oral contract is that it is more difficult to prove what was agreed to, whereas a written agreement is easier to substantiate. For those who follow Jesus, there ought to be no difference between written and spoken promises. If we say that we are going to do something our commitment is binding.

As a young pastor, a couple from our church was preparing for ministry and studying at a seminary. It was a huge struggle for them financially. They had friends who told them they had become convinced God was asking them to provide financial support. They had an old bus they wanted to sell, and made a promise that when it sold, they would give the proceeds to pay the seminary fees of their friends. For several months the bus did not sell, but when it did the couple selling it changed their minds as to what they would do with the proceeds. They said that God had told them to put the money to another use and they reneged on their promise. The couple studying at the seminary were understandably devastated.

According to Jesus: a promise is a promise, and an oath is an oath. Whether in writing or by invoking the name of God, in the presence of a hundred witnesses or none, it does not matter. For the man or woman who follows Jesus, their word is their bond.

2. DO NOT COMPARTMENTALIZE YOUR LIFE

That is what the people of Jesus day were doing. They were saying that some aspects of their life were "God-parts," and others were "ordinary." In those parts that involved or invoked God, a different level of integrity was required—different rules for various situations. They differentiated between promises or commitments that invoked the name of God from those that did not. If they swore an oath in the name of the LORD, they did not want to cross him, so there was greater motivation to follow through or be honest. However, if God was not explicitly mentioned or involved in the wording of the original contract, their motivation for honesty and integrity was lessened. It is as if their lives were represented by a series of pigeon-holes or compartments, signifying different aspects of their being. In those compartments that mentioned God, they were honest and spiritual; in those that did not mention God, they behaved differently.

Sadly, some Christians are like the little chameleon lizard that changes its color to blend in with the surrounding environment, to avoid being noticed. When a chameleon is on a green leaf, its body appears green; on a brown tree trunk, its body appears brown. For Christian chameleons, when in the presence of God or God's people they are spiritual and godly, however, in the secular world of business, sport, politics or their local neighborhood their behavior is altogether different. If God is not directly involved, they behave differently.

When Jesus talked about heaven being God's throne, earth his footstool, Jerusalem his holy city, or our head as the source of human life, the point he was making was that God is present and active in all areas of our being. There is no such thing as "sacred" or "secular." For the follower of Jesus, everything is sacred, because God is intimately involved in everything they do. He is with them in all life's compartments and pigeon-holes. They do not honor God in the "God-parts" and dishonor their commitments or lower their integrity in, say, their business environment. Wherever they go, and whatever they do, they behave as if Jesus is with them.

3. SACRED OATHS ARE NOT NECESSARY

[37] All you need to say is simply 'Yes,' or 'No'; anything beyond this comes from the evil one.

Matthew 5:37

Some have interpreted Jesus saying it is wrong, even sinful, for Christians to swear an oath in the name of God or on the Bible. Based on this verse, they refuse to swear an oath in a court of law or at a formal investiture ceremony. Jesus, they say, forbade such action. But that was not Jesus' intention. He was not so much forbidding the making of an oath, as suggesting that they are unnecessary as a motivation to keep one's word. Christ-followers live a life that exemplifies honesty and commitment to promises made. They are known as people whose word is as good as the most binding of contracts. Clement of Alexandria, one of the early church fathers in the second century, put it wonderfully: "Christians must lead such a life and demonstrate such a character that no one will ever dream of asking an oath from them."[7]

Why are legal contracts needed in our day and age, in situations such as the sale and purchase of property, defining terms of employment, or as an affidavit attesting to truthfulness? Is it not for the same reason Jesus needed to address this issue in his day? Is it not because some people are still dishonest, unfaithful or corrupt? A contract or an oath is predicated by distrust. If a person does not make or sign one, their obligation to follow through is somehow perceived to be not as high. Not so in the Kingdom of Heaven. The follower of Jesus keeps his or her word. An oath or a signed contract might be helpful in some instances, but it ought to be superfluous. A Christian's reputation in his or her community should be such that when they say "YES," people know they mean "YES," and when they say "NO," people know they mean "NO." Anything more than that suggests there is reason to distrust their integrity.

Jesus younger brother, James, established this as a core principle of Christian life when he wrote:

> [12] Above all, my brothers and sisters, do not swear—not by heaven or by earth or by anything else. All you need to say is a simple "Yes" or "No." Otherwise, you will be condemned.
>
> James 5:12

In closing this chapter, a humorous story to make you smile. Driving home from her office one hot summer's day, a woman noticed four places within 500 yards of her home where she could stop and buy a five-cent glass of lemon-flavored ice-tea. Each little stand had two or three youngsters behind it all eager to serve any customer who came their way.

During the next two weeks, the woman managed to stop at each of the stands to encourage these young entrepreneurs. In each case the tea tasted very good, was served in a real glass, and small talk revealed that

---

7. Clarke, *Pipeline (Salvation Army)*, 7

all the youngsters were selling tea made by their mothers who used real tealeaves and real lemons in making the tea.

Then one day the woman discovered only one stand was operating. Behind it was a new kid on the block. She stopped and ordered a glass of tea. It was served in a paper cup, and it cost ten cents. The conversation brought out the fact that the young man's father was a lawyer who specialized in mergers, which had inspired the boy to buy out his competitors, bartering with sports cards, marbles and stuff he had lying around his garage. His first act, he explained, was to raise the price of the ice-tea and cut costs. He was using a powered lemon-tea mix from the supermarket, he said, which eliminated buying real lemons, as well as the bother of squeezing them or putting them in the juicer. He did not have to brew real tea either. He had plans to cut costs further, and with his competitors out of the market, he expected sales to grow. Intrigued the woman made half a dozen more stops at the stand over the next few days and became aware that the tea was getting weaker and weaker. One day the young man confessed that sales were dropping, and he attributed this to the fact that he was using less and less of the powered tea mix. Then one day, he went out of business as attempts to turn things around failed.

The moral of the story: *honest-tea is the best policy!*

SMALL GROUP DISCUSSION QUESTIONS

Matthew 5:33–37

1. Do you think people are more, or less, honest these days compared to previous decades?
2. What experience have you had of being treated dishonestly? How did it affect you?
3. Is there ever an occasion when telling the truth is unnecessary or not required?
4. Some people (Christians among them) use the name of "God" or "Lord" as a figure of speech—and sometimes as an expletive. How appropriate is this?
5. The people of Jesus day were guilty of "frivolous" and "evasive" swearing. What might be twenty-first-century equivalents to this?
6. Why do you think Jesus says that sacred oaths are unnecessary for the Christian?

7

Living in a World Full of Nasty People

We live in a world full of pain and hurt. Human beings have the capacity for unbelievable love and kindness, yet also the ability to inflict unimaginable cruelty and injustice. It is the same for everyone. Each day we associate with people who can bless us or hurt us deeply. Responding to those who show us kindness and warmth is easy; but how do we cope when people behave towards us in ways that are mean and hurtful or deeply offensive? It was an issue Jesus addressed in his sermon on a Galilean hillside:

> [38]"You have heard that it was said, 'Eye for eye, and tooth for tooth.' [39]But I tell you, do not resist an evil person. If anyone slaps you on the right cheek, turn to them the other cheek also. [40]And if anyone wants to sue you and take your shirt, hand over your coat as well. [41]If anyone forces you to go one mile, go with them two miles. [42]Give to the one who asks you, and do not turn away from the one who wants to borrow from you."
>
> Matthew 5:38–42

It would have been fascinating to see the looks on the faces of the people who heard Jesus say these words. What he said probably made them do a double-take. Jesus' advice on how to respond to offense or injustice was so different from the cultural norm of his day. It is counter-cultural in the contemporary age as well.

There is a principle here that deserves emphasis before we delve into all that Jesus said in these verses. The values and worldview of the kingdom of God are often very different from the values and worldview of the kingdoms of this world. To be a follower of Jesus involves so much more than the adoption of a personal belief system about God—as if it were merely an internal philosophy to which we subscribe. It affects the way a person thinks and behaves, and especially the manner in which they interact with others. It changes us; there is a price to be paid. Living the Jesus way requires daily choices to adopt and live by the values of God's kingdom. And when kingdom values clash with the culture in which a person has been shaped, the follower of Jesus needs to make a conscious choice to be transformed and re-align themselves so that their lives reflect the rule of God.

It has been suggested that there are few passages in the New Testament that contain more of the essence of Christian ethics or attitude than these verses.[1] To begin with, Jesus draws attention to the ancient law or principle of retribution: "An eye for an eye, and a tooth for a tooth" or Lex Talionis—retaliation authorized by law.[2] That is, the injured party has the right to repay the wrong action a person commits against them, with a similar action. The people of Jesus' day would have often heard this principle expounded. Three times in the *Law of Moses*, it is referenced. For instance:

> [19]Anyone who injures their neighbor is to be injured in the same manner: [20]fracture for fracture, eye for eye, tooth for tooth. The one who has inflicted the injury must suffer the same injury.
>
> Leviticus 24:19–20

This was not only a principle the Jews had lived by since the time of Moses. The concept of equal retribution is found in the earliest known record of human law, the Code of Hammurabi, dating back to ancient Babylon, which predates the Law of Moses by 400 years. Hammurabi was the sixth king of ancient Babylon, and his code of conduct and behavior is dated at 1754BC. Virtually every human society since has had a similar concept of fair retribution for wrongs done against a person. If someone does something that injures or disadvantages another, it is only just and

---

1. Barclay, *The Gospel of Matthew, Volume 1*, 163
2. Plaut, *The Torah—A Modern Commentary*, 571ff

equitable that some measure of revenge or retaliation be made that evens the score.

However, its inclusion of this principle in the *Law of Moses* is arguably unique and often misunderstood. Moses couched it as more than the principle of retribution. An eye for an eye and tooth for a tooth was not, as many people think of it, a license for revenge. It was intended to constrain the extent of revenge. Behind the principle of an "eye for an eye" was the concept of mercy—retribution and punishment were limited to the same measure as the actual offense committed.

Without such a law there might have been the kind of situation caricatured in movies about organized crime, when the toes of the local Mafia boss are trodden on, or perhaps his wife has been insulted, he takes revenge by putting out a "contract" on the offender's life. Moses' law sought to limit the retribution to the actual value of the original crime. If toes are trodden on, the offender can expect the same treatment in return, but should not find himself at the bottom of the harbor wearing a pair of concrete slippers! That would be a punishment that went well beyond the severity of the original crime

In other words: *Let the punishment fit the crime*. In fact, Jesus went on to suggest an even higher principle—two wrongs do not make a right. He did not actually contradict the Law of Moses, but he did introduce a new aspect of Kingdom life that went a whole lot further:

> [39]But I tell you, do not resist an evil person . . .

Here is a classic example of the behavior and values of the Kingdom differing from the behavior and values of the World.

My first experience of traveling to a foreign country was in 1982. I was invited to speak at a conference in Papua New Guinea. In Papua New Guinea there is a long-established cultural tradition of revenge that, to the outsider, looks rather primitive. It is known as "payback" and is grounded in a logical theory of economic parity. If a person from one tribe or family is injured or killed, even in an accident, that person's tribe seeks to inflict the same injury or death on the tribe of the person who caused the original offense. Consequently, if a person knocks someone over while driving their car in Papua New Guinea, the last thing they should do is stop to help the injured person. Instead, they should drive as fast as possible to the nearest police station and ask to be locked up—as protection from payback! Thankfully, these days revenge of this nature tends to be sorted out in financial terms, or through the exchange of livestock, rather than by spilling blood. Nevertheless, it is basically the same law of tit for tat—an eye for an eye and a tooth for a tooth.

Something similar happened amongst the ancient Israelites. Rather than take the law literally, the eye for an eye and tooth for a tooth principle was interpreted metaphorically, and the infliction of punishment was calculated in economic terms. A system for reckoning damage was developed, and the process was administered through the legal or judicial system. This was not a form of vigilante or summary justice, where an offended party might act as judge, jury and executioner inflicting revenge independently of others. It was a system assessed and enacted within a judicial process.

Jesus, however, was teaching that the way of the Kingdom is quite different. Instead of revenge or payback, his followers were to show love and forgiveness. When his original audience first heard him say this, many probably thought he was out of his mind. "Come on Jesus . . . you can't be serious!" The cultures of our world are so consumed with the seeking justice for wrongdoing or standing up for one's rights, that it is not regarded as fair that evil behavior goes unpunished or un-responded to. However, Jesus proclaimed that the culture of God's kingdom is completely different from the cultures of our world in this respect. That is not to say that there is no place for standing up for righteousness and justice and exposing corruption. There is a very definite place for that kind of prophetic stand. However, there are also times when anger, evil and oppression are best met with forgiveness and non-retaliation rather than seeking revenge. To get his point across, Jesus suggested some real-life scenarios where this Kingdom principle of non-retaliation might be applied. To fully grasp the impact of what he was saying, we need to read ourselves into the culture in which Jesus lived.

1. IF SOMEONE SLAPS YOU ON THE RIGHT CHEEK, TURN TO HIM THE OTHER ALSO

What did Jesus have in mind when he said this? Contrary to popular opinion, Jesus was not talking about pacifism or non-aggression. He was addressing the way people cope with insults. Suppose two people stand facing each other; since the majority of people are right-handed, how would one person strike another on the right cheek? The only way to do this is with the back of their right hand. Jesus original audience would have caught his drift straight away. In those days, striking a person with the back of one's hand was an act of extreme insult. It was one thing to hit someone with an open hand or fist, but to slap a person with the back of the hand was a deeply demeaning insult or put down.

In a metaphorical sense, the backhanded slap could mean something literal or something figurative, like in words. Jesus was talking about the way people react or respond when they are insulted. When one person receives abuse from another, even of the most demeaning kind, whether a backhanded slap or a verbal lashing with the tongue, the Christian response is not retaliation. More than that, the Christian is to turn the other cheek even at the risk of further insult.

Perhaps this principle can be applied to physical violence and the practice of pacifism. But Jesus was going further than suggesting a passive response to physical injury. Many pacifists loudly campaign for non-aggression and non-violence, yet they can be extremely vicious and violent with their tongues. One bruises and breaks on the outside; the other bruises and crushes the spirit on the inside. Both are wrong.

The Christ-follower, in the face of insults and abuse, exercises self-restraint, not retaliation. To be sure, this runs counter to the way the world spins. When someone says or does something offensive and hurtful, the way of the Kingdom, Jesus said, is to absorb the insult, and to leave revenge or retaliation in the hands of God, who guards our reputation.

This is the model Jesus demonstrated in the face of insult. People misunderstood his motives and his theology. They called him a glutton and a drunkard because he spent time at parties with sinners. They called him a friend of prostitutes and tax-collectors. They slandered his reputation and accused him of being a servant of the devil. But Jesus did not retaliate or slap back at the face of those who insulted him. Even at his trial before Jewish high priest Caiaphas, King Herod Antipas and the Roman governor Pilate, and his subsequent crucifixion, Jesus remained still and absorbed the insults thrown at him.

Early Christians were labeled bloodthirsty cannibals because they talked of eating and drinking the body and blood of Jesus. They were accused of incestuous behavior and orgies because they spoke of their love for brothers and sisters in the family of God. They were regarded as traitors to the state because they refused to call Caesar "LORD." How did they respond—with counterarguments and equally vicious insults? No, they took it on the chin and left their reputation in the hands of God, who has the power to change the hearts of evil men. It was Jesus who said:

> [10]Blessed are those who are persecuted because of righteousness, for theirs is the kingdom of heaven. [11]Blessed are you when people insult you, persecute you and falsely say all kinds of evil against you because of me. [12]Rejoice and be glad, because great is your reward in heaven, for in the same way they persecuted the prophets who were before you.
>
> Matthew 5:10–12

2. IF SOMEONE WANTS TO SUE YOU AND TAKE YOUR SHIRT, LET HIM TAKE YOUR COAT AS WELL

Some have extrapolated from this statement the need for Christians to encourage and be generous in their dealings with people—giving more than is requested or demanded. That is not a wrong principle to live by, but within the culture of Jesus' day it is more likely he was referring to an individual's legal rights. The illustration he used was associated with the way legal contracts were formalized.

The "shirt" or "tunic" that Jesus refers to was the long sack-like inner garment that men wore, made of cotton or linen. Even the poorest of men had a change of shirt. The "coat" or "cloak" he refers to was a big blanket-like outer garment, which a man wore as a robe during the day, and then used as a blanket to keep himself warm at night. Most men would have had just one coat. A man's shirt was sometimes put up as a form of collateral in the formalizing of an agreement. Giving of one's shirt or tunic was a sign of personal integrity or surety that an obligation would be fulfilled. But the law was quite specific that a man's coat or cloak was never to be held or retained for any length of time as a form of collateral.

> [26]If you take your neighbor's cloak as a pledge, return it to him by sunset, [27]because his cloak is the only covering he has for his body. What else will he sleep in? When he cries out to me, I will hear, for I am compassionate . . .
>
> Exodus 22:26–27

In other words, the *Law of Moses* put a limit on how much a person could extract from someone else who was defaulting on a contract. Regardless of what they have done, or how much they owed, a person's cloak was not to be held back from them. Over the years, the ownership of one's coat or cloak became a symbol of the most basic of human rights. A person may not have much in the way of possessions, dignity or pride, but every man had the right to the protection of the coat which kept him warm at night.

If this was the background of Jesus' statement, and if his original audience heard him talking about fundamental human rights, what was the point he was making? *Be prepared to give them up!* The follower of Jesus is willing to forgo his or her rights in life if it helps serve God's cause.

In those days, there was only one class of people who did not possess the dignity or rights associated with having their own coat. Even this most basic human right was denied these people. They were regarded more as chattels or human machines than people—*slaves*. They belonged to another and lived to please their masters rather than themselves. When Jesus spoke these words, perhaps this is what he was alluding to. To be a Christian is not to be at the top of the pile but at the bottom. Rather than being served *by* others, those who follow Jesus are to be a servant *to* others. It was Jesus who said that greatness in the Kingdom of God comes through being a servant—a concept completely contrary to the ways of the world.

Contemporary culture is almost paranoid about protecting human rights, and perhaps not without cause. There are many instances of exploitation and injustice in our world; people have been ripped-off or oppressed. Scripture encourages the people of God to be prophetic and active in campaigning for the rights of the poor, the oppressed and the disenfranchised. The gospel restores the stature and rights of people, which have been stolen by the evil one. Nevertheless, there is a sense in which people can play on, or demand too many rights. It is possible to be dominated by a litigious or assertive mentality that is aggressive and angry, lest personal rights are infringed. Whereas the way of God's Kingdom is not dominated by rights, but by responsibilities. The way of the kingdom is less about preserving human dignity, and more about giving up our rights in order to be a servant to others.

Christ-followers emulate the one who announced that he came not to be served, but to serve, and to give his life as a ransom for many.[3] They follow the one who set an example by washing the feet of his disciples.[4] All of which raises the question: Are we willing to give up our rights for the sake of God's cause—even toward those who insult us and treat us harshly?

3. Mark 10:45
4. John 13:1–17

3. IF SOMEONE FORCES YOU TO GO ONE MILE, GO WITH THEM TWO MILES

In the days of Jesus, the nation of Israel was an occupied country. It had been conquered, subjugated, and as part of the Roman Empire, was governed by the Roman army. Conquering and occupying regimes do not usually enjoy the favor of the local people. They are more typically hated. In those days, the rule of law was the rule of the sword or spear. If a Roman soldier tapped your shoulder with his spear and asked you to do something, you had to do it—if you wanted to see out the rest of the day. A common form of bullying or forced labor that a Roman soldier could engage in was compelling a person to carry his bag or armor, up to a mile in the opposite direction to which he was heading. The local people lived in constant fear that they might be conscripted like this. It is not hard to imagine how "joyfully" and "willingly" they would have obliged. They did as they were asked—it would have been suicide not to—but inside their hatred would have simmered and boiled toward the Romans occupiers.

You can just imagine the ripples that would have gone through the crowd when they heard Jesus suggest, "Don't just go one mile . . . Go two miles! Serve them willingly!" It would have sounded like a collaboration with the enemy. Once again, Jesus was illustrating the fact that a relationship with God means servanthood. The Christian serves others, even those who are his or her enemies.

However, maybe there was another point in what Jesus was suggesting. The way we respond to oppression and injustice can either change the heart of the oppressor or make him more determined. The natural reaction to tyranny, bullying or oppressive behavior is to fight back. Give them as much as they are giving; an eye for an eye and a tooth for a tooth. Tit for tat! Stand up to injustice and stare it in the face! The problem is, it hardly ever works. Conflict is seldom resolved that way.

When anger is met with corresponding anger, the angry person tends to become angrier! When we behave begrudgingly toward those who give us orders, those with power tend to become more determined to make us do what they want us to do. However, when anger, bullying, tyranny or oppression is met with compliance, love and a willingness to serve, it becomes increasingly difficult for that tyranny to continue. The bully begins to lose interest. It's no fun anymore. Paul put it this way in Romans 12:17–19:

¹⁷Do not repay anyone evil for evil. Be careful to do what is right in the eyes of everybody. ¹⁸If it is possible, as far as it depends on you, live at peace with everyone. ¹⁹Do not take revenge, my friends, but leave room for God's wrath, for it is written: "It is mine to avenge; I will repay," says the LORD.

According to Jesus, the way of the kingdom is vastly different from the ways of the world. When people do as Jesus suggests, "Do not resist an evil person . . ." they disempower the bully's wrath, and they show forth the Kingdom of God here on Earth. Likewise, when generosity is shown toward the person who wants to borrow from us (*v.40*), then generosity, kindness, graciousness, and willingness gives birth to like behavior.

Maybe some reading this chapter live or work amidst or under what might be termed unjust tyranny. It feels to them as if their personal rights are being infringed, and that their experience of being bullied is mean and unfair. What might happen if in the week ahead they tried an experiment? If instead of meeting injustice with a spirit of indignation, seeking retribution or behaving in a passive-aggressive way—they implemented Jesus' advice—taking it seriously, turning their cheek and giving less thought to protecting their personal rights, leaving revenge in the hands of God, (who is so much better at it than we could ever be); what would the result be? Jesus' advice here will be a bitter pill for some to swallow.

But what if it works . . . ?

SMALL GROUP DISCUSSION QUESTIONS

Matthew 5:38–42

1. Following Jesus means living by a different set of values to the world in which we live. What are some examples of that difference from your experience?

2. What do you understand to be the meaning of the phrase: "An eye for an eye, and a tooth for a tooth"?

3. Does v.39 mean that Christians should always be pacifists?

4. How would you explain Matthew 5:10–12 to someone who was a brand-new Christian?

5. Jesus reference to tunics and cloaks in v.40 implied forgoing our rights for the sake of others. What is an example of waiving rights in our twenty-first-century context?

6. Is there a legitimate place for standing up for justice and fighting back when we're offended?

7. What is the best way to disempower someone who is bullying you?

8

Rising above Offense

Corrie ten Boon and her family were committed Christians living in the Netherlands at the beginning of the Second World War. As a family, they showed love and compassion toward Jews fleeing the Nazi regime and hid them within their home. When this was discovered, they were arrested and sent to different prisons and concentration camps. Corrie and her sister Betsie were incarcerated together. The conditions in their concentration camp were harsh and cruel. Corrie became extremely bitter and resentful over their treatment, especially over how Betsie was handled when she became ill. Betsie's illness grew steadily worse, and she eventually died. Yet throughout her illness, she maintained grace and serenity that deeply challenged and contrasted with the anger of her sister. Through the process of Betsie's death, Corrie was profoundly touched by God particularly as she watched her sister show love and respect toward her enemies, even as she was dying.

Some years after the war, Corrie ten Boon wrote a book, "The Hiding Place,"[1] about her ordeal and how she battled with the bitterness and anger it caused. She developed a powerful speaking ministry and toured the world, preaching on how the power of God is able to turn the hatred of enemies into love. But it was not always easy. She wrote about a particular occasion when she came face to face with one of the former concentration camp guards:

---

1. Ten Boon, *The Hiding Place*.

"It was a church service in Munich that I saw him, the former SS man who stood guard at the shower room door in the processing center at Ravensbruck. He was the first of our actual jailers that I had seen since that time. And suddenly it was there—the room full of mocking men, the heaps of clothing, Betsie's plain blanched face. He came up to me as the church service was emptying, beaming and bowing, "How grateful I am for your message, Fraulein," he said. "To think that, as you say, Christ has washed my sins away!" His hand was thrust out to shake mine, and I, who had preached so often to people in Bloemendaal the need to forgive, kept my hand at my side. Even as the angry, vengeful thoughts boiled through me, I saw the sin of them. Jesus Christ had died for this man; was I going to ask for more? "LORD Jesus," I prayed, "Forgive me and help me to forgive him." I tried to smile; I struggled to raise my hand. I could not. I felt nothing, not the slightest spark or warmth or charity. And so again I breathed a silent prayer; "Jesus I cannot forgive him. Give me your forgiveness". As I took his hand, the most incredible thing happened. From my shoulder along my arm and through my hand, a current seemed to pass from me to him. While into my heart sprang a love for this stranger that almost overwhelmed me. And so, I discovered that it is not on our forgiveness that the world's healing hinges, any more than on our goodness, but on Christ's. When he tells us to love our enemies, he gives, along with the command, the very love itself."

The Imperative of forgiveness and love toward those who do us harm was one of the radical teachings of Jesus. In his sermon on a Galilean hillside, he made a statement about how to live above offense, and the response he expected his followers to demonstrate toward those who treat them badly:

> [43]"You have heard that it was said, 'Love your neighbor and hate your enemy.' [44]But I tell you, love your enemies and pray for those who persecute you, [45]that you may be children of your Father in heaven. He causes his sun to rise on the evil and the good and sends rain on the righteous and the unrighteous. [46]If you love those who love you, what reward will you get? Are not even the tax collectors doing that? [47]And if you greet only your own people, what are you doing more than others? Do not even pagans do that? [48]Be perfect, therefore, as your heavenly Father is perfect.
>
> Matthew 5:43–48

Once again, Jesus alludes to the oral teaching people had received about the *Law of Moses*, and how that teaching had been skewed somewhat with pedantic situational technicalities and legalism. Definitions were added to the original teaching, supposedly to clarify, but often altering the intent of the original Scripture. So, Jesus gave essential clarity about how the *Law of the* LORD was initially intended to be understood.

In this instance, there was an understanding amongst the people of the day that having enemies was inevitable and perfectly natural, therefore a person was allowed to treat them in a derogatory way: "Love your neighbour and hate your enemy."

However, nowhere in the original *Law of Moses* was that kind of license ever given. In several places, there are references to the first half of the saying, about loving your eighbour. But nowhere in the Bible are we ever encouraged to hate our enemies. This is a classic example of how popular teaching in Jesus' day was missing the mark.

On the contrary, the ancient Old Testament said things like:

> [4]"If you come across your enemy's ox or donkey wandering off, be sure to return it. [5]If you see the donkey of someone who hates you fallen down under its load, do not leave it there; be sure you help them with it.
>
> Exodus 23:4–5

> [21]If your enemy is hungry, give him food to eat; if he is thirsty, give him water to drink.
>
> Proverbs 25:21

In other words, the people of God were encouraged to live in such a way that they might possibly turn their enemies into friends. Their conduct and treatment of other people were to be such that it generated respect, rather than entrenching animosity.

That stated the Bible does indicate, in several places, that a certain measure of hostility and opposition toward those who take their relationship with God seriously is unavoidable and perhaps inevitable. To have enemies does not necessarily imply that a Christ-follower has done something wrong or that ill-will toward them is warranted or justified. For Christians, to have enemies or people who oppose and hate them is not necessarily a sign of sin or bad conduct. Sometimes enmity occurs for no reason other than that a person follows Jesus' approach to life. Take, for example, this cheerful encouragement from Jesus:

> [18]"If the world hates you, keep in mind that it hated me first. [19]If you belonged to the world, it would love you as its own. As it is, you do not belong to the world, but I have chosen you out of the world. That is why the world hates you. [20]Remember what I told you: 'Servants are not greater than their master.' If they persecuted me, they will persecute you also. If they obeyed my teaching, they will obey yours also. [21]They will treat you this way because of my name, for they do not know the one who sent me.
>
> John 15:18–21

Indeed, sometimes receiving a hard time or being disliked and despised for being a follower of Jesus is something of a compliment—less a sign of failure; more an inevitable consequence. There can be many reasons why this happens. In some instances, it might be that the choice a Christian makes to follow or adopt God's values makes them stand out from the values of the world around them. They do not go along with the dominant view of their culture, and such a position is not always appreciated. On other occasions, hostility has no apparent or logical reason. It can even be purely spiritual, in the sense that the evil one stirs up people to oppose Christ-followers and make life difficult for them. That may have been what the apostle Paul had in mind when he wrote to the Christians in Rome: "If it is possible, as far as it depends on you, live at peace with everyone."[2] Sometimes, it is not up to us, because hostility or enmity is not always within our control. While Christians are not to hate and despise anyone, there are times when they may not be able to account for the attitude of others.

What, then, is a Christian response toward those who oppose and treat us as their enemies? Jesus offered some practical advice:

1. TREAT YOUR ENEMIES THE WAY GOD DOES

Love them as God does! What did Jesus mean by that? Taken at face value, this may not have sat well with some of Jesus' original audience. Remember, the Jewish people of Jesus' day were an oppressed and conquered

---

2. Romans 12:18

nation, and the rule of law was administered by armed Roman soldiers, whom people loved to hate. How is it possible to love someone who is mean, cruel or malicious?

Firstly, be clear about what Jesus meant here by the word *love*. In the English language, we have one word for "love" which can mean different things in different contexts. In New Testament Greek language, there were at least four different words; each describing a specific type of love. Firstly, there was *storgé*, which described love within a family—the kind of love a parent has for a child, or a child has for their benevolent grandparent. Secondly, there was *erōs*, which described sexual passion between two lovers that finds its expression in intimacy and touch. Thirdly, there was *philia*, which expressed the love or companionship which exists between close friends. This kind of friendship is characterized by reciprocity and loyalty. Fourthly, there was *agape*, which described the type of love that goes out of its way to care for the wellbeing of another person. It is a benevolent, caring and unconditional love, which always wants the best for its recipient. This is a love that is not dependent on being loved back; it seeks nothing less than the highest good.[3]

Agape is used for the kind of love that God demonstrates toward us, and it was this word for love that Jesus used when he encouraged his followers to love their enemies. This kind of love persistently sees and wants the best for other people. It is a love that stops by the side of the road and in compassion bandages the wounds of the injured, as in Jesus' parable of the Good Samaritan.[4] This love acts even if the injured person is an enemy. In essence, *agape* describes the character of God and is the motivation for the gracious way he treats people—fairly, without partiality, and independently of their response to him.

When a person lives life the Jesus way, his or her worldview is altered. They begin to see things differently. Perhaps instead of seeing only a person's angry exterior, they begin to notice the pain or sense the motivation behind the hostile behavior. They start seeing people the way God sees them. And how does God treat people who oppose him, insult him or reject his friendship? He is patient and kind, not capricious, spiteful or easily offended. He goes on loving those who reject him and continually desires what is best for them. Surely, this is the experience of every Christ-follower, whom God continued to love even when they were his

---

3. Barclay, *The Gospel of Matthew, Volume 1*, 173–174.
4. Luke 10:30–37

enemies? This is the standard of love he now calls his followers to demonstrate toward others.

To the people of Jesus' day, the expression of love and kindness was something they handled with careful discrimination. They tended to put people into categories. To those who are neighbors or friends—show love and kindness. But to those who are your enemies—do not give them even the time of day! Jesus challenges those who only show kindness towards those who reciprocate: "even the pagans do that." There is nothing unique or unusual about loving those who love us back. However, those who are now a part of God's Kingdom are called to live by a different set of values. Their attitude and response to hostility should be quite different. The way of the Kingdom is to love people indiscriminately, regardless of whether they reciprocate. This was the point behind Jesus statement:

> [45]He causes the sun to rise on the evil and the good, and sends rain on the righteous and the unrighteous . . .

Many have misunderstood this, believing it to be a statement about how all people, whether good or evil, go through good times and bad times; sometimes it rains, sometimes it shines, such is life. This statement is much more significant than that. The shining of the sun or the falling of rain were regarded as symbols or metaphors of God's supply and provision. Crops need both rain and sunshine. Jesus was saying that God is benevolent or caring toward all humankind, not discriminating according to whether they are for or against him. He does not make the sun to shine, or rain to fall more on a Christian's crop because he is a Christian; and less on a non-Christian's because he is an atheist. All men and women are loved (*agape*) equally by God. Further, now that the Christ-follower has been adopted into God's family, they are called to treat other people, even their enemies, in the same way God does. To be sure, this runs against the grain of human nature and the values of this world and that is precisely the point—those who follow Jesus are no longer part of this world! Their allegiance has changed, and they belong to another kingdom. With the Holy Spirit residing within them, their nature is being changed. They are in the process of being spiritually modified!

An old eastern fable tells of a holy man engaged in his morning meditation under a tree whose roots stretched out over the riverbank. During his meditation, he noticed the river was rising, and a scorpion caught in the roots was about to drown. He crawled out onto the roots and reached down to free the scorpion, but every time he did so, the scorpion struck back at him. An observer came along and said to the holy man, "Don't you know that is a scorpion, and it is in the nature of a scorpion to want to sting?" To which the holy man replied; "That may well be so, but it is in my nature to save, and must I change my nature because the scorpion does not change its nature?"[5] The way of the world is retaliation or revenge—a snub for a snub, and an insult for an insult. The way of God's Kingdom is unconditional love—good for evil, kindness to those who would do us harm.

2. PRAY FOR THOSE WHO PERSECUTE YOU

Are there people who give you a hard time? Jesus' advice: "Put them on your prayer list." No doubt one of the reasons for this instruction is that it is difficult sustaining feelings of anger and hostility toward someone for whom you are praying. When people are unkind, hostile and treat others as an enemy, the natural reaction is to wish harm upon them in return. After all, they need to be repaid for what they have done. Some might even be tempted to pray to call down God's judgment and wrath upon them—perhaps even praying more specifically for an experience of calamity or failure. However, when a person spends any time with God in prayer, it is not easy to hold on to selfish and retaliatory motivations. When people spend time with God, they begin to think his thoughts after him. They start to see situations and people as he does and make requests for the things they believe God would want.

Another old rabbinic fable tells of how the Egyptians drowned in the Red Sea chasing Moses and the Israelites at the time of their Exodus. As the fable goes, while the Egyptian army was drowning, the angels in Heaven began to sing and shout in praise. But God told them off, and said sorrowfully: "The work of my hands are sunk in the sea, and you would sing before me?"[6]

When Jesus suggested praying for our enemies, maybe he was mindful that such a discipline would also change a person's perspective or worldview. Bringing people before the throne of grace tends to diminish the pain and sting of our relationship with them. It is not easy to be angry at someone while standing in the presence of Jesus. So, Jesus' invitation to pray for those who are obnoxious or offensive was not only for

---

5. Anderson, *God Tracking Through The Year—Year Two*, 145.
6. Barclay, *The Gospel of Matthew, Volume 1*, 173 176.

their benefit, because they need the touch of God on their lives. Praying also provides good therapy for one's own soul.

3. SHOW THE FAMILY LIKENESS

Jesus uses two phrases referring to characteristics shared within the family of God. Jesus says that those who love their enemies, and pray for those who persecute them, are "children of [their] Father in heaven." The actual words Jesus used translate literally as "sons of your Father in heaven," which was not a reference to gender, but an idiomatic way of describing the attributes or characteristics of a person. In the idiom of the English language, a person who is very much at peace with him/herself might be characterized as a *peace-ful* person. In the Hebrew language of Jesus' day, they would use the phrase: "a son of peace." This was the equivalent of an adjective used to describe a specific personality or character trait—as if they are children or offspring of that quality. For instance, the New Testament church leader, Barnabas, was given the nickname "son of encouragement" because he had a reputation for being an encourager.[7] Jesus gave the two brothers, James and John, the nickname *Boanerges* meaning "sons of thunder," presumably because they had a reasonably boisterous or thunderous personality.

When Jesus said that loving our enemies signified our being "children of our Father in heaven," it was a way of saying that a God-like person (godly) is a person who loves his or her enemies. Loving, instead of hating, an enemy is to reflect the character of God—to show the family likeness.

The second phrase concerning family characteristics that Jesus alludes to is:

48Be perfect, therefore, as your heavenly Father is perfect.

Matthew 5:48

At first glance, this might look like a pretty tall order. Who of us can ever hope or claim to be perfect? The Greek word translated as "perfect" (*teleios*) does not convey the same ideas as our concept of perfection today. Perfection is maybe thought of as something without moral or ethical flaws—without blemish or defilement, but Jesus was not asking us to be perfect in that sense. He knows we cannot attain that kind of perfection—at least not in this life.

7. Acts 4:36

Teleios denoted the idea of fulfillment, completion, or an end accomplished as the effect of a process.[8] Jesus' concept was more about attaining maturity or having grown up. It described someone becoming complete or fulfilled, as opposed to someone who is immature, half-grown or incomplete. In the culture of the day, someone or something was regarded as being perfect if it fully realized or fulfilled the potential for which it was created.

When Jesus asked his followers to be perfect, he was asking them to grow into the new nature or capacity that they have as God's children. Going back to the creation story, human beings were created by God after his own image. We, therefore, have within us both the potential and the purpose of reflecting his glory and character in our world. The apostle Paul said that Christians are the "body of Christ." They embody the values, attitudes and conduct of their heavenly Father before others. Jesus calls his followers to be "perfect," which might be translated as an instruction to, *"grow up!"* Fulfill the potential within you, and represent the Kingdom, and the King, to whom you swear allegiance.

And when it comes to people who give Christ-followers a hard time, who treat them as their enemies, or who persecute and defile their name, the best response is the way of our Father in heaven. As the apostle Paul put it, ". . .the love of God has been poured into our hearts, by the Holy Spirit, whom he has given to us."[9] Deposited within every Christ-follower is everything required to treat other people the way God does—even, if not especially, those who treat us as enemies. It is a potential within all of God's children. All we need to do is activate it and show the family likeness.

Stephen Olford told this famous story about a pastor during the American Revolution, Peter Miller, who lived in Ephrata, Pennsylvania and enjoyed the friendship of George Washington. In Ephrata, there also lived a man called Michael Wittman. He was an evil-minded man who apparently did all he could to criticise and humiliate the pastor in front of others. It is unclear what had happened between these two men, but Michael Wittman did all he could to oppose Peter Miller.

One day Michael Wittman was arrested for treason and sentenced to die. Peter Miller traveled seventy miles on foot to Philadelphia to plead for the life of a traitor.

---

8. Vine, *An Expository Dictionary of New Testament Words*, 847
9. Romans 5:5

"No, Peter," General Washington said. "I cannot grant you the life of your friend."

"My friend!" exclaimed the old pastor. "He is the bitterest enemy I have!"

"What!" cried Washington. "You have walked 70 miles to save the life of an enemy? That puts the matter in a different light. I will grant you your pardon".

And he did. Peter Miller took Michael Wittman back home to Ephrata—no longer an enemy but a friend.[10]

---

10. Larson, *750 Engaging Illustrations for Contemporary Illustrations for Preachers, Teachers and Writers*, 327

SMALL GROUP DISCUSSION QUESTIONS

Matthew 5:43–48

1. What experience have you had (that you feel comfortable sharing) of struggling to forgive someone who has deeply offended you?
   - What happened?
2. Are Christians allowed to have enemies?
3. John 15:18–21 speaks of hatred for Christians. Why have Christians been persecuted over the centuries?
4. How does God actually give us the love that he wants us to show toward others—even our enemies?
5. When Jesus suggested that we pray for our enemies, for what in particular should we pray?
6. How would you explain v.48 to someone new to the Christian faith?

9

How to Be Generous

The Mazatec Indians in southwestern Mexico are renowned for at least three interesting things. One is their artistic creativity. A second is their consumption of the hallucinogenic mushrooms that grow in their area, which apparently helps their creativity. The third is an interesting approach to sharing (or more particularly, not sharing) their blessings and good fortune with other people.

According to a missionary named Eunice Pike, who worked with the Mazatec Indians for more than forty years, they seldom wish someone well and are hesitant to teach one another any skills they might have acquired. For instance, when she asked the village baker, "Who taught you to bake bread?" He answered, "I just know," meaning he acquired the knowledge without anyone's help. This odd cultural behavior evidently stems from the concept of *limited good*. They believe there is only so much good, so much knowledge, so much love to go around. To teach another means you drain yourself of knowledge, or to love a second child means having to love the first child less. To wish someone well, for example, "Have a good day," results in giving away some of your own happiness, which cannot be reacquired.[1]

It is unclear how the worldview of Mazatec Indians developed, but it is the opposite of a core-value the Bible teaches, that of being generous—especially toward those who have less than you or are in need of extra help. Jesus had an important point to make on the topic of generosity during his famous Sermon on a Galilean hillside. In particular, he spoke

1. May, *Learning to Trust*.

of motive and having the right attitude in acts of religious worship if they are to be received by God:

> ¹"Be careful not to do your 'acts of righteousness' in front of others, to be seen by them. If you do, you will have no reward from your Father in heaven.
> ²"So when you give to the needy, do not announce it with trumpets, as the hypocrites do in the synagogues and on the streets, to be honored by others. Truly I tell you, they have received their reward in full. ³But when you give to the needy, do not let your left hand know what your right hand is doing, ⁴so that your giving may be in secret. Then your Father, who sees what is done in secret, will reward you."
>
> Matthew 6:1–4

When Jesus spoke to the people of his day, he was speaking to those who understood that there were three types of religious behavior that were regarded as signs of righteousness. If people were serious about God and devout in their spirituality, they did at least these three things:

- They gave to people in need (or almsgiving)
- They said prayers (or did specific acts of focused worship)
- They fasted from food (or disciplined their body)

Each of these acts of spiritual devotion had their roots in the *Law of Moses*. The popular understanding was that by doing them, a person earned a reward or the blessing of God's favor. Not doing these things was to be regarded as a backslider or someone moving away from God.

However, over the years, and especially in the period leading up to the time of Jesus, each of these three acts of religious devotion had lost its intended focus. Rather than people practicing their acts of devotion for an audience of One, that is for the eyes or pleasure of God, they tended to be performed for in order to be noticed by others. People would give to needy causes or pray lengthy prayers in public, or make people aware that they were fasting, as a way of proving their spirituality to others.

Jesus addresses each of these acts of religious devotion in turn and points people back to the original reason for them. In this chapter, the first practice of giving to the needy is discussed. In summary Jesus said, that the motive behind acts of worship (or spiritual disciplines) is the most important thing. What is the purpose for which they are performed? Are they actions to be seen or noticed by others, and in the process, enhance one's reputation, or are they done solely to be noticed or appreciated by God?

It is worth noting that Jesus does not say that these historical symbols of religious worship are wrong or inappropriate. He does not discourage giving to needy causes. Nor does he suggest we stop praying and fasting. These are worthy and important expressions of faith for those who follow him. However, the right reason or motive behind each discipline is the all-important factor.

While Jesus words here were spoken initially to a specific group of people, some timeless principles can be extrapolated and applied, to every generation of Christ-followers. Here are three in particular:

1. THE PRINCIPLE OF GENEROSITY

From the earliest days of the Christian church, there has been an understanding that followers of Jesus are to share their excess with those who are poor or struggling. Helping people in need is a fundamental characteristic of godliness or god-likeness. Of course, Christianity does not own this value all to itself. Jews, Muslims, and Buddhists—even secular communists—would all see this as something they should do as well. But for followers of Jesus, acts of generosity are of particular importance.

Indeed, a real Christian worldview regards everything about life—our time, our talents, and our resources—as belonging to God, rather than to one's self. Christians act as stewards or administrators of God's resources, rather than as owners. And if God wants to redistribute some of what now belongs to him, then the Christian's role as steward is merely to cooperate with that act of generosity.

At the time of Jesus, there was a saying amongst some of the Jewish rabbis: "Greater is he who gives alms than he who offers all sacrifices!"[2] Feeding, clothing or housing the poor was deemed a more meritorious act of worship than other sacrifices or words of praise.

Indeed, the earliest Christians took giving generously to those in need very seriously. The leader of the first Christian church in Jerusalem around the middle of the first century, was James, the younger brother of Jesus. When he wrote about what it means to be a follower of Jesus, he had some powerful words to say about the practice of generosity:

---

2. Montefiore and Loewe, *A Rabbinic Anthology,* 429

> ²⁷Religion that God our Father accepts as pure and faultless is this: to look after orphans and widows in their distress and to keep oneself from being polluted by the world.
>
> James 1:27

In other words, a genuine relationship with God is less about the words a person speaks to God, or that they might read in the Bible, and more about the evidence of how well they care for people in need. A little further on in his letter he went even further:

> ¹⁴What good is it, my brothers and sisters, if people claim to have faith but have no deeds? Can such faith save them? ¹⁵Suppose a brother or sister is without clothes and daily food. ¹⁶If one of you says to them, "Go in peace; keep warm and well fed," but does nothing about their physical needs, what good is it? ¹⁷In the same way, faith by itself, if it is not accompanied by action, is dead.
>
> James 2:14–17

In many contemporary church circles, the temperature of spirituality and devotion to God has been measured by a person's consistency in Bible study and participation in corporate times of worship. These are both valuable and important, and not to be neglected, but James would say that if participation in that kind of activity does not lead or result in tangible, practical care for the poor and needy, it misses the point. It is empty religion.

The writer of the book of Proverbs captured the idea of caring for the poor like this:

> ³¹Whoever oppresses the poor shows contempt for their Maker, but whoever is kind to the needy honors God.
>
> Proverbs 14:31

> ¹⁷Those who are kind to the poor lend to the LORD, and he will reward them for what they have done.
>
> Proverbs 19:17

> ⁹The generous will themselves be blessed, for they share their food with the poor.
>
> Proverbs 22:9

The first generations of Christians demonstrated a different attitude toward the poor and needy than that often found in the contemporary church. To be sure, back then there were not the social welfare safety-nets that exist in many parts of the world today. There were no pensions for unemployment or sickness or retirement. In those days, without a source of income, the plight of the poor was significantly more direr. Many were forced to beg to survive. Widows and orphans were particularly vulnerable, and Christian communities felt they had a direct responsibility to care for such people. The situation described at the beginning of Acts 6 points to a systemic ministry for the care and feeding of widows and their families in the first church of Jerusalem. This was also a core feature of Christian communities that developed over subsequent years around the known world. For instance, by the year AD250, the Christian church in Rome had a register of one-thousand-five-hundred needy persons that they supported.[3]

A century before, the Christian apologist and historian, Aristides, wrote this description of Christian community:

> "They walk in all humility and kindness, and falsehood is not found among them, and they love one another. They do not despise widows and they do not grieve orphans. He that has distributes liberally to him that has not. If they see a stranger, they bring him under their roof, and rejoice over him, as if he was their own brother; for they call themselves brothers and sisters, not after the flesh, but after the Spirit and God; but when one of their poor passes away from the world and any of them see him, he provides for his burial according to his ability and if they hear that any of their number is imprisoned or opposed for the name of their Messiah, all of them provide for his needs; and if it is possible that he may be delivered, they deliver him. And if there is among them a man who was poor and needy and he has not an abundance of necessaries, they fast two or three days that they may supply the needy with the necessary food."[4]

We also know that it was the persistent generosity and care of needy people by Christians that eventually turned the tide of popular opinion within the Roman Empire—to the extent that by the middle of the fourth century there were more Christians in the empire than not. As

---

3. Martin, *Property and Riches in the Early Church*, 42–44

4. Aristides, quoted in Martin Hengel, *Property and Riches in the Early Church*, 42–43

previously mentioned, the last of the pagan Roman emperors was Flavius Claudius Julianus (often referred to as Julian the Apostate). A relative of the converted Constantine, during his two-year reign (AD361363) he unsuccessfully attempted to turn Rome back from Christianity as the favored religion and to restore the ancient pagan religions. He grudgingly commented to a pagan friend: ". . . the godless Galileans (Christians) feed not only their poor but ours also . . . those who belong to us look in vain for the help that we should render them."[5]

However, amongst Jesus' original audience on that Galilean hillside, the expressions and practices of righteousness had gone somewhat awry. Clearly, people were giving to needy causes, but in many cases, their motives for giving alms were corrupt. It was more about their own reputation in the eyes of onlookers than a response to the need of the recipient. That said, they did at least give. It has been suggested that if Jesus were delivering his *Sermon on the Mount* to contemporary believers, his emphasis might be a little different. The question might not be so much the motivation with which people give to the needy, but whether they give anything at all! Perhaps in our generation, more energy is given to analyzing why it is that the poor are poor—in order to sooth our consciences with the notion that the plight of poor people is mostly self-inflicted. "The poor are poor because they are lazy . . . Why should I give to them if they made bad choices or squandered their opportunities?"

While Jesus said that giving with the right motivation is important, so too is the principle of *actually* giving or sharing our own blessings with those less fortunate so that the Christian church might again become renowned for its generosity.

2. THE PRINCIPLE OF ANONYMITY

Jesus spoke to the process of giving to the needy:

> [2]So when you give to the needy, do not announce it with trumpets, as the hypocrites do in the synagogues and on the streets, to be honored by others . . . [3]But when you give to the needy, do not let your left hand know what your right hand is doing, so that your giving may be in secret.
>
> Matthew 6:2–3

---

5. Neill, *A History of Christian Missions*, 37–38

Whether Jesus was literal about people blowing loud trumpets in the synagogue, or whether this was hyperbole spoken in order to make a point, is moot. In either case, what Jesus vividly described is that some were giving to the needy in such a way that it drew attention to themselves. People wanted their generosity observed and recognized, with the hope that others would be impressed and think well of them. "If no one notices or acknowledges my gift or thanks me, was it worth the effort of giving at all?"

Telethons are not as popular these days as they were a few decades ago, but they have been a fun way of raising money for charitable causes. Pledges were made, on the proviso that the donor's name was read out on air? Sometimes people would make a pledge and challenge their friends or colleagues to do the same. As if to say: "I'm giving this much; I dare others to be as good as I think I am!" Contemporary fundraising theory still operates along similar lines in acknowledging and listing the biggest donors or sponsors to a cause or charity. Those who give the most might get their names on the program, the best seats in the house, or some other form of avoured treatment.

This was the kind of practice Jesus was challenging. If our motivation for giving is personal acknowledgment and recognition, a line has been crossed. In my home country of New Zealand, a local congregation published the list of annual donor pledges from congregational households. The idea of collecting household pledges each year can be helpful for a church as it budgets for expenditure in the following year, but this church took it a step further. They had the names of the congregation households printed on a large sign in the church foyer, listing, in descending order, the names and amounts of what was pledged! Every time a person entered the church building, this list confronted them. Those who gave the most, perhaps because of their greater income, had more influence in the church than those who were only able to give a little.

Jesus responded to those motivated to give only because there might be recognition or an accolade in return, by suggesting a strategy of giving in secret! That way, no one else would know except God. Such giving could not be from mixed motives, it would be from a genuine desire to meet the need or support the cause to which it was given, and therefore be a genuine act of worship toward God.

Some have taken this principle as a reason for not declaring charitable giving when filing their tax returns. This is obviously a matter of personal conviction, but there are valid arguments for re-giving rebated money back to a charitable cause. In any case there are legitimate questions to consider. Is our giving to charity coupled with an expectation or calculation of rebate entitlement (a tax right-off)? Might there be room for Jesus to question the motive for such giving? Or to examine the purity of our motives another way, if the IRS rules were to change next year, so that tax deductibility was no longer offered for charitable donations, would our giving to support needy causes diminish?

The story is told of a Jewish rabbi who, whenever he gave alms to beggars in the street, always did so by dropping the money behind his back. That way he could not see who picked it up, nor gain credit from anyone. He merely recognized the need and shared from his excess, and that was sufficient motivation.

Might this issue of anonymity in charitable giving have been a cause for discussion within the very first church when it started caring for the people amongst them who were poor and needy? At the end of Acts 2, there is a challenging description of the level of love and fellowship that people enjoyed in this prototype church.[6] Some people were quite wealthy, and other people were quite poor. It was not uncommon for people with more means to liquidate assets and give the proceeds to those amongst them who were in need. This was not an isolated instance either. Two chapters on, at the end of Acts 4, we read again about a similar practice in that first church. Only this time the method of distribution had changed:

> [34] . . . there were no needy persons among them. For from time to time those who owned land or houses sold them, brought the money from the sales [35] and put it at the apostles' feet, and it was distributed to anyone who had need.
>
> Acts 4:34–35

In Acts 2, people gave directly to those in need as they came across them. The recipients knew who their benefactors were. By Acts 4, the apostles or church leaders received the donations and disbursed them amongst the neediest causes. In other words, the recipients probably did not know where the gift had come from, nor did the donor know where their donations went. The donors merely gave as unto the LORD, and the recipients recognized their help as coming from God, rather than specific people.

---

6. Acts 2:42–47

Again, the point Jesus was making was this: when giving to those in need, let it be with the right motivation and not for a kickback in terms of reputation or acknowledgment. The best way to protect one's self from wrong motives, is to give in secret—not letting the left hand know what the right hand is doing.

3. THE PRINCIPLE OF REWARD

Jesus pointed to two sources or types of reward that come to those who are generous. He said they are mutually exclusive; you can have one or the other, but you cannot have both.

The first reiterates the reward received through the recognition of other people. This was a big issue in Jesus' day. People were doing their religious acts of righteousness in front of other people with the hope or expectation that they would be seen as generous, and therefore as righteous. The reward could come in two ways. There was the potential for reward in the form of gratitude from the recipient. The benefactor could enjoy the satisfaction of hearing someone say "thank you" for the help given to them.

Of course, expressions of gratitude on the part of a beneficiary can also mask another emotion—a feeling of frustration (even resentment) at being in a position of needing to be helped in the first place. Sometimes well-intentioned charity can have an unintended toxic effect—making the needy person feel more despondent, humiliated, beholden, and patronized about their predicament. By contrast, when donations are given anonymously, the recipient is more likely to give thanks to God, than to feel bad about themselves. Perhaps there is a place for the Christian community to facilitate giving that protects the emotions and motivations of both the giver and the recipient.

The second kind of reward received through onlookers is from those who get to see, and note, what is given and because of this think well of the donor. Such benefactors give to a needy cause, sure, but their real motivation is to garner favor from those who will notice and admire them. They are playing to the crowd, rather than genuinely sharing their excess with the poor. There is a famous story along these lines about Henry Ford, who was once asked to donate money for the construction of a new medical facility. The billionaire pledged to donate $5,000. The next day the newspaper headline read, "Henry Ford contributes $50,000 to the local hospital." The irate Ford was on the phone immediately to complain to the fund-raiser that he had been misunderstood and misquoted. The fund-raiser replied that they would print a retraction in the paper the following day to read, "Henry Ford reduces his donation by $45,000." Realizing the poor publicity that would result, Ford reluctantly agreed to the $50,000 contribution in return for the following: That above the entrance to the hospital was to be carved the biblical inscription: "I came among you, and you took me in!"[7]

Again, Jesus makes the point that if giving occurs with the thought of reward, recognition or advancing our reputation among those who see or know what we give, then that will be all the reward we get. There might be a sense of glory and accolade for a little while, but it does not last. People forget and accolades pass. The original Greek word for reward in this passage referred to an account that was paid in full.[8] It was a word employed in the world of business or commerce, describing a payment made and receipted, that was full and final. There would be nothing more paid, nor due to be paid. The account is closed. This, Jesus said, would be the experience of those who give charitably with the mixed-motive of being recognized and honored by others.

By contrast, Jesus suggested a more valuable type of reward, the reward that comes to those who give in secret. Giving with anonymity means that only God sees. But that is actually what Jesus wanted his followers to grasp: *GOD SEES WHAT WE DO!* When people do righteous acts such as giving to those in need solely because this is what God desires, God knows, and he rewards them with his blessing and pleasure. Sometimes those rewards might come in this life; sometimes the reward is not until the life that is to come. However, Jesus wanted his followers to know that it is not possible to have it both ways. The two types of reward or recognition, that from other people and that from God, are mutually exclusive. Which begs the question: Whose reward or recognition is most valuable?

In closing, a story from the life of the famous British pastor, Charles Hadden Spurgeon. Spurgeon and his wife reared chickens, and they would sell, but refused to give away, the eggs their chickens laid. Even close relatives were told, "You may have them if you pay for them." As a result, some people unkindly labeled the Spurgeons as greedy and grasping. Mr. & Mrs. Spurgeon accepted these criticisms without ever

---

7. *Bits & Pieces*, March 3, 12
8. Barclay, *The Gospel of Matthew, Volume 1*, 186.

defending themselves. It was only after Mrs. Spurgeon died that the full story was revealed. Apparently, all the profits from the sale of eggs went to support two elderly widows. Because the Spurgeons were unwilling to let their left hand know what the right hand was doing (as Jesus instructed), they endured attacks on their character in silence—attacks that came from fellow believers, who should have known better!

SMALL GROUP DISCUSSION QUESTIONS

Matthew 6:1–4

1. How do you assess which kinds of charitable causes you support?

2. Some people have interpreted v.1 as suggesting that faith is a purely private matter and not something others should see. What was the point Jesus was making in that verse?

3. Is it always wrong if someone else sees or notices our acts of righteousness—like giving to needy causes?

4. In Acts 2:44–45 and Acts 4:34–35, we read of the amazing sharing of resources (wealth) that existed in the first generation of the church. How applicable to our situation in the twenty-first century are these verses?

5. How important is it to know where donated money to charitable causes goes and how it is used?

6. How do you personally apply the principles Jesus talks about in these verses?

10

Learning to Pray

During a time of intense warfare, a soldier was hauled before his commanding officer and accused of communicating with the enemy. He had been seen emerging from an area where enemy troops were known to patrol. The young man explained that he had slipped away to spend an hour alone in prayer. "Have you been in the habit of spending an hour in private prayer?" demanded the officer.

"Yes, Sir," he replied.

"Then," said his Commander. "Never in your life have you been in more need of prayer than now. Kneel down and pray aloud so that we all may hear you."

Anxious because he was being accused of treason and conspiring with the enemy, which was a summary capital offense, the soldier dropped to his knees and poured out his heart to God. His prayer immediately revealed an intimacy with his heavenly Father. His fluency, his humble appeal for divine intervention, and his evident trust in God's goodness told unmistakably that he regularly came before the throne of grace.

When the soldier finished his prayer, his commanding officer said: "You may go. No-one could have prayed that way without a long apprenticeship. No-one could pray like that unless it was a frequent habit."

Prayer is the currency which people use to transact with God. It should be no surprise then that Jesus addressed it in his sermon on a Galilean hillside. When Jesus talked about prayer, it was not anything new to the people of his day. They thought they knew a lot about prayer. For the strict and devout amongst them, there were set prayers that needed to be recited at specified times of each day, and on special ceremonial occasions.[1] However, the practice of prayer and the way many perceived it should be done, had gone off track. Rather than being an expression of intimacy and a means of communicating with God, the typical pattern of prayer had become a performance to be observed and to create a positive impression on others.

Sadly, for many contemporary Christians, whenever the subject of prayer is raised, one of two reactions occur. The first is a tendency to tune out because the concept of prayer has a boring ring to it. The other is to feel guilty because we do not pray enough. If you are experiencing the second of those reactions, and are perhaps tempted to skip this chapter as a result, you are in good company. Indeed, it is very hard to find any follower of Jesus who really believes they have an adequate prayer life. That would be a bit like a husband or a wife feeling they love their spouse enough. There is always room for improvement or growth.

At its core, prayer is simply the intimate communication that a person has with God. God is perpetually and willingly available to us when we talk to him. How he manages this, with billions of people all around the world vying for his attention, is a mystery. Thankfully though, God does not respond to our prayers via a telecommunications call-center. Imagine praying and receiving a response like this:

> "Thank you for calling my Father's house. Please select one of the following four options:
> Press 1 for requests.
>> Press 2 for thanksgiving.
>> Press 3 for complaints.
>> For all other inquiries, please stay on the line, and an angel will be with you shortly. Your prayer is really important to us. All the angels are helping other customers right now. Your prayer will be answered in the order in which it was received. Please stay on the line."

Be grateful that prayer is not like that. Whenever we turn our thoughts in God's direction, he is always available and listening. Neither is struggling with the issue of prayer something new to our generation. It was obviously an issue for the people amongst whom Jesus lived and he offered great advice on how to go about it:

---

1. Barclay, *The Gospel of Matthew, Volume 1*, 194–95

> [5]"And when you pray, do not be like the hypocrites, for they love to pray standing in the synagogues and on the street corners to be seen by others. Truly I tell you, they have received their reward in full. [6]But when you pray, go into your room, close the door and pray to your Father, who is unseen. Then your Father, who sees what is done in secret, will reward you. [7]And when you pray, do not keep on babbling like pagans, for they think they will be heard because of their many words. [8]Do not be like them, for your Father knows what you need before you ask him. [9]"This, then, is how you should pray: 'Our Father in heaven, hallowed be your name, [10]your kingdom come, your will be done, on earth as it is in heaven. [11]Give us today our daily bread. [12]And forgive us our debts, as we also have forgiven our debtors. [13]And lead us not into temptation, but deliver us from the evil one.'"
>
> Matthew 6:5–13

As noted in Chapter 9, in the culture of Jesus' day prayer was one of three meritorious *acts of righteousness* that people performed to demonstrate their supposed spirituality. If a people were truly right with God, they would give to the poor and needy, they would pray, and they would fast. Some people, however, were evidently using prayer as a means of showing off. They used words and language that sounded as if they were talking to God, but really their words were for the ears and the good impression of those listening in. Jesus had strong words for such people. He called them hypocrites! The original Greek word in this text, *hupokrites*, was used by Jesus at least seventeen times throughout the Gospels and described someone who played a role that was not sincere.[2] It meant literally an actor—someone who puts on a mask or plays a role, for the benefit of others. Jesus suggested that such people who flaunted their prayer-life in this way were play-acting.

Perhaps you have had the experience of engaging in conversation with someone in a crowded room, and they keep looking over your shoulder and greeting other people while you are talking to them? They are supposedly conversing with you, but really, they are playing or working the room. It is an unnerving experience when the person you are talking with is insincere or does not really want to stop and chat. This type of experience is what Jesus had in mind when he spoke of people praying prayers in the synagogues or on street corners to be seen by others. They were supposedly engaged in a conversation with God, but all

---

2. Vine, *An Expository Dictionary of New Testament Words,* 572

the while their minds were on others listening in, and the impression being given to them.

That said, it is important not to misunderstand what Jesus was saying. He was not criticizing public prayer *per se* or inferring that prayer only really connects with God when a person prays in private. Jesus' point was that the perceived audience of the person praying is critical. Prayer is either a means of "horizontal" communication to other people or a "vertical" communion with God. Put simply, this means that if a person claims to be talking to God in prayer, then God should be the sole focus of his or her attention.

I recall once being horribly embarrassed at a meal with friends. The husband gave thanks before we ate but failed to mention in his prayer specific gratitude to his wife, who had cooked the meal. The wife was visibly offended by this failure to mention her and sulked through the rest of the evening. Now, there is nothing wrong with thanking the cook for a meal (in fact, it is a custom to be encouraged!). However, doing so in the middle of giving thanks to God may not necessarily be the appropriate place. If a person is talking to God, let him or her be talking to God.

Bill Moyers, a former Baptist Pastor, worked as a White House Press Secretary and special assistant to President Lyndon Johnson. One day he was asked to say grace before a meal in the family quarters of the White House. As Moyers began praying softly, the President interrupted him: "Speak up, Bill! Speak up!" The former pastor stopped in mid-sentence and, without looking up, replied steadily: "I was not addressing you, Mr. President."

Then there are those who speak with ordinary vernacular speech and tone of voice, when in general conversation, but the moment they start to pray audibly they adopt an altogether different tone. The volume goes up and with it a sense of pomp and ceremony. As if this is the proper way one is supposed to address God, rather than in ordinary conversational tones. To be sure, some may choose to address God in honorific tones and words, as an expression of respect, but Jesus seemed to suggest God equally understands our everyday speech just fine.

There are also those who use open times of prayer to preach a little sermon or communicate information they think others have not yet heard. Like the man at a prayer meeting who prayed, "Dear LORD as you doubtless read in this morning's New York Times . . ." If there is news to share, or a burning conviction that something should be done, it may be better to stop the prayer meeting and share it. It is inappropriate to mix in with a prayer to God an underlying motive of communication or challenge to other people listening in.

Another issue Jesus singled out for special mention are those who recite religious words that do not have any meaning to them:

> ⁷And when you pray, do not keep on babbling like pagans, for they think they will be heard because of their many words. ⁸Do not be like them, for your Father knows what you need before you ask him . . .
>
> Matthew 6:7–8

What was Jesus getting at here? Jesus wanted his followers to see prayer as a personal communication from the heart of a pray-er, rather than mere recitation of pre-prepared statements. What kind of marriage would it be where a husband walks in the door and reads his greeting to his wife off a script: "Hello darling, it is good to see you, how was your day?" And the wife responds, reading her prepared text: "My day was wonderful. Tell me, how were things at your place of work?" When two people know and love each other, they do not need the help of a *Hallmark* greeting card to compose words of affection. They speak freely out of their hearts. If a person loves God, talk to him as freely and spontaneously as they would to someone they know and love.

By contrast, the pagan idea of prayer in Jesus' day was very different. It was more akin to "wearing down" or "wearying" the gods (Latin: *fatigare deos*) through long and repetitive prayers. The prophets of Baal called on the name of their God from morning until noon, crying, "O Baal, answer us."[3] The writer of the book Acts describes the Ephesian mob who challenged Paul and sought to shout him down: "they all shouted in unison for about two hours: "Great is Artemis of the Ephesians."[4] To the pagan way of thinking, the gods are reluctant to hear prayers unless the prayers are long, and only when petitioners have proved themselves sincere by calling out to him for a long time, will the gods begin to listen.

Some have wondered whether Jesus' challenge about "babbling prayers" calls into question the use of prayer-books or fixed liturgies as used by some Christian traditions. Is Jesus inferring that these kinds of set prayers are inappropriate or like pagan babbling? Noted Anglican theologian, the late John Stott, raised this about his own denomination's

---

3. 1 Kings 18.26
4. Acts 19:34–35

prayer books. "Are Anglicans guilty of babbling and meaningless prayers" where their "set forms of prayer permit an approach to God with the lips while the heart is far from him?"[5] On the other hand, for many Christ-followers, the carefully prepared prayers in a fixed liturgy, or prayer book, are profoundly moving. They capture heart-sentiments and express ideas in a profound and meaningful way. Sometimes free-church traditions, where prayers are almost always extemporaneous, are weaker for their insistence on informality and spontaneity.

Jesus' point was this: the people of his day went through the motions of ritual spirituality, but it clearly did not connect with their hearts. The same could be said for other world religions where words of worship are recited in a foreign language, that the ordinary people do not fully understand. When living in Bangladesh, I recall observing large gatherings of Bengali men listening to, and participating in, rituals of Muslim worship—all conducted in Arabic, rather than their mother-tongue, which almost none of them understood. The same could be said for certain Catholic traditions that only hold their worship liturgies in Latin as if this is the primary language of God. Such forms of ritualistic meditation and prayer are nothing short of sterile religious rituals.

Jesus invites his followers to talk with God in their own language. Rather than just reciting someone else's words, God loves to hear us speak with our own words—even if they are not as precise or measured as those that are specially prepared. Whatever language a person speaks, God is proficient in that tongue!

Jesus also offered a suggestion about where we pray:

> [6]But when you pray, go into your room, close the door and pray to your Father, who is unseen. Then your Father, who sees what is done in secret, will reward you . . .
>
> Matthew 6:6

Once again, it is important to avoid misunderstanding Jesus' point here. He was not suggesting that praying in groups or in front of others is wrong, as if the only valid or genuine prayer is that offered on one's own. That would contradict other statements of Jesus where he encourages us to listen to each other and to agree in prayer together. It was Jesus who suggested that when two or three agree in prayer, it has more effect.[6] Jesus'

---

5. Stott, *The Message of the Sermon on the Mount*, 144
6. Matthew 18:19

point was about focus. If a person is tempted to use communication with God as a means of bolstering their spiritual ego, or gathering kudos from others listening in, then the best way to deal with that temptation is to pray on one's own—with no-one else present to hear. Prayer is not talking *about God*; it is communicating *with God*. When a person prays on their own, with no one else listening in, the degree of intimacy, honesty and confidentiality between themselves and God is greatly enhanced. There is no pretence. God becomes less a bystander observing the communication, and more a participant actively engaged in relationship with the person addressing him.

Taking Jesus' advice seriously, what should a person do when they get alone with God in these times of prayer? Jesus went on to give his followers a simple agenda for personal times of prayer.

> [9]"This, then, is how you should pray: "'Our Father in heaven, hallowed be your name, [10]your kingdom come, your will be done on earth as it is in heaven. [11]Give us today our daily bread. [12]Forgive us our debts, as we also have forgiven our debtors. [13]And lead us not into temptation, but deliver us from the evil one."
>
> Matthew 6:9–13

These verses are among the most well-known and recited in the whole of the Bible. Nevertheless, it might be that a lot of Christians misunderstand entirely the point Jesus was making when he spoke. We often refer to these verses as the LORD's *Prayer*, and in many churches, it is taught by rote to children and recited weekly as part of the liturgy. In the secular high school I attended; we would recite the LORD's *Prayer* every week in our school assemblies. However, did Jesus ever intend this to be a recited prayer at all? Was he instead laying out an agenda for prayer? After all, Jesus has just been talking about how prayer needs to be personal and heartfelt, and not mindless. In many instances today, people recite the LORD's *Prayer* in a way reminiscent of the babbling pagans. The words roll off their tongue, but the sentiment behind each phrase has little impact or depth of meaning. By contrast, when these words are treated as a prayer agenda, they offer profound truth. Jesus was not so much teaching us *"what* to pray," as *"how* to pray."

The first thing he addresses is the manner in which God is addressed: "Our Father in heaven . . ." In other words, when speaking with God, the Christ-follower speaks in tones of intimacy, as one talks with a parent. Prayer is coming before God with a sense of family relationship.

Christians do not pray to some far-off uninterested deity, nor to a god whose anger needs to be appeased. Talking with God does not require rehearsed or pre-prepared statements. It is communication with someone with whom we already have a relationship.

When little children of a king or queen, or the political leader of a country, sit down for dinner with their father, do they refer to him formally as Your Majesty or Mr. President? Or do they call him "daddy." This is how God invites his children to come before him in prayer. Not with formal speeches and stuffy protocol, or having to choose words carefully, lest the wrong thing is said. In prayer, it is merely talking with "Dad." Jesus modeled this in the Garden of Gethsemane, on the night that he was betrayed. As he prayed, he asked if the cup of suffering he was about to face could pass from him. He addressed his prayer to "Abba Father." That word *"Abba,"* which the apostle Paul also used in his letters to the Christians in Rome and Galatia,[7] literally means "Daddy." It expresses the love and intelligent confidence of a young child.[8] In the context of prayer, it is not just addressing *the* Father, but *our* Father; and more particularly: *My* Father. Followers of Jesus have been adopted into God's family. In the same way that a human parent knows the intimate history of his or her children, so too, our Heavenly Father knows all about our past and what we are really like. Nothing is hidden from him, and genuine communication and prayer begin with that realization of intimacy and that knowledge.

Having taught us how to approach God in prayer, Jesus goes on to suggest seven specific topics or agenda items that are good for us to pray about:

AGENDA ITEM #1 — "HALLOWED BE YOUR NAME . . ."

The Good News Bible translation renders this phrase: "May your holy name be honoured." In other words, when praying to *Daddy* (in the familial sense of our relationship), keep in mind who he actually is and the scope of his capacity. God is holy or distinct from the things of this world. God transcends human existence. While God is not approached as someone to be feared or appeased, it is important that he is not treated with irreverence or flippancy. To put that another way, prayer starts with a recognition and expression of God's honor and the worship due to him.

---

7. Romans 8:15; Galatians 4:6
8. Vine, *An Expository Dictionary of New Testament Words*, 1

AGENDA ITEM #2—"YOUR KINGDOM COME..."

When praying, Christ-followers seek to align themselves with God's big picture and purpose, rather than hoping God will fit into theirs. Throughout his ministry, Jesus preached the coming or establishment of God's kingdom on earth. The kingdom exists wherever, and over whomever, God reigns as King. In that sense, the nature of the *Kingdom of God* is perpetually intent on growth and expansion. So, to pray for the coming of God's kingdom is to pray that more people, and more territory, will submit to the rule and reign of God. In other words, pray for the growth of God's mission and the impact of his rule throughout the world. In the apostle John's vision of the future, at the end of this age, he saw a day when our prayers will realise the completion of the Kingdom of God:

> [15]The kingdoms of this world have become the kingdom of our God, and of his Christ, and he shall reign forever and ever...
>
> Revelation 11:15

AGENDA ITEM #3—"YOUR WILL BE DONE ON EARTH AS IT IS IN HEAVEN..."

This agenda item goes hand in hand with the coming of God's kingdom, for where the kingdom or rule of God is established, there his will is done. The most obvious place where this happens at present is in the place where God dwells—in heaven. There the will of the King is carried out completely. It is God's expressed objective that the situation in heaven is emulated here on earth. Among all the other things brought before God in prayer, Christ-followers are to pray for the fulfilment of God's desire and intentions within the world. Pray for issues of righteousness, justice and peace within the world—both near and far. Pray for courage to live out the will of God personally, especially when that differs from the ways of the cultures which surround you.

AGENDA ITEM #4—"GIVE US OUR DAILY BREAD..."

Christ-followers bring before God their daily needs for survival. To put that another way, God is not only interested in listening to words of worship and praise. He is also vitally interested in the affairs of a Christian's everyday life. Talking to God about the provision of food and the basic necessities in life is not carnal or selfish. Some have mistakenly thought so and felt reluctant to bother God with personal needs. No! Such matters God cares about and is interested in responding to. We are the object of God's love and care, and the invitation to present our daily needs before him is perpetually open. Ask God to supply your daily needs.

AGENDA ITEM #5—"FORGIVE US OUR DEBTS AS WE ALSO FORGIVE OUR DEBTORS . . ."

Jesus encourages his followers to confess their sins to God and ask his forgiveness openly. To confess essentially means to own up to, or to agree or admit to.[9] Concerning sin, the Christ-follower concurs with God's assessment. Rather than trying to mitigate or deny their guilt, they own up to actions, words or attitudes that they know are disobedient to the will of God. In the same way that offensive or deceitful ehaviour interferes with ordinary relationships, clear communication with God is interfered with when there are outstanding issues. So, in times of 'alone' prayer, admit failures and where you have fallen short of God's standards, and ask his forgiveness.

Jesus went further than this: he placed a rider on asking for forgiveness. He said that it is only possible to ask for or expect God to forgive us, to the extent we are willing to forgive others who have sinned against us. At the end of this prayer agenda, Jesus came back to this particular point and gave additional commentary:

> [14]For if you forgive men when they sin against you, your heavenly Father will also forgive you. [15]But if you do not forgive men their sins, your Father will not forgive your sins.
>
> Matthew 6:14–15

In other words, it is not possible to ask God to forgive more than we are willing to forgive others. Or to put that the other way around, if a people refuse to forgive others, and continue to hold resentment and grudges against them, their own sins will not be forgiven.[10]

---

9. Vine, *An Expository Dictionary of New Testament Words*, 216
10. See Jesus parable of the Unmerciful Servant—Matthew 18:21–35

AGENDA ITEM #6—"LEAD US NOT INTO TEMPTATION..."

This is not a suggestion that God might himself do the tempting. The Bible is clear on that point—God tempts no one. James 1:13 makes that clear:

> ³When tempted, no one should say, "God is tempting me." For God cannot be tempted by evil, nor does he tempt anyone...

This is a request for God's help to withstand temptation. Are there areas of weakness or vulnerability that you have toward particular types of sin? Make these items for prayer. Ask God for the courage and character not to give in, and for his help and protection. The more such issues are made the subject of prayer, the less likely it is the Christ-follower will put him or herself into those types of places and situations where such temptation can occur.

AGENDA ITEM #7—"DELIVER US FROM THE EVIL ONE..."

Followers of Jesus have an enemy. The devil's stated desire is corruption and destruction of those who love God. One of the greatest weapons we have in standing firm against him is prayer.[11] Among all the other things to pray about, ask God for strength and protection from evil.

In closing, a word to those who might think they do not have time in their busy schedules to take Jesus' advice, and find a quiet place to pray and nurture their relationship with God. In Stephen Covey's book, "The Seven Habits of Highly Effective People," his seventh habit includes a story of a man coming across a woodcutter feverishly sawing down a tree.

> "You look exhausted! How long have you been at it?"
> "Over five hours," the woodcutter replied. "And I am beat. This is really hard work."
> "Maybe you could take a break for a few minutes and sharpen that saw. Then the work would go faster."
> "Oh, no. No time," the man said emphatically. "I am far too busy sawing to stop and do that."[12]

---

11. Ephesians 6:13; 18–20
12. Covey, *The 7 Habits of Highly Effective People*, 289

Some people think they do not have time for God, and so they labor through life with a blunt saw. Abraham Lincoln reputedly once said: "Give me six hours to chop down a tree, and I will spend the first four sharpening the ax." Maybe the best thing a person can do when coping with the rigors and stresses of life, is to stop cutting and sharpen their connection with Jesus by spending time alone in prayer.

SMALL GROUP DISCUSSION QUESTIONS

Matthew 6:5–15

1. Jesus talks about people who do their "acts of righteousness" for the notice of others as "hypocrites." Is there a difference between hypocrisy and sinful failure, or are they the same thing?

2. Why does Jesus suggest praying in secret, as opposed to praying in public?

3. Why do so many (all!) Christians say they do not pray enough? How much is enough?

4. What might a contemporary example of v.7 be in our day and age?

5. V.8 suggests that God knows what we need before we ask him. Does that negate the need for us to pray? How would you explain this idea to a new Christian?

6. How have you benefited (or otherwise) from praying the LORD's Prayer regularly throughout your life?

7. What was Jesus primary intention in v.9–13?

8. How do verses 14 & 15 challenge you?

11

Going Without

Each year the Islamic community engage in a month-long fast, called *Ramadan*. It is celebrated during the ninth month of the Islamic calendar and commemorates the first revelation that came to Mohammed. During *Ramadan*, Muslims are called to fast (i.e., go without food or drink) each day from dawn (literally: when it is light enough to distinguish white bread from black bread) through to sunset.[1] Some individuals, such as breastfeeding mothers and pregnant women are exempted, while others such as soldiers or travelers are permitted to defer their fast to another time.[2] For the rest, fasting is the order of the day. Living in the Muslim country of Bangladesh, one quickly learned to watch where one was walking during *Ramadan*; since not even saliva was allowed to be swallowed and was consequently spat out on the ground. Fasting during the month of *Ramadan* is very important to Muslims, although technically, it is more a deferment of eating during daylight hours because they tend to feast after sunset.

Ceremonial or ritualistic fasting is certainly not limited to Muslims. Other religions have rituals and practices along the same lines. For the Jewish people of Jesus' day, 600 years before the prophet Mohammed, there were similar cultural rules around religious fasting. Fasting was regarded as one of three essential *acts of righteousness* that a genuine son or daughter of Abraham would perform. If a person were true to the faith

---

1. Qur'an, 2:185

2. There are other exceptions, including children, menstruating women, the sick and elderly.

and righteous before God, he or she would give to the poor, recite prayers at certain times of the day, and practice fasting.

However, as we have learned, by the time of Jesus many would practice each of these disciplines in ways that other people would notice and consequently think well of them. The original intent of God's people giving, praying, and fasting was not wrong or inappropriate, but it needed to be done from genuine motives—as physical acts of worship toward God. By time of Jesus, the original intent of the *Law* had been lost in transmission—distorted by the pedantic and legalistic experts so that rather than doing their *acts of righteousness* for God's eyes, many religious people tended to do them for the eyes or notice of others.

The whole idea of "doing things for others to notice" was something that Jesus challenged. According to Jesus, motive and manner were the important factors, either accrediting or discrediting the validity of the worship. In the previous two chapters of this book, the practice of giving and prayer have been discussed; here is what Jesus had to say about the practice of fasting:

> [16]"When you fast, do not look somber as the hypocrites do, for they disfigure their faces to show others they are fasting. Truly I tell you, they have received their reward in full. [17]But when you fast, put oil on your head and wash your face, [18]so that it will not be obvious to others that you are fasting, but only to your Father, who is unseen; and your Father, who sees what is done in secret, will reward you."
>
> Matthew 6:16–18

People were play-acting or putting on a role that was insincere and once again, Jesus employs the word "hypocrite." His point was clear and straightforward. If a person is worshipping or making a sacrifice unto the LORD, then let it be done unto the LORD. Perform for an audience of One, rather than for the recognition of others.

The practice and philosophy behind fasting, amongst the people and culture of Jesus' day, obviously stemmed back to the *Law of Moses*. For instance, there was one compulsory fast-day for every Jew once a year, on the Day of Atonement (or *Yom Kippur*). This was the holiest day of the year:

> [29]"This is to be a lasting ordinance for you: On the tenth day of the seventh month you must deny yourselves (i.e. fast) and not do any work—whether native-born or a foreigner residing

among you—³⁰because on this day atonement will be made for you, to cleanse you. Then, before the LORD, you will be clean from all your sins. ³¹It is a day of sabbath rest, and you must deny yourselves (i.e., fast); it is a lasting ordinance."

Leviticus 16:29-31

There were many fasting times and days. In Jesus' time, the typical days of the week for fasting were Mondays and Thursdays, which also happened to be market days in most towns and villages. If the motive was to be noticed and thought of as spiritual, these were prime opportunities to demonstrate one's self-sacrifice and piety because the town would be crowded with people. There were some who, as they fasted, would walk through the streets with their hair deliberately unkempt and disheveled, or their clothes wrinkled and scruffy. Some even went to the trouble of whitening their faces to look anemic or to accentuate their pallor, as a result of going without food. "Notice me . . . Notice me . . . See how righteous I am . . .!"

Jesus' condemnation was unequivocal. Such behavior rendered the act a sham or display and negated the spiritual discipline. His prescriptive advice was straightforward and practical. If a fast was intended as an act of worship unto God, then fast so that you do not draw attention to yourself. Faces should be washed, hair combed, and oil applied, as one would typically do before going out in public. Others ought not to be able to tell by looking that a person is restricting his or her food, and then God, who sees what is done in secret, will respond.

As noted with each of the three *acts of righteousness*, there are two types of reward a person could receive: recognition or kudos in the eyes of others who notice and are hopefully impressed, or the reward that comes from God in response to genuine worship. There may be one or the other, but there cannot be both.

Understanding the point Jesus was making here is not difficult. Purity of motive is the most important thing. However, two thousand years on from the time of Jesus, there is another question that begs an answer: Why do it all? What is the point or the purpose of fasting? How does it help or achieve the desired end? Understanding the necessity of giving to the poor and needy is not obscure, and it is certainly not difficult to grasp the point of prayer. But what does fasting actually achieve? It does not sound like a particularly pleasant practice, nor something to put on a glossy brochure advertising the Christian faith. Neither is it a spiritual discipline that gets a lot of airtime in the contemporary church. When was the last time you heard a talk on fasting during a service?

Yet, when one looks through the Bible, those who choose to practice the discipline of fasting are in pretty good company. As will be noted later, there is no shortage of role models to draw upon: Moses the lawgiver, David the King, Elijah the prophet, Esther the Queen, Daniel the dream-interpreter, Ezra the priest, Jehoshaphat the king, Anna the prophetess, Jesus the Son of God, Paul the Apostle, Barnabas and the elders of the church in Antioch. . . All practiced fasting as an expression of their worship and devotion to God. Throughout church history, there is an even longer list of people who deliberately practiced this discipline.

Neither, as we have noted, is the act of fasting exclusively a Judeo-Christian practice or religious discipline. Greek philosophers like Plato, Socrates, and Aristotle described how and when they fasted. Muslims, Buddhists, and Hindus also practice fasting.

Fasting has also been something to which whole nations have been called. In 1756, the king of England called for a day of solemn prayer and fasting because of a threatened invasion by the French. John Wesley wrote this in his journal on February 6th:

> "The fast day was a glorious day, such as London has scarce seen since the Restoration. Every church in the city was more than full, and a solemn seriousness sat on every face. Surely God heareth prayer, and there will yet be a lengthening of our tranquility..."[3]

Then in a footnote in his diary, he wrote a little while later:

> "Humility was turned into national rejoicing for the threatened invasion by the French was averted..."[4]

There are numerous examples throughout the Bible describing when, why, and how people fasted. The occasions tend to fall into two categories: *repentance* or *mourning* over the realization of sin, and *prayer*—especially inquiring of the LORD about a particular course of action. For instance:

- Judges 20—the Israelites were losing badly in a battle. The whole army went to Bethel and sat before the LORD, fasting for the whole day, as they inquired of him what they should do.

---

3. Wesley, *The Journal of the Reverend John Wesley*, 147.
4. Foster, *Celebration of Discipline*, 44.

- 1 Samuel 7—the Israelites assembled at Mizpah where they fasted as an act of contrition, confessing their sin in worshipping false gods.
- Nehemiah 9—Ezra and Nehemiah sought to reintroduce obedient worship and the Israelites fasted, wore sackcloth, and put ash on their heads as an act of repentance.
- Jonah 3—the city of Nineveh heard Jonah's prophesy concerning God's impending judgment and the king, as an act of repentance, called a city-wide fast from food—including deprivation for all their animals, sheep and cattle.
- Esther 4—Queen Esther faced an extraordinary crisis that could have resulted in her own death. She asked Mordecai to have the Jewish people join her in fasting and prayer for three days.
- 1 Kings 21—King Ahab recognized his sin against the LORD and tore his clothes, put on sackcloth and fasted as a sign of his repentance.
- Luke 2—Anna the elderly prophetess, who was present in the temple when Jesus was consecrated as a baby, was in the habit of worshipping night and day through fasting and prayer.
- Luke 4—Jesus, while enduring a period of intense testing at the hand of the devil, fasted for a period of forty days.
- Acts 13—the leaders of the church in Antioch were seeking the mind of the LORD about a particular course of action so they fasted as they prayed.

While the Bible does not define precisely when and why one should fast, by taking a composite view of these examples, a picture or pattern emerges. In each instance, they are linked with an act of worship or submission toward God. People would fast as a physical discipline that demonstrated sorrow and repentance for wrongdoing, or they would fast as a physical expression of earnest prayer and seeking to understand the mind of the LORD.

The Bible also offers different examples of fasting. Some fasts lasted a day, others three days, and some even up to forty days. Most fasts were only from food, but there are a couple of examples where those fasting abstained from food and water. There are even examples of partial fasts, as when Daniel, Shadrach, Meshach, and Abednego abstained from certain types of food during the Babylonian captivity, as an act of submission or reverence toward God.[5]

Perhaps we could understand Christian fasting as being all about heightened *focus*. It is a physical discipline that people practice in order to sharpen the focus of their attention upon God. It is a way of bringing the mind and body into the act of communion with God, and perhaps also a way of demonstrating a person's seriousness or willingness to be subject to his will when seeking his guidance or help. "When the body is most disciplined, the mental and the spiritual faculties are most alert."[6]

However, as with any physical act of worship, there is always opportunity for it to be corrupted or misused. This was the issue in Jesus' day. People did the technical act, but with mixed motives. Fasting, as an expression of sorrow, mourning or penance for sin, can sometimes lead to people depriving themselves physically, without it really meaning anything spiritually. The physical act becomes a substitute for actual commitment and submission. For instance, it is entirely possible to give something up for Lent, without it really creating a focus in preparation for Easter. The outward form becomes mechanical or ritualistic, rather than a genuine desire to engage seriously with God. This was why the prophet Zechariah wrote:

> [4]Then the word of the LORD Almighty came to me: [5]'Ask all the people of the land and the priests, "When you fasted and mourned in the fifth and seventh months for the past seventy years, was it really for me that you fasted? [6]And when you were eating and drinking, were you not just feasting for yourselves?
>
> Zechariah 7:4–6

In seeking to understand the point and purpose of fasting in the contemporary age, there are several things worth noting that fasting is not:

- dieting—either to lose weight or for ideological reasons. (It may be a good thing to do as a weight-loss strategy or a preparation for surgery or to cleanse one's liver, etc., but going without food is different from a spiritual fast.)
- a hunger strike or a means of protesting.

---

5. Daniel 1
6. Barclay, *The Gospel of Matthew*, Volume 1, 234.

- able to make a person more holy or righteous. (It might actually make them grumpy and ornery for a while!)
- earning a person merit in heaven. (Those who fast are not better, per se, than those who do not.)
- a way of manipulating (intentionally or otherwise) God into answering one's prayers. (As if God listens and acts more to those prayers that are accompanied by fasts, than those that are not.)

Some people have questioned whether fasting is a practice that every Christian should observe, or whether it is optional. When Jesus' gave advice about fasting in his Sermon on the Mount, he certainly was not prescribing a new practice. Nor was he dissuading existing practice as if it was no longer necessary. Jesus did not say: *"if"* you fast, but *"when"* you fast, implying that his followers would do so. His position seems to assume that people would fast at significant points in their spiritual journey—either weekly, monthly or at certain times of the year. Jesus point was that when fasting, it is important to do so with the right motive.

An answer to the question about whether or not fasting is a command may be influenced by the tradition a person comes from, and given certain medical conditions, fasting may not be appropriate for everyone. However, the best answer to this question might be to say that it is a discipline more people should try than who currently do. It is a physical expression of worship that costs something. Words of praise are easy and cheap; self-denial is more costly. If it has not been a part of your routine or repertoire of worship, it might be something worth exploring.

One other model of fasting warrants a mention. This model from early church history is not usually thought of when exploring the discipline of fasting, but perhaps it should be. In the first few hundred years of the Christian church, there was a tangible sense of community amongst followers of Jesus. They cared for each other in times of need. Christian fellowship (*koinonia*) was more than just sharing a cup of coffee and a cookie after church or having parties in each other's homes. It was palpable, tangible and costly. In the first generation of the church was known for its practice of sharing wealth and excess with those who were poor.[7] People with more than they needed would sell property and possessions to support those within the church who were in dire straits.

---

7. Acts 2:42–47; 4:32–37; 9:36

A further example of this form of practical love comes from the second century. A historian by the name of Aristides wrote a letter to Emperor Hadrian in defense of the Christians and the hard time they were experiencing. He wrote about the culture of the Christian church around AD125 and the costly love that members of the church showed toward people in need. At the end of his statement were these challenging words:

". . . And if there is among them a man who was poor and needy and he has not an abundance of necessaries, they fast two or three days that they may supply the needy with the necessary food."[8]

Might this be a model of fasting that shifts it beyond self-serving or self-promoting motivations? Rather than fasting to get something, or to be noticed by others, what if Christians were to deliberately fast in order to resource others who are in need? Rather than fasting with the subtle motive of manipulating God into answering our prayers (in the way or timing we want) instead of purchasing a bottle of wine, or making an upgrade on our car, or staying in a really fancy hotel or a buying a new pair of shoes, or a new set of golf clubs . . . people chose (as an act of worship) to drink water, or to stay cheaper, or stick with an older model for another year, and instead give the equivalent cost to a brother or sister in need? Maybe that kind of fast might be a valid and acceptable expression of worship that gains approval from the LORD. The prophet Isaiah certainly seemed to think so:

> [2] . . . They ask me for just decisions and seem eager for God to come near them.
> [3]"Why have we fasted,' they say, 'and you have not seen it? Why have we humbled ourselves, and you have not noticed?'
> "Yet on the day of your fasting, you do as you please and exploit all your workers.
> [4]Your fasting ends in quarreling and strife, and in striking each other with wicked fists. You cannot fast as you do today and expect your voice to be heard on high.
> [5]Is this the kind of fast I have chosen, only a day for people to humble themselves?
> Is it only for bowing one's head like a reed and for lying in sackcloth and ashes? Is that what you call a fast, a day acceptable to the LORD?

---

8. Aristides, quoted in Martin Hengel, *Property and Riches in the Early Church*, 42–43

> ⁶"Is not this the kind of fasting I have chosen: to loose the chains of injustice and untie the cords of the yoke, to set the oppressed free and break every yoke?
> ⁷Is it not to share your food with the hungry and to provide the poor wanderer with shelter—when you see the naked, to clothe them, and not to turn away from your own flesh and blood?
>
> Isaiah 58:2–7

Given that fasting is fundamentally an act of sacrifice and "giving up" something, it raises the sticky question: *What has it really cost us to be a follower of Jesus?* One thing fasting does is to underscore the concept of self-sacrifice. Genuine Christian faith, according to the Bible, is more than a philosophy or a belief system. It is not merely something added to a portfolio of spiritual beliefs. It is more than a ticket into heaven or a get-out-of-hell-free card. Genuine faith in Jesus Christ is a radical act of surrendering ourselves and the leadership of our own lives to another. It is akin to an act of abdication. We stop acting and existing only for our pleasure and instead live our lives to please and honor God. Jesus put it like this in Luke 9:23

> ²³Whoever wants to be my disciple must deny themselves and take up their cross daily and follow me . . .

At the core of genuine Christian faith is the notion of self-denial. What does that mean for us in the twenty-first century? In some parts of the world, it has a very literal definition, as those who choose to become a Christian face severe and literal persecution. They lose their family, their home, and their employment—sometimes even their health. In other parts of the world, where there is religious tolerance enshrined in a country's law, faith in God might draw the odd comment or snigger of ridicule, but the physical cost is much less.

Jesus seemed to imply that there needs to be a cost to our discipleship if it is real. Rather than trying to fit Jesus into our way of living; we must be bent, trimmed and squeezed into His mold. We cannot continue to live self-indulgent lives, but rather we submit to his LORDship. Our worship and allegiance to Him is supposed to cost us something. Perhaps this is where fasting comes into play. If it has not been something we have ever done before, perhaps we should give the discipline of fasting a try. Maybe starting small and giving up a meal once a week to instead spend time in prayer. Or perhaps going without food for a day or two or three, as a way to focus our body, mind, and spirit on Jesus.

Whatever action is chosen, and for however long it is done, make sure it is done unto God. Not, Jesus said, for the notice or recognition of others. Then our Father, who sees what we do in secret, will reward us . . .

SMALL GROUP DISCUSSION QUESTIONS

Matthew 6:16–18

1. What is your experience personally (historically) with fasting? How did it affect you?
2. If you had to explain the point of fasting to someone unfamiliar with the Bible, what would you say?
3. What was the main point(s) Jesus had in his comment on fasting in Matthew 6:16–18?
4. What is the primary challenge you take from Zechariah 7:4–6?
5. The early Christians used to fast in order to raise funds for brothers and sisters in dire need. How might that principle be applied in the church today?
6. What does a verse like Luke 9:23 say to you? What have you "denied yourself" to be a follower of Jesus?

12

Treasure Hunter

A cruise ship docked near a small Mexican village. A tourist came ashore, complimented a local fisherman on the quality of his fish, and asked how long it took him to catch them.

"Not very long Señor," answered the fisherman.

"But then why don't you stay out longer and catch more fish?" asked the tourist. The fisherman explained that his small catch was sufficient to meet his needs and those of his family.

The tourist persisted "But what do you do with the rest of your time?"

"I sleep late, fish a little, play with my children, and take a siesta with my wife. In the evenings I go into the village to see my friends, have a few drinks, play the guitar, and sing a few songs. I have a full life."

The tourist interrupted, "Sir, I have an MBA from a prestigious university, and I can really help you! If you start by fishing longer every day, you can sell the extra fish you catch to buy a bigger boat. With the extra money you earn from the larger boat, you will be able to buy a second one and a third one and so on, until you have a fleet of fishing trawlers. Then, instead of selling your fish to a middleman, you can negotiate directly with the processing plants, and maybe even open your own plant. You can leave this little village and move to the capital city and live in a really up-market home. From there, you can direct your huge enterprise."

"How long would that take Señor?"

"Twenty, perhaps twenty-five years," replied the tourist.

"And after that, Señor?"

"Afterwards, that's when it gets really interesting," answered the tourist laughing. "When your business gets really big, you can start selling stocks and make millions of dollars!"

"Millions! Really Señor? And after that?"

"Well, after that you'll be able to retire to a tiny village near the coast. You will be able to sleep late, play with your children, catch a few fish, take a siesta every day, and spend your evenings drinking and enjoying your friends . . ."

Throughout human history, many have written about their struggle to understand the meaning and purpose of life. What is the point of all that consumes our time and energy, and that keeps us so busy? Does it really add value to our lives or result in happiness? Or are we merely spinning our wheels, like the proverbial hamster running an endless race in a cage?

One such philosopher was King Solomon, king of Israel (990–931BCE). The ancient book of Ecclesiastes records his wrestle with the point or purpose of working hard, earning lots of money, amassing a fortune, only to finally die leaving a heap of assets for lazy (and possibly ungrateful) children to enjoy—who did not work hard to get it. He concluded that such toil and anxious striving was meaningless and vanity.[1]

Solomon is not alone in asking these kinds of questions. What is the point, or end result, of all that consumes our time and money and energy? Is it worth the effort? Is striving to earn more, so more can be purchased, actually producing a happier and more successful life?

Jesus had some interesting comments to make along these lines. In particular, he challenged people to think about the long-term yield from all the time and money we invest in life:

> [19]"Do not store up for yourselves treasures on earth, where moth and vermin destroy, and where thieves break in and steal. [20]But store up for yourselves treasures in heaven, where moth and vermin do not destroy, and where thieves do not break in and steal. [21]For where your treasure is, there your heart will be also. [22]"The eye is the lamp of the body. If your eyes are healthy, your whole body will be full of light. [23]But if your eyes are unhealthy, your whole body will be full of darkness. If then the light within you is darkness, how great is that darkness! [24]"No one can serve two masters. Either you will hate the one and love the other, or

---

1. Ecclesiastes 2:17–23

you will be devoted to the one and despise the other. You cannot serve both God and money."

Matthew 6:19-24

Jesus had a knack for making people think in ways that were not always comfortable or appreciated. He challenged popular paradigms of life; the models for living that people thought were fixed and immutable. In these verses, he asks people to consider what in life they regard as most valuable. Are all those things they invest their energy and time to acquire worth it? Are they truly lasting?

One way to look at the challenge Jesus gives in these verses is to consider what will be accomplished with the resources that will pass through typical household accounts over the next ten years. For most households in the wealthy western world, if we were to take the combined annual household incomes (e.g., salaries, investments, capital-gain on property, accumulating pension funds) and multiply it by ten, then the majority would see more than a million dollars pass through their accounts over the next decade! At the end of that period, what will they have to show for it?

Jesus was keen for his followers to understand their eternal status. If life here on Earth is finite (i.e., it ends or ceases at the point of mortal death), then earthly treasure or material possessions—personal wealth, fancy homes and flash chattels which make that life more comfortable—are all worthwhile acquisitions. If dying marks the cessation of a person's existence, then they might as well burn up their energy and resources in the accumulation of such treasure. This is as good as it gets!

On the other hand, if life on Earth is not finite, but a doorstep that a person passes over or a prelude to a new world of everlasting life, then another set of values is called for. If life continues past the point of death, then that reality needs to be kept in mind when it comes to evaluating all the trappings this world regards as worthwhile.

A Polish rabbi, Chofetz Chaim, was once visited by an American tourist, who was astonished to see that the rabbi's home was only a simple room filled with books, a table, and a bench. The tourist asked: "Rabbi, where is your furniture?"

"Where is yours?" replied the rabbi.

"Mine?" asked the puzzled tourist. "But I am a visitor here. I am only passing through."

"So am I," said Chofetz Chaim.

It has been wisely said: "The world is like a bridge. The wise man passes over it, but he does not stop to build his house on it." For the follower of Jesus, their real home or heartland is not tied up in the affairs of this world. When a person becomes a follower of Jesus, their citizenship or status is changed. Their primary citizenship is no longer in this world or in the country of their birth. They become citizens of another kingdom—the kingdom of God—and the values they are called to live by, within that kingdom, are dramatically altered.

In Chapter 7, I mentioned a visit I made to Papua New Guinea, to speak at a conference. It was my first visit outside of my home country and culture. Understandably, it was fascinating learning the value or treasure that the tribes of Papua New Guinea placed upon pigs. The number of pigs a man owned was used as a means of measuring a man's wealth or status. In fact, some years earlier pigs had been the official currency of the country. As a native of the so-called developed world, pigs are dirty, smelly creatures—delightful to eat, but not to have around your home. However, to the Papua New Guineans, they were a precious treasure and a valuable asset. (There were even stories of PNG women nursing orphan pigs on their breast!) The western worldview that I had grown up with is very different from the tribal worldview of Papua New Guinea.

That is the point Jesus wanted his followers to grasp. Followers of Jesus no longer have their primary citizenship in the countries and ethnicities of this world. They are technically foreigners. Their real citizenship is now in the kingdom of God. The values and treasures and precious things that "natives" of this world prize become foreign values. As Christians grow in their relationship with God, they find that their values are no longer a neat fit with the values and ethos of this world.

In the Old Testament, when the Jewish nation was divided and exiled, their focus was always on their real homeland. Daniel, for instance, as an exile in Babylon, deliberately opened windows in his house that faced Jerusalem as he prayed. Whenever a synagogue was built in a foreign land, it was constructed in such a way that as people entered it, they were facing Jerusalem. When the apostle Peter wrote his first pastoral letter, he addressed it: "To God's elect, strangers in the world." Peter referred to Christ-followers as "aliens and exiles."[2] In other words, their focus is more on their homeland than where they presently live.

---

2. 1 Peter 1:1; 2:11

After traveling abroad, many people accumulate a collection of currency in coins and notes acquired from different countries they have visited around the world. These are legal tender in their respective countries but are of absolutely no value in one's home country. Jesus challenged his followers to ponder whether the wealth that they were amassing in this life would retain its value in the next.

Jesus addressed three types of treasure that are certain to depreciate:

1. TREASURE THAT MOTH CAN DESTROY

One of the common symbols of wealth in the culture of Jesus' day was the possession of fine or expensive clothes. Wealthy people wore garments that were woven with refined and colorful thread or were so beautifully ornate that they were obviously a cut above what the ordinary citizen could afford. If you wanted to impress your community and make them aware of your status, you bought elaborate apparel.

Contemporary culture is probably not too far removed from this. Every year fashion designers tempt us with new and the latest designs, accompanied by a not-so-subtle inference that we should keep pace with the most recent available wardrobe. Clothes remain symbols of financial prosperity, social status, and the ability to keep pace with current trends. Often, the tiny label in the collar carries more value than the actual material of the garment itself. If anyone doubts that this is true, ask any family trying to clothe teenagers!

Jesus suggested that in God's kingdom, such treasure is a poor investment. It is horribly short-lived. Moths and insects are no respecter of person or value; they eat holes in the most expensive garments, or the cheapest, regardless of the quality. The nail sticking out of the garage wall, or the spilled glass of red wine can ruin an expensive piece of apparel just as well as something cheap. Those relying on these kinds of treasure or valuing this kind of recognition might well be let down.

The old proverb says: "Clothes maketh the man!" and alludes to how dressing well accounts for the quality of a person's character. An inversion of that proverb might be a greater truth: "Man maketh the clothes!" If Jesus were walking amongst us in the 21st century, he might say: "Don't put your sense of value in perishable garments that will not last." This is not to suggest people should go around in scruffy clothes, looking drab and unkempt. But many people are driven by desire and addicted to extending their own elaborate wardrobe. Jesus called such pursuit "false treasure."

2. TREASURE THAT VERMIN CAN DESTROY

The literal meaning of the word translated as "vermin" (*brōsis*) was that which "eats away."[3] Some English translations use the word "rust" to capture the idea of something decaying or wasting away. However, the imagery probably originally brought to mind a stockpile of grain that has gone bad or become polluted or infected by rats and mice. Jesus told stories of a farmer's bumper-crops and barns filled with stockpiled food as a metaphor of prosperity. He counselled his hearers not to regard perishable things which may not prevail or survive adverse conditions as treasure. He warned them not to be tricked into investing their time and energy into acquiring things that look nice today, but by tomorrow are rotten or eaten away.

The newly built house, worth hundreds of thousands of dollars more than another the same size, but a few years older, decays and rots in the same way. The expensive brand-new car and the sense of status associated with it, does not transport us from place to place any better than the second-hand car that costs half the price . . . Nor does the cheaper car devalue by $5,000 as soon as it is driven off the lot and around the block. Investing in depreciating assets is not smart.

Again, this is not to suggest that assets like cars and houses are unnecessary or unimportant. However, living with a sense of kingdom values makes the Christ-follower question the pressure our culture puts upon us to continually upgrade to the latest or most expensive model. Christians should think differently about treasure and pleasure than those who are not citizens of God's kingdom. They are to think less about acquiring status symbols, and more about how to wisely use the resources entrusted to them.

3. TREASURE WHERE THIEVES BREAK IN AND STEAL

The original word translated here as "break in" (*diorussō*) meant "digging or breaking through."[4] Houses in the Middle East in Jesus' day were not

---

3. Vine, *An Expository Dictionary of New Testament Words*, 982
4. Vine, *An Expository Dictionary of New Testament Words*, .140

constructed with wooden siding or bricks and mortar. They were often made of baked clay; a material that could be picked at or dug through. The imagery is of the person who stored money or gold within his or her house only to find burglars had dug through a wall and stolen it all.

Hopefully, modern-day banks and investment companies are a little more secure when it comes to guarding money, but there are all sorts of ways treasure is taken from them as well. Stock markets can crash, companies go into bankruptcy, steady sources of income can disappear, and house values plummet.

Jesus' point was that these forms of worldly treasure are vulnerable or fickle. They are not consistent, durable or guarantees of happiness. Many people have chased after elusive happiness or security by amassing different forms of worldly treasure, only to find themselves feeling empty and frustrated as if it has all been a waste of time. Indeed, it has been suggested there are more suicides amongst the rich than there are amongst the poor. Or as the Psalmist put it: "Surely everyone goes around like a mere phantom; in vain they rush about, heaping up wealth without knowing where it will finally end."[5]

Jesus' advice is clear. There is a sense in which material possessions will always be important; it is not possible to survive without them. However, they must not be viewed as a treasure that will guarantee security or protection in adversity or that has an intrinsic value so that it becomes an end in itself. Such a treasure is fickle and temporary. If people are going to strive for something of value, Jesus urges them to make an investment in eternal, inflation-proof bonds:

> [20]But store up for yourselves treasures in heaven ... [21]For where your treasure is, there your heart will be also.
>
> Matthew 6:20–21

What does that mean? What exactly is treasure in heaven? To be clear, Jesus was not suggesting a blanket prohibition on material possessions, or savings, or retirement investment. These are far from being inherently wrong. Nor was he proposing that people don't choose wisely—even expensively—when making a purchase. Buying second-hand is not necessarily more meritorious than paying more for brand-new. Sometimes value means "we get what we pay for." No, Jesus point was about the selfish heart of those who chase after wealth and riches.

---

5. Psalm 39:6

The phrase "treasure in heaven" was familiar to the people of Jesus' day. It was associated with heavenly rewards for good deeds done during a person's life. It was based on an understanding that God rewards acts of generosity toward others, and especially expressions of compassion and care for people in need—particularly widows and orphans, and those who were suffering. Those who were generous and gave to the needy, in an unselfish manner, were said to be storing up treasure in heaven. Their eyes and their hearts were fixed on using their resources for causes that really matter. This is likely what Jesus alludes to in v.22–23:

> 22"The eye is the lamp of the body. If your eyes are healthy, your whole body will be full of light. 23But if your eyes are unhealthy, your whole body will be full of darkness. If then the light within you is darkness, how great is that darkness!

These words seem quite cryptic and scholars offer various interpretations as to Jesus' meaning. The most logical meaning is a reference to that which fills a person's vision. Light enters the eye, enabling a person to see. When they look at the world around them, what does a person notice? Do they see that which they can purchase or acquire for themselves? Or do they see people and situations of need where they can assist? In the Jewish world of Jesus' day, the eye was regarded as a gateway into a person's heart or mind.[6]

The word that is translated as "healthy" (*haplos*) carried the idea of liberality and being generous.[7] In other words, people with a healthy vision of their world see need in others and respond with generosity; those with unhealthy vision see through a lens of selfishness and self-interest. The light in their eyes is darkness, Jesus said, and how great that darkness becomes.

There is a parable of a rich man who died and went to heaven. He was being shown around by one of the angels. They came across a huge mansion, and the rich man asked the angel, "Who lives here?" When told it was his gardener, the man got very excited, thinking that if this was the mansion his gardener lived in, the kind of house he would live in was beyond what he could imagine. They walked down another street, and there was another large and beautiful house. "Who lives here?" the man asked. The angel replied that it was a missionary who gave 40 years of her life serving the poor. Again, the man was very excited as to the kind of

---

6. Tasker, *The Gospel According to St. Matthew*, 75
7. Vine, *An Expository Dictionary of New Testament Words*, 662

house in which he would live. They went down another street, and there they found a ramshackle old tin shed with a front door and no windows. The man was shocked and said, "Who lives here?"

The angel replied, "This is your house."

The man was stunned. "How come I get to live in a place like this, when my gardener lives in opulence?"

To which the angel replied, "We are sorry about this, but this was all we could build with what you sent ahead."

There is an old Spanish proverb: "There are no pockets in a shroud."

In Luke 18, there is the record of a conversation Jesus had with a wealthy young businessman who wanted to know how to acquire eternal life. They talked about several issues of religious lifestyle and theology, but in the end, Jesus focused in on this young man's wealth. It is a rather uncomfortable passage to read, although Jesus was not saying that having a lot of money or material possessions was a problem. The issue was the high value this young man assigned to his resources. They were a bit like a god to him. Jesus said to the young man, on this occasion: "Sell everything you have and give it to the poor ... and you will have treasure in heaven."

Here is the deal for the Christ-follower: if they genuinely value treasure in Heaven, as opposed to treasure on Earth, they will also value the Christ-like expression of unselfishness, generosity, and servant-hood. These are in stark opposition to selfishness, personal ambition, and greed.

It is not hard to imagine how through statements along these lines, Jesus tended to "rattle the cages" of the wealthy in his day. They still do today. There is a sense in which the gospel of Jesus is good news for the poor, and not such good news for the rich and selfish. Jesus' teaching raises uncomfortable questions for people in cultures and demographics that are wealthy. Do individuals belong to the kingdoms of this world, or do they truly belong to the Kingdom of God? Do their values, or those things that they treasure in life, reflect where their citizenship lies? That is the point Jesus makes in v.24. Their sense of value or treasure betrays who or what is their master:

> 24"No one can serve two masters. Either you will hate the one and love the other, or you will be devoted to the one and despise the other. You cannot serve both God and Money.

In the original language, there is a more graphic picture than we might initially recognize. The word translated as "serve" is not someone such as an employee, restaurant-waiter or volunteer. No, the original word implied slavery—the lowest and most comprehensive form of servitude—with no rights or freedom. Likewise, the word translated as "master" described more than just an employer, foreman or supervisor. It was used to describe a person with complete power and authority over another—a slave owner. Jesus was alluding to whom (or what) it is that his followers are in bondage or servitude to.

In other words, Christ's followers must determine what or whom, he or she will serve. Will it be the gods of treasure and riches of this world? Or will it be the God of Heaven and the treasure of his reward for eternity? If they choose the latter, their attitude toward money and what it can buy must be transformed.

This was a harsh word from Jesus, and I suspect not everyone listening to him liked it. In fact, it might be that many people, then and now, are not sure Jesus got this quite right. John Stott offers a fascinating reflection:

> "Some people disagree with this saying of Jesus. They refuse to be confronted with such a stark and outright choice and see no necessity for it. They blandly assure us that it is perfectly possible to serve two masters simultaneously, for they manage it very nicely themselves. Several possible arrangements and adjustments appeal to them. Either they serve God on Sundays and mammon on weekdays, or God with their lips and mammon with their hearts, or God in appearance and mammon in reality, or God with half their being and mammon with the other half."[8]

Many people in the time of Jesus were initially attracted to what he had to say and the movement he was beginning. However, when they came to a fuller understanding of the cost of being one of his followers, some began to fall away. Jesus made it explicitly clear. If the choice is made to belong to God's kingdom, the things regarded as most important in life will differ from the culture of the world in which one lives. In place of selfish ambition, will be selfless sacrifice. Rather than storing up treasure on Earth for our own comfort, or the comfort of our children, or those who will inherit their estate, the way of the kingdom is to store up treasure in heaven through sharing of our resources with people in need and causes close to the heart of God. Indeed, it has been suggested, "There is only one thing we can take with us to heaven: people!"

---

8. Stott, *The Message of the Sermon on the Mount*, 158

A story to close:

"One day, a wealthy old man with a miserable disposition visited a rabbi who took the man by the hand and led him to a window. "Look out there," he said. The rich man looked out into the street. "What do you see?" asked the rabbi.

"I see men, women, and children," answered the rich man. Again, the rabbi took him by the hand and this time led him to a mirror.

"Now, what do you see?" The man replied that he could see himself.

Then the rabbi said: "Behold, in the window there is a glass and in the mirror, there is a glass, but the glass in the mirror is covered with a little silver, and no sooner is the silver added than you cease to see others, and you see only yourself."

SMALL GROUP DISCUSSION QUESTIONS

Matthew 6:19–24

1. In what ways are Christians "different" or "not of this world" compared to those who are not Christians?
2. What are some examples of decisions or life choices you have made that represent our different "citizenship" as a Christian?
3. How would you explain the concept of "treasure in heaven"?
4. How do you respond to Jesus' suggestion that our heart is where our treasure is? What might this mean for you?
5. Read the story of the rich young ruler—Luke 18:18–29.
   - What was his problem?
   - Was it wrong for him/us to be rich?
   - How would you explain Jesus teaching here?
6. How important is it that we drive a nice car or dress well or live in a good neighborhood or house?
7. Identify three things you could do this week that could be classified as "storing up treasure in heaven"?

13

Antidote to Worry

J. Arthur Rank, a British industrialist, and filmmaker decided to do all his worrying on one day each week. He chose Wednesdays. When anything happened that caused him anxiety, and irritated his ulcer, he would write it down, put it in his "worry box," and forget about it until the following Wednesday. The interesting thing was that when, on the next Wednesday, he opened his worry box, he found that most of the things that had disturbed him during the previous six days were already settled. They turned out to not be worthy of worry after all.

Every person experiences anxiety at some stage. Many issues keep us awake at night, worrying and feeling anxious. Perhaps money issues, conflict at work, or maybe problems within the family. No one is exempt. It has been calculated that for the average person:

- 40% of our anxiety is over things that will never happen
- 30% of our worry is over stuff in the past that cannot be changed
- 12% concerns criticism by others, most of which is untrue
- 10% is about health issues which, in turn, become greater because of stress
- Only 8% of our anxiety is about real problems that will ever be faced.

Of course, another theory suggests that worry actually works. When was the last time you really worried about something, becoming anxious only to find that that which you worried about never came to pass? Perhaps "worry" is a strategy to stop bad things happening to us!

ANTIDOTE TO WORRY

Two thousand years ago, Jesus had great advice to offer on the subject of worry. In his famous sermon on a Galilean hillside he said this:

> [25]"Therefore I tell you, do not worry about your life, what you will eat or drink; or about your body, what you will wear. Is not life more than food, and the body more than clothes? [26]Look at the birds of the air; they do not sow or reap or store away in barns, and yet your heavenly Father feeds them. Are you not much more valuable than they? [27]Can any one of you by worrying add a single hour to your life? [28]"And why do you worry about clothes? See how the flowers of the field grow. They do not labor or spin. [29]Yet I tell you that not even Solomon in all his splendor was dressed like one of these. [30]If that is how God clothes the grass of the field, which is here today and tomorrow is thrown into the fire, will he not much more clothe you—you of little faith? [31]So do not worry, saying, 'What shall we eat?' or 'What shall we drink?' or 'What shall we wear?' [32]For the pagans run after all these things, and your heavenly Father knows that you need them. [33]But seek first his kingdom and his righteousness, and all these things will be given to you as well. [34]Therefore do not worry about tomorrow, for tomorrow will worry about itself. Each day has enough trouble of its own.
>
> Matthew 6:25-34

The first word in this passage is: *"Therefore . . ."* As a general rule, when studying a passage of Scripture that begins with the word *"therefore,"* it is important to understand what that word is *"there for."* It is a link word, connecting what has been said immediately beforehand, to what comes after. In this instance, the preceding verses (Chapter 12), record Jesus speaking about values, priorities, and the kinds of things people treasure in life. In particular, he spoke of the lure of money and possessions. He suggested that the things many people regard as treasure are fickle or temporary, and he contrasted this with the accumulation of a treasure in heaven which is truly valuable and lasting. Jesus challenged his followers to take their eyes off earthly treasure that drives the desire to acquire more and more "things" in this life that distract from God's purpose. In the kingdom of God, we live by a different set of values.

In the verse immediately preceding the word "therefore," Jesus made, what some would have thought, an outrageous suggestion that trust in money and trust in God are mutually exclusive.

> ²⁴No one can serve two masters. Either you will hate the one and love the other, or you will be devoted to the one and despise the other. You cannot serve both God and Money.
>
> Matthew 6:24

Quite possibly, this was one of those *hear-a-pin-drop* moments as people heard and processed what Jesus was saying. It was an extremely radical and uncomfortable statement. Those who follow him, Jesus said, must decide who or what will control their lives. Will it be God and his purposes, or will it be the pursuit of money and all that it can buy?

When it comes to the emotion of anxiety, the kinds of issues that generate worry will differ from person to person. But it is probably safe to assume that the types of money worries that Jesus spoke about in his day are generic, and so will be equally applicable today. Most will identify with the sticker I once saw on the back of a car: "How come there's so much month left at the end of my money?" There are few people in our culture who wish their salary could be reduced from year to year. Concern for how to feed one's family, educate our children, clothe ourselves, or provide warm, safe shelter, is something familiar to all. These are universal, perhaps even appropriate, points of anxiety for most people in the world. If Christ-followers are not to chase after earthly treasure which might meet their material needs, how are they to survive? In response, Jesus highlights four eternal principles:

1. GOD CARES FOR AND PROVIDES FOR HIS CREATION

One of the Hebrew titles for God, *Jehovah-Jireh*, means: "The LORD will provide." An essential aspect of the character of God is to provide for and sustain, that which he has created. There are many weird and wonderful constructs of God's nature and attributes, that exist in the world. Some have a misinformed concept of the relationship between God and his creation. They believe and act as if he made the world and all that inhabits it, inserted a couple of celestial long-life batteries, and then threw the switch that sent it spinning through time and space. Subsequently, God sits passively in heaven and watches his creation unfold. Eventually, when humankind went off course, he sent Jesus amongst us to get us back on track, and this is about the only interference God has had with the course of events in our world.

Suffice it to say; the Bible paints a very different picture of what God is like. The concept of God described in the Bible is of a creator continually interested in the progress of his world and in our welfare. He is continually restoring, replenishing, and re-creating his creation. That care and promise of provision are never truer or more evident than his interventions for the human race. The Bible describes the creation of humanity as the pinnacle of God's creative activity. Of all that he created, human beings are the only ones fashioned in his image or likeness. It is true that God calls us to care for and nurture the whole of his creation, but this does not diminish the hierarchy inherent in God's created order. God's interest concerning the welfare of men and women exceeds his interest in the care and well-being of all the rest of his creation.

This is why Jesus suggests looking at the birds of the air or the flowers of the field. Notice how wonderfully God sustains them, cares for them, feeds them, and clothes them. They do not bother storing up treasure for themselves in order to survive or to be comfortable. God looks after all their needs. Jesus says:

> [26]Are you not much more valuable than they . . . ? [30]If that's how God clothes the grass of the field that's here today and tomorrow is thrown into the fire, will he not much more clothe you . . . ?
>
> Matthew 6:26;30

Martin Luther suggested the Gospel of Jesus made the helpless sparrow a theologian and teacher of the wisest of men.[1] Or as the nineteenth-century poet, Elizabeth Cheney, put it:

> "Said the robin to the sparrow,
> 'I should really like to know,
> Why these anxious human beings
> Rush about and worry so.'
> Said the sparrow to the robin,
> 'Friend, I think that it must be,
> That they have no heavenly Father
> Such as cares for you and me.'"

What did Jesus mean by his analogy of flowers and grass having a short life, and then being thrown into the fire? Most likely it was a

---

1. Stott, *The Message of the Sermon on the Mount*, 158

reference to the way a cook could instantly increase heat in an earthenware oven, by throwing dried grass into the flames. That which once looked beautiful in the fields, is dead the next day and consumed in fire. Jesus point? If God cares for and adorns the flowers of the field which are here today and fit only as fuel tomorrow, how much more will he care for those created in his image.

2. TRUSTING IN ONE'S OWN RESOURCEFULNESS IS FOOLISH

If God has promised to provide for our needs, surely it is foolishness to ignore him and seek to look after ourselves, without his help. Clearly, God is far better at doing so and has far more experience than we have. Yet this is precisely what most of us tend to do: we ignore God's promise of provision and try to take care of all our own needs. That is, until our resources are exhausted, and then we start to worry about how we will cope. In contrast, Jesus says:

> [25]I tell you, do not worry about your life, what you will eat or drink; or about your body, what you will wear. Is not life more important than food, and the body more important than clothes?
>
> Matthew 6:25

Here is advice for the workaholic, or the greedy person with an insatiable thirst for more. According to Jesus, it is better to live in a dilapidated house, wear second-hand clothes, drive a rusty old car, but have a great relationship with your children, than it is to work all day and half the night, to amass all the treasure in the world, and in the process lose the love of your spouse and the respect of your children. How many successful businesspeople on their deathbed lament: "My greatest regret in life is that I did not spend more time at the office!" compared to those who say: "I wish I had spent more time with my kids!"

Work ethics in different parts of the world have been contrasted in this way. In poorer and less developed parts of the world, men and women simply: "work in order to live," while in developed countries, men and women too often: "live in order to work." A person's self-identity and vocation are intertwined because, from an early age, the culture, economy, and education system shapes and influences their mode of employment and the quest for career success.

To be clear, Jesus' advice here is not a license for laziness. Trusting in God to provide a person's needs does not mean sitting back with our feet up—expecting God to provide everything on a platter. In the Garden of Eden, God told Adam, that it would be by the sweat of his brow that he would eat his food.[2] Paul encouraged the leaders of the Thessalonian church to challenge those who were idle and to not associate with those who were lazy.[3] Perhaps though, western culture has taken this to an unhealthy extreme. Personal time, communication and relationships, healthy recreation, and family time are too often sacrificed to gain a few little luxuries, that are so short-lived. Jesus, in effect, says: "Do not trust in your own resourcefulness, trust in God. He is better at this than you are anyway."

3. WORRY IS AN EXPRESSION OF DISTRUST IN GOD

One way to comprehend the main point of a passage in Scripture is to note repetitive words or phrases. In this instance, it would be difficult to miss the repeated word and command. On six occasions, Jesus uses the term "worry," and on three occasions, he prefaces it with the words "Do not." The original Greek word, translated as worry, did not mean not to bother doing anything—as if one need not bother to work, Rather, it meant not to be anxious or fretful or to worry anxiously.[4] The follower of Jesus is not to stew, or become anxious or fretful, about the provision of their daily needs. Instead they are to trust that the care God shows in meeting the needs of the birds and flowers of the field, will extend even further to meet the needs of those created in his own image and likeness. To fret or to become anxious is an expression of distrust in God's promised provision and protection. Worse than that, Jesus said it is the kind of thing heathens or pagans (those without faith in God) do.

As a humorous aside, the story is told of the husband who was awakened often by his wife because she became anxious and distressed about hearing strange noises, possibly a burglar, downstairs in their home. This went on for several decades. One night, as usual, the husband got up and went grumpily down the stairs, not expecting to find anyone. But this time, he found himself staring down the business end of a gun!

2. Genesis 3:19
3. 2 Thessalonians3:6–15
4. Barclay, *The Gospel of Matthew, Volume 1,* 255.

A burglar had, in fact, broken into their home and now ordered him to hand over all the household valuables. When the burglar started to leave, the husband said: "Please sir, before you leave, I would like you to come upstairs and meet my wife. She has been expecting you every night for the last thirty years!"

When a person frets about their daily provision they view themselves as solely responsible for the affairs of their life and believe (even though they might not admit it) that God cannot or will not fulfil his promises. This is why it is possible to say that worry is essentially an expression of distrust in God's ability to provide.

Again, that does not mean a license to go out and spend-up-large on one's credit card, trusting that God will mysteriously provide the necessary resources to meet the bills. Obviously, God's promise of provision is limited to those who walk in obedience to his will. God does not bail us out from the consequences of sinful activity. However, those who do seek to live in obedience and are righteous before God enjoy the promise of God's provision.

Robert J. Burdette was a Baptist Minister and a Newspaper Humorist who died in California in 1914. He once wrote the following:

> There are two days in the week upon which, and about which, I never worry—two carefree days kept sacredly free from fear and apprehension. One of these days is yesterday . . . with its cares and frets and pains and aches . . . all its faults, all its mistakes, and blunders have passed forever beyond my recall. It was mine; it is now God's.
>
> The other day I do not worry about is tomorrow. Tomorrow with all its possible adversities, its burdens and its perils, its large promise and poor performance . . . is as far beyond my mastery as its dead sister—yesterday. Tomorrow is God's day.
>
> There is left for myself, then, but one day in the week—today. Any man can fight the battles of today; any woman can carry the burdens of just one day . . . It is not the experience of today that drives us mad; it is the remorse of what happened yesterday and fear of what tomorrow might bring. These days are God's days—leave them to Him.

Or as Jesus put it:

> [34]Therefore do not worry about tomorrow, for tomorrow will worry about itself. Each day has enough trouble of its own.
>
> Matthew 6:34

4. GOD'S MONEY-BACK GUARANTEE FOR SUCCESS

Everyone has purchased a product that had a money-back guarantee. The manufacturer promised the product would do certain things or fulfill specific promises, provided the product is used in a manner consistent with how the manufacturer designed it. If the purchaser chooses to not comply with the manufacturer's instructions and specifications, the guarantee is voided. It could be argued that Jesus applied that very principle to life and God's provision:

> [33]But seek first his kingdom and his righteousness, and all these things will be given to you as well.
>
> Matthew 6:33

As the creator, God says to the people of this world: "I guarantee you will be provided for, that all your needs will be met—provided you obey my conditions."

What does the phrase, "seek first the kingdom of God," mean? In its most concise definition, it means to seek, to be, or to live under the authority of God. It calls for a person to put God's desires and God's interests, first and foremost in all the plans and the activity of his or her life. The kingdom of God exists wherever God is king. What, then, does it mean to, "seek his righteousness?" The word "righteous" is a significant word in the Bible and is used in a variety of ways. It can refer to being "right" (as in a right relationship with God), and it can also be rendered "just" (as in doing life in a "just" and truthful or fair way). It fundamentally describes what God is like with respect to his authority and attributes. To seek after God's kingdom and righteousness means to seek after God's rule and behave in accordance with his character, making it our own. It describes moral conduct that is "right" before God.

Of course, the status of achieving "righteousness" with God is not something a person can ever attain just by being good. Nor can it be earned by being kind and generous to other people. Righteousness is a mark or a stamp of approval, the Bible says, that God puts upon those who place their faith or trust in him. It is a status God gives when a person chooses to become one of his followers.[5]

Jesus' point here is clear: If a person obeys God's money-back manufacturer's specifications and conditions, God guarantees that all

---

5. Romans 1:17; 3:22; 4:3–24

the other things needed in life will be added to them. Maybe for some that might mean putting worship ahead of wages. For others, it might mean serving God's kingdom ahead of promotion, or tithing before purchasing treats and trinkets. Maybe it means working fewer hours in order to give more time to the people they are responsible to care for. For some, the cost of righteousness is a lower-income—maybe lower than they think their budget can afford. How exciting to give God room to prove himself!

Being a follower of Jesus requires a personal relocation from the driving seat to the passenger seat. It implies a cessation of control over one's destiny, in favor of allowing God an opportunity to carry his or her burden. Seeking first God's kingdom and his righteousness is a way of describing what it means truly to become a follower of Jesus. One stops being in charge. They abdicate from ruling or controlling their own affairs, and future, in favor of submitting themselves to God's will for their life.

A story to close:

Once there was a man of worry. He worried about everything in life. He hardly went out because he worried about the dangers he might encounter in the outside world—accidents, diseases, pollution and people he did not want to see. He also worried about his personal finances, work, domestic affairs, and a range of trivial matters. This state of anxiety really made him extremely unhappy.

But one day, he changed into a different person. He became happy and carefree. He always smiled and hummed songs. His friends were so amazed by the changes and went to ask him the secret.

"I am not anxious anymore." he said to his friend.

"It is good to see you so happy, but how can you do that?" his friend asked him.

"Well, it is easy, I am now hiring a man to do the worrying for me, so I do not have to." he said.

"That is a good idea. But how much do you pay him?" his friend asked.

"Ten thousand dollars a month." he said.

"That is a lot of money, how can you find the money pay him?" his friend asked.

"Well, that is his job to worry about," he said.

SMALL GROUP DISCUSSION QUESTIONS

Matthew 6:25–34

1. How much money would you require to be really happy or contented in life?
2. What do you believe to be the impact of wealth on a person's faith in God?
3. Does God have a priority for those who receive his provision or assistance?
4. Share experiences you have had of God providing for your needs—perhaps when your own resources were exhausted?
5. Is worry a sin?
6. What are three ways that you will "seek first God's kingdom and righteousness" in the coming week?

14

The Unqualified Critic

A woman was waiting at an airport one night.
With several long hours before her flight,
She hunted for a book in the airport shop,
Bought a bag of cookies and found a place to drop.

She was engrossed in her book, but happened to see,
That the man beside her, as bold as could be,
Grabbed a cookie or two from the bag between,
Which she tried to ignore, to avoid a scene.

She read, munched cookies, and watched the clock,
As the gutsy "cookie thief!" diminished her stock.
She was getting more irritated as the minutes ticked by,
Thinking, "If I weren't so nice, I'd blacken his eye!"

With each cookie she took, he took one, too.
When only one was left, she wondered what he'd do.
With a smile on his face and a nervous laugh,
He took the last cookie and broke it in half.

He offered her half, as he ate the other.
She snatched it from him and thought, "Oh brother,
This guy has some nerve, and he's also rude,
Why, he didn't even show any gratitude!"

She had never known when she had been so galled,
And sighed with relief when her flight was called.
She gathered her belongings and headed for the gate,

Refusing to look back at the "thieving ingrate."

She boarded the plane and sank in her seat,
Then sought her book, which was almost complete.
As she reached in her baggage, she gasped with surprise.
There was her bag of cookies in front of her eyes!

"If mine are here," she moaned with despair,
"Then the others were his, and he'd tried to share!"
Too late to apologize, she realized with grief,
That she was the rude one, the ingrate, the thief![1]

It is easy to form an opinion of someone, perhaps based upon first impressions, only to find out later they have been wholly misjudged. Sometimes judgments and conclusions about people are minor; other times, they can lead to severe consequences. Forming judgments, and critiquing the character of others, is something Jesus warned his followers not to do. So often, the person criticizing fails to see their own glaringly obvious faults:

> [1]"Do not judge, or you too will be judged. [2]For in the same way you judge others, you will be judged, and with the measure you use, it will be measured to you.
> [3]"Why do you look at the speck of sawdust in your brother's eye and pay no attention to the plank in your own eye? [4]How can you say to your brother, 'Let me take the speck out of your eye,' when all the time there is a plank in your own eye? [5]You hypocrite, first take the plank out of your own eye, and then you will see clearly to remove the speck from the other person's eye.
>
> Matthew 7:1–5

It has been suggested that of all the commands and instructions of Jesus, none have been more often broken and neglected than this.

The place to start is in defining what the word "judge" or "judgment" means. There are several ways that such a word is employed in the English language. At one end of the spectrum, it calls to mind a courtroom scene with an imposing judge behind an elevated bench, gavel in hand, passing sentence on a guilty person. In a more competitive context, it refers to someone who determines the winner of a prize, or perhaps the outcome of a sporting event. The original Greek word had a legal connotation and stemmed from the Greek word *krino*, meaning "separating" or

---

1. Cox, *A 3rd Serving of Chicken Soup for the Soul.*

"selecting" of someone or something into a category.[2] It implied forming an estimate of value; or assessing usefulness or potential. An extension of the word *krino* is the Greek word *criterion*, from which stem words like criteria, critique, or criticism. Some recent English translations actually use the word "criticize" instead of the word judge.

Jesus was speaking about critiquing or criticizing the life and character of people and sorting them under different labels or into category boxes. To use a different analogy, he was talking about judging of a book by its cover, or determining the character of a person by his appearance, forming an assumption that a person is "one of those," based upon how they dress, behave, talk, the color of their skin, or ethnicity.

Another old-English word, which captures the concept of judging that Jesus was talking, about is censorious. "The censorious critic is a fault-finder who is negative and destructive toward other people and enjoys actively seeking out their failings."[3]

Not only does Jesus suggest that judging other people like this is not a good idea, but he also offers a stern warning about what happens to those who do so. The way we assess or judge other people is precisely the way we can expect other people will categorize or judge us.

Before the days of computer-assisted-drawing software and photocopiers, there was an apparatus that draftsmen used to help them copy, or duplicate plans of a drawn object. Its technical term was a *pantograph*. One end of the device was fixed, and in the middle was a central point where the operator held a pencil. At the other end of the device, another pencil was attached to a long arm. Wherever the pencil in the hand of the operator moved, a copy was made by the pencil at the outer end. By tracing over an original drawing, a duplicate was made. Such was Jesus' warning to those who judge others. When formulating or making a critical assessment on the worth or caliber of others, a duplicate pattern is drawn allowing others to evaluate the character of the judge.

It is not uncommon for those with a severe inferiority complex (those who fear that everyone is criticizing or talking about them behind their back), to be the worst offenders in maligning others and passing critical judgment. Often the reverse is also true. Those most looked up to and admired, are typically people who only speak kindly of others and refer to them in deferential ways. Jesus said the manner with which a

---

2. Vine, *An Expository Dictionary of New Testament Words*, 610
3. Stott, *The Message of the Sermon on the Mount*, 176

person judges another forms a script for how they themselves will be judged. Or as Paul put it in his letter to the Christians in Galatia: "A man reaps what he sows."[4]

One of the reasons Jesus spoke firmly on this issue, is the powerful effect such judgments have upon people, both for good and for bad. It is possible to dramatically affect the formation of a person's character and decision making, especially if they hear about the opinion or judgment made. On the one hand, knowledge of an affirmative judgment can provide them with confidence to keep going in difficult circumstances or release them from a destructive perception of themselves. On the other hand, judgmental and critical words spoken about a person, can destroy their self-confidence, and often have the effect of crushing or breaking their spirit. Many people become what others say they are.

As a principle, this is never truer than for those who work with children and young people. Teachers are encouraged to take special care with the words recorded on school report cards because they can have a powerful impact on the future development of a child.

In ancient cultures, naming a child was often accompanied or guarded by careful traditions. The Jews, for instance, believed the name given to a child would influence or develop the character of the person. They would become the name they were given. The sound would go into the ear, then into the bloodstream, and emerge in the personality. A name given was information as to what that person would be like—*in formation*.

Therefore, when Jesus spoke on this subject, he was not introducing something new to the people of his day. Jewish rabbis often warned people against judging others. There was a popular teaching around that time that suggested there were six great works which brought a person credit in this world, and profit in the world to come:

- Study
- Visiting the sick
- Hospitality
- Devotion in prayer
- Education of children in the Law
- Thinking the best of other people.[5]

---

4. Galatians 6:7
5. Barclay, *The Gospel of Matthew, Volume 1*, 261

In addition to those points already mentioned, there are three crucial reasons why the making of judgments about other people is off-limits for the Christ-follower:

1. WE NEVER KNOW ALL THE FACTS OR THE WHOLE PERSON

The colloquialism above of "judging a book by its cover" can have serious consequences when applied to people. Measuring the worth of people or stereotyping them by what is seen externally—perhaps by their dress, or their race, or their language—is grossly unfair. People are complex creations; many-faceted beings. Great men and women of history have been wrongly judged by others, based upon a superficial view and an ill-informed or unqualified opinion.

Collie Knox was a well-known British author and journalist who wrote about his experiences in World War II. He once wrote of a sad and unpleasant experience he and a friend had on the day his friend died in a plane crash. Earlier on the day of the accident, his pilot friend had been decorated for gallantry and bravery at Buckingham Palace by King George. He was honored as a hero. However, after the official function, the two men changed from their Air Force uniforms into civilian clothes and had lunch at a well-known London restaurant. A young woman in the restaurant saw these two young men in civilian clothes and formed a judgment that they must be conscientious objectors. She went up to them, presented them with a white feather (as a sarcastic symbol of cowardice), and then with indignation turned and walked out of the restaurant. It was a shocking misjudgment on her part that affected the concentration of the pilot.[6] Later on that day, his mind was distracted, and the plane he was flying crashed.

Formation of a quick opinion, or summation of a person by a superficial understanding of his or her character, can have disastrous consequences. Attitudes reflected in sayings like: "You can tell the character of a man by the strength of his handshake;" or "First impressions are usually right," conflict with the teaching of Jesus. The apostle Paul offered a corrective statement along these lines:

---

6. Barclay, *The Gospel of Matthew, Volume 1*, 263

> ¹⁶From now on we regard no one from a worldly point of view. Though we once regarded Christ in this way, we do so no longer.
>
> 2 Corinthians 5:16

Racism and racial profiling are heinous sins, and all too prevalent. By definition, racial profiling refers to: "the act of suspecting or targeting or assuming a person of a certain race is or will behave in a certain way based upon assumed characteristics or behavior of a particular racial or ethnic group." By contrast, in God's kingdom, people are treated as individuals, fashioned after the image of God, and full of redeemable potential. There is a crystal known as the *Labrador Spar*. In most lights, it looks dull, ordinary, and without luster. However, if it is turned around into different positions, it suddenly comes into an angle where the light sparkles off it with radiant beauty. People are like that. Perhaps at first impression, a person appears dull. But then a new glimpse of the person is caught in a different light and his or her character and potential—not at first visible—comes into view.

The famous preacher, F.B. Meyer, once made a poignant comment about forming judgments too quickly.

> "When we see a brother or sister in sin, there are two things we do not know: First, we do not know how hard he or she tried not to sin. And second, we do not know the power of the forces that assailed him or her. We also do not know what we would have done in the same circumstances."[7]

2. IT IS IMPOSSIBLE TO BE TOTALLY IMPARTIAL IN OUR JUDGMENT

A fair judgment requires impartiality. An honest judge is someone not intimately connected to a particular person or situation. During international sporting matches, the usual pattern is to bring in referees from a different homeland (or state) to either of the competing teams to ensure impartiality. Those qualified to judge are people whose values and perspective are not prejudiced by past-history or bias. Defense lawyers are permitted to "challenge" potential jurors who might have grounds for partiality at the beginning of court proceedings. A defendant might not

---

7. Brown, *Christianity Today*, April 5, 1993, 17

otherwise be given a fair trial. In ancient Greek courts, when a particularly important or difficult trial was being held, it was sometimes conducted in the dark. That way, the judge and the jury could not see the person on trial and be influenced or prejudiced by their appearance.

The Greek historian, Herodotus, once recorded a grim story about a famous judgment by Cambyses, a Persian king in the 6th Century BC. A corrupt judge in his kingdom, by the name of Sisammes, accepted a bribe from a man on trial, and as a result, let him off. When King Cambyses heard of this, he was so incensed that he not only had the judge put to death. He had his body flayed, and his skin used to cover the judges' bench so that his successors would sit upon it and be reminded of the need for impartiality.

When it comes to assessing another person's value, no one is capable of being completely impartial or objective and therefore fair. Perceptions of importance or worth might be colored by the environment in which people live, or perhaps by what they have experienced or personally like or dislike. Accurately assessing the value or potential of another person is something only God is qualified to do. He sees their possible future, irrespective of where they have failed in the past. Human judgment is much more clouded and suspect. It does not have God's capacity for making objective, equitable and just determinations.

3. NONE OF US ARE GOOD ENOUGH TO JUDGE ANOTHER

Look again at what Jesus said:

> ³"Why do you look at the speck of sawdust in someone else's eye and pay no attention to the plank in your own eye? ⁴How can you say, 'Let me take the speck out of your eye,' when all the time there is a plank in your own eye? ⁵You hypocrite, first take the plank out of your own eye, and then you will see clearly to remove the speck from the other person's eye.
>
> Matthew 7:3-5

The only person who has the right to assess faults in another is one who is without fault. If they are not perfect in their own life, what right do they have to judge or put down someone else for not being perfect in their life? This truth could be applied to those on the sidelines of the sports field or the couch-critic watching a T.V. sports broadcast. People become vehement and articulate judges of good and bad plays on the field or court, and none of them, of course, come close to the ability of the sportsmen and women they are criticizing.

The judgments of sideline critics are probably not critical. However, Jesus treats with deep seriousness someone adopting a *holier-than-thou* attitude, or criticizing and passing judgment on another person's character. Once again, Jesus uses the term *hypocrite* or pretender to describe that kind of attitude or behavior. Only the faultless have the right to criticize or to judge. This qualifies God alone and disqualifies everyone else.

Some might wonder whether these words of Jesus contradict another principle which he was to subsequently address. Jesus definitely encouraged his followers to go and identify the faults they saw in others. Doesn't that imply a level of judgment? Consider these words of Jesus:

> [15]"If a brother or sister sins, go and point out the fault, just between the two of you. If they listen to you, you have won them over. [16]But if they will not listen, take one or two others along, so that every matter may be established by the testimony of two or three witnesses. [17]If they still refuse to listen, tell it to the church; and if they refuse to listen even to the church, treat them as you would a pagan or a tax collector."
>
> Matthew 18:15–17

Paul said something similar:

> [1]Brothers and sisters, if someone is caught in a sin, you who live by the Spirit should restore that person gently. But watch yourselves, or you also may be tempted.
>
> Galatians 6:1

How are these two scriptures able to be reconciled with what Jesus said about not judging? On the surface, this looks like a paradox or a contradiction. On the one hand, Jesus says not to judge; on the other hand, he says to confront a brother or sister who is doing something wrong.

But is this really a contradiction? When Jesus used the (probably humorous) analogy of specs of dust, and planks of wood, in respective eyes, he was not actually placing a prohibition on recognizing wrong or sinful behavior. This was not an encouragement to be like those three ubiquitous (Japanese) monkeys, "See no evil, hear no evil, speak no evil," which are sometimes referenced as an excuse for doing nothing. Such people hide behind the idea of not being qualified to judge, rather than caring enough to confront or challenge blatant sinful behavior. No, Jesus was referring here to why and how one goes about it. One of the greatest kindnesses a person can offer a friend is taking the risk of helping him see and confront an unresolved flaw or fault in his character.

Jesus' statement in Matthew 7 qualifies his later statement in *Matthew 18*. By taking to heart Jesus' words about not judging the faults in others, and addressing the motivation and manner in which a confrontation is handled, a person begins to cultivate for him or herself a cloak of humility. Before addressing the sin in another, they need to deal with sin in their own life. And when they remove the dirty-great-log from their own eye, they can more effectively and compassionately help remove the speck from another's eye.

Jesus words in Matthew 18 are certainly not a license to go around as spiritual law enforcement officers, issuing infringement notices on the faults and failures of other people. That was something the religious leaders in Jesus' day were known to do and has also been an oppressive behavior in some legalistic churches in more recent times. Jesus' objective was primarily one of love and restoration. The point of going to see the person, first on one's own, and then secondly (if they did not respond) with a witness, was always with the objective of restoring the relationship. The aim is not to point the finger, uncover sin and kick them out of fellowship. Even if the process failed, the church was to regard them as they would an unsaved or non-Christian person, not to shun them or stop loving them.

Jesus' words in Matthew 7 teach Christ-followers to humble themselves, as people who also have many deficiencies and flaws. As children are renowned for reciting: "Every time you point your finger at someone else, there are always three fingers pointing back at you!"

The way of the Kingdom is this: Christ-followers are not to judge. They are not to form definitive conclusions about people. Invariably, when looking at people and situations in life, opinions will form. Perhaps that is normal. Certainly, there is a little saying that justifies this: "Everyone is entitled to his or her opinion!" However, in light of Jesus' advice, maybe that little saying is not accurate? Everybody may well have (or form) an opinion, but are they entitled to it? Do they have the right to hold it? No one knows all there is to know about a given person or situation. No one is sufficiently unbiased, and none have the right quality of life or spiritual qualifications to pronounce a verdict. When people do judge others, they open themselves to being judged in return.

The famous Bible scholar and theologian, Harry Ironside, once told the story of Bishop Potter, who was crossing the Atlantic on a large ship. When he went on board, he found he was to share his cabin with another person. After viewing his accommodations, he came up to the purser's desk and inquired if he could leave his gold watch and other valuables in the ship's safe. He explained that ordinarily he never availed himself of that privilege, but he had been to his cabin and had met the man who was to occupy the other berth. Judging from his appearance, he was afraid that he might not be a very trustworthy person.

The purser accepted the responsibility for the valuables and remarked, "It's all right, bishop, I'll be happy to take care of them for you. The other man has been up here and left his valuables with me for the same reason!"[8]

---

8. Ironside, *Illustrations of Bible Truth,*.111

SMALL GROUP DISCUSSION QUESTIONS

Matthew 7:1–5

1. Tell of an experience you have had of wrongly judging the character of a person, only to find out later that they are someone to admire?
2. What experience have you had of being unfairly judged or criticized? How did it impact you?
3. What kind of attitude or behavior might be the opposite of judging?
4. Why is judging another person so strongly warned against by Jesus?
5. In what ways do you think 1 Corinthians 5:16 might apply to everyday life?
6. If Jesus used the analogy of "specks of sawdust" and "planks" in our twenty-first-century context, what might he have in mind?

15

How Approachable Is God?

The city of Kolkata (West Bengal, India) has a special place in my heart. I estimate I have visited it around thirty times since 1991. The broader metropolitan area of Kolkata has a sprawling population approaching sixteen million people—give or take a few million. A former national capital, it was once described as the jewel of India. Today it is a city in chaos and decay, and home to some of the poorest people in the world. Kolkata is about as different to cities in the western world as it is possible to be. Like the rest of India, it is intensely religious, in fact India is one of the most religious countries in the world. The vast majority of people unashamedly profess belief in God. However, their understanding or construct of God is very different from that of most people in the western world. Within the Hindu majority worldview in India, there are literally thousands and thousands of different gods or deities that people defer to and worship. One of the more significant in the history and culture of Kolkata is the Hindu god Kali, and at a place called Kalighat, there is a temple to her honor. Kali represents a rather gruesome incarnation of the god of death and destruction.

It was in the suburb of Kalighat that Mother Teresa's *Missionaries of Charity* ministry first began. Right next door to the Kali Temple is her famous *Home for the Destitute and Dying*. Over the years, I have taken many teams to visit Kalighat. One visit was particularly memorable. My wife and I were showing some close friends around Kolkata, and we visited the Kali Temple—as tourists, not as worshippers. This particular morning, the Temple area was wall-to-wall people. You had to push your way through the narrow alleyways. The annual *puja* celebrations were about to take place. Ten thousand people crammed into an area about the size of two basketball courts. Goats and chickens were being sacrificed, and their blood sprinkled as symbols of submission and supplication. People crammed into a tiny inner-temple area (dating back seven hundred years) where the main effigy of Kali is found. In the outer courts, various shrines to other Hindu deities were worshipped. Little children were presented to Kali and made to drink a vile looking milky substance in the hope that it would bring health and prosperity. In addition to the sacrifice of chickens or goats, people were ritualistically bowing down and kissing grotesque inanimate effigies of a god (in the form of a phallic symbol) who might grant them fertility or protect them from harm. The scene was absolute chaos.

You could tell from the dress of the worshippers that they represented a cross-section of Indian society. There were the very poor and illiterate, but there were also those with means and reasonably sophisticated education. The perception of god or the divine that I saw that day at Kalighat left an indelible imprint on my mind. It seemed dark, futile and devoid of any sense of compassion. The theological construct of god observed in the actions of these Kali worshippers seemed so distant and uncaring, not loving, kind, or even present in the worshipper's life. Their god was aloof, distant, and feared, apparently needing to be appeased or placated through sacrifice, lest something terrible happen. I often find myself wondering what Jesus would say or do if he personally visited a place like Kalighat.

When it comes to the ministry of Jesus, one of his main purposes or missions in life was helping people gain a more complete and accurate understanding of the nature of God. The picture he painted could not have been more different from the temple worship of the Hindu god Kali, that I witnessed. No doubt, like the worshippers in Kolkata, people of Jesus' day thought they had a pretty complete understanding of God, developed from thousands of years of experience and teaching from religious leaders. However, Jesus often found himself clarifying significant misunderstandings. Take, for instance, these words that Jesus spoke in his famous address on a Galilean hillside:

> [7]"Ask and it will be given to you; seek and you will find; knock and the door will be opened to you. [8]For everyone who asks receives; those who seek find; and to those who knock, the door will be opened. [9]Which of you, if your son asks for bread, will

give him a stone? ¹⁰Or if he asks for a fish, will give him a snake? ¹¹If you, then, though you are evil, know how to give good gifts to your children, how much more will your Father in heaven give good gifts to those who ask him!

Matthew 7:7–11

Where does one begin in attempting to explain the nature of God? What character traits or attributes best describe what he is like? The age in which we live is intensely spiritual, despite what many people think. Church attendance in western countries might be declining, but that is not to say that people are no longer spiritually inclined. Numerous studies reveal quite the opposite. There is a deep and profound hunger for spiritual reality. Most people, even in western countries, still believe in the existence of God or the concept of deity. They simply do not have a uniform perception of God's nature and character.

On an international scale, this diversity is amplified by many different world religions. Those with no religious affiliation hold the view that all religions are essentially the same and reach the same conclusion—that they are merely different pathways to the same end. Others disagree. They say that their particular path to God is the right or only one. Christians, especially those who take the Bible seriously, are among those who believe that Jesus Christ is the exclusive way to God.

Others seem (intentionally or inadvertently), to design their own version of God. In fact, some who call themselves Christians are among those who believe in a kind of self-styled *designer-deity*. They build their perception of God according to their personal preferences. God originally made humankind after *his* image. These people have returned the favor and have reshaped or fashioned a God after *their* image. "If he exists, let him fit into how I see the world and life and spirituality." Back in the 1960s, some openly claimed that God, as we have known him, is dead. TIME magazine ran a cover story to that effect in April 1966.[1] Some while believing he still exists, tend to view him as an angry, stern judge, or something akin to a celestial "wet blanket" who squashes fun. Others feel he is more like a cuddly old Santa Claus, who gives good gifts to everybody, and in his benevolence will let everyone into heaven in the end. Some see God in everything that exists, while others define their

---

1. TIME Magazine, Volume 87, No.14, April 8, 1966

"higher power" according to whatever they chose him or her to be. And so, it goes on.

The different ways that people perceive the character and existence of God is reminiscent of John Godfrey Saxe's famous nineteenth century poem, "The Six Blind Men of Indostan." Six blind men had an individual encounter with an elephant, from which they "saw," or could describe, its shape and nature. One of them touched the *side* of the elephant and was quite convinced the elephant was like a wall. Another felt the *tail* and was convinced the elephant was like a rope. Another touched the *trunk* and believed the elephant was like a snake. Another touched the *tusk* and thought it to be like a sword. Another felt the *leg* and said it was like a tree. And the other touched the *ear* and was quite convinced the elephant was like a large fan. As the poem goes on, they argued that what they encountered was an accurate description of the nature and characteristics of an elephant. In one sense, each perception was correct; in another sense, each was woefully incomplete.

Which perception of God, on this buffet table of religious beliefs, is accurate? For those who hold to a historical Christian worldview, Jesus of Nazareth is their authority in defining the nature of God. By his life and teaching, clarity on God's nature and character is explained. More than that, he claimed that anyone who has seen him had seen the Father in heaven.[2] For the Christ-follower, Jesus is the true or authoritative expression of the character of God. He came from heaven and lived amongst us, and he returned to sit at the right hand of the Father in heaven. The Bible defines him as part of the Godhead and the only means of entering into relationship with God. By implication, therefore, all revelation of God's nature and personality before the time of Jesus, and all understanding of God apart from Jesus, is deemed limited or incomplete. The pages of the Old Testament and God's dealings with his chosen Jewish race are now read through the *interpretive lens* of Jesus in order to gain an accurate perception of God. While the existence of God through the wonder and complexity of creation is recognizable,[3] it is through the life, ministry, and teaching of Jesus, and the subsequent illumination of the Holy Spirit,[4] that one acquires an accurate picture of God's character.

---

2. John 6:38; 6:46; 10:30; 14:9; Mark 14:62
3. Romans 1:19–20
4. John 14:15–22

In the verses above, Jesus offers three classic insights into not only what God is like, but also how he invites us to relate to him.

1. GOD IS ALWAYS APPROACHABLE

God is never too busy or preoccupied to bother with us. He is always constantly available. No person is ever so bad or so embroiled in evil that God would determine to have nothing to do with them. No matter what the circumstances, his door is always open.

> [7]"Ask and it will be given to you; seek and you will find; knock and the door will be opened to you . . ."
>
> Matthew 7:7

With the advent of cell phones, e-mail, and direct-dial phone numbers, it is possible to be a little too available. Time management theory has developed a range of ways to manage availability to people, and ways to avoid distractions. Encouragement is given to turn these devices off, or to switch them to an automated answering service. Some workplaces have a code system to indicate staff availability. If a person is unavailable and cannot be interrupted, their office door is shut. Conversely, if they are available, the office door is not fully closed. If the door is closed, and they need to be seen urgently, a colleague may knock on the door, but if there is no response, they do not go in. That person is unavailable.

Jesus' invitation to *ask, seek* or *knock* is an indication that God's office door is always ajar. Whenever he is wanted or needed, he is available and approachable.

As an illustration of God's character, this becomes clearer when we understand the original Greek words translated as *ask, seek,* and *knock.* The translated words are accurate, but the original tense of the verbs can be missed. The original Greek words are in the *"present imperative"* tense, as distinct from the *"aorist tense."* They were not describing a single action that one does and then stops doing. They referred to a continuous and persistent action. Jesus was saying: "Keep on asking . . . Keep on seeking . . . Keep on knocking . . ." He paints a picture of God as one continually inviting people to approach him and make their requests known. God never gets sick of people or tired of their interruptions. He is not deaf or lethargic so that he has to have things repeated several times before he acts. Instead, he continually invites approach—and then encourages us to keep on coming back time and time, and time again.

The two key Protestant Reformers captured this concept of God's availability in prayer. John Calvin wrote, "... nothing is better adapted to excite us to prayer than a full conviction that we shall be heard."[5] Martin Luther suggested, "... He knows that we are timid and shy, that we feel unworthy and unfit to present our needs to God ... we think that God is so great and we are so tiny that we do not dare to pray ... that is why Christ wants to lure us away from such thoughts, to remove our doubts, and to have us go ahead confidently and boldly."[6] The writer of the book Hebrews had a great way of expressing this idea of God's approachability when he said:

> [16]Let us then approach the throne of grace with confidence, so that we may receive mercy and find grace to help us in our time of need.
>
> Hebrews 4:16

This is not a picture of God as angry, distant, uncaring, or made of stone. The Christian view of God's nature distinguishes it from other religions. Jesus throughout his ministry introduced God as someone who welcomes and invites contact with us ... Keep on asking, keep on seeking, keep on knocking.

2. GOD IS ALWAYS FAITHFUL AND DEPENDABLE.

When he invites his followers to approach him and make known their requests, he does not frustrate them by not responding. Jesus declared the character of God as one who fulfils his promises.

> [8] ... everyone who asks receives; those who seek find; and to those who knock, the door will be opened ...
>
> Matthew 7:8

Now, it might be possible to take this to an illogical extreme and presume more than Jesus was saying. When he promises God's response to presented requests, Jesus was not offering the company "credit card"

---

5. Calvin, *Commentary on a harmony of the evangelists, Matthew, Mark and Luke*, I, 351

6. Luther, *The Sermon on the Mount*, 234

to go out and pray up large! While the Bible teaches that God always answers prayer, it also teaches one or two riders to those requests. Those who are genuine or sincere in their approach to God can expect God to be genuine or sincere in his response. Those who are disingenuous or asking from selfish motives should have a different expectation of God's response. Being told to ask and expect to receive, does not give license to ask for selfish things, with the expectation that God will jump to our beck and call. For those who feel frustrated because they are not receiving answers to their prayers, James asserted:

> ³When you ask, you do not receive, because you ask with wrong motives, that you may spend what you get on your pleasures.
>
> James 4:3

God is not to be confused with a kind of celestial vending machine, where a prayer is inserted and the answer to the request is automatically forthcoming. Asking God for a $500,000 car, for instance, because it would be nice to have the fanciest car in the eighbourhood, is not a request one should expect to be answered. The motives are questionable and contravene God's values around pride, stewardship and selfishness. Jesus gave a clear statement on how requests of God are processed:

> ¹³I will do whatever you ask in my name, so that the Son may bring glory to the Father. ¹⁴ You may ask me for anything in my name, and I will do it.
>
> John 14:13–14

Three words in this verse are key: "In my name." Whatever requests made "in the name of Jesus" can expect an affirmative response. What does that mean? When the Bible uses 'name' in phrases like the "name of the LORD," or the "name of Jesus," it refers to the characteristics of the person to whom the name belongs. It means to do as he would do, or to be as he would be; to think, and to pray and request as he would. Therefore, to pray "in the name of Jesus" is to pray for those things that Jesus would pray for, were he in our situation.

Sticking with the company credit card analogy, the holder of the card is limited to purchases that are within company policy. To pray "in the name of Jesus" means to pray with God's sense of values, priorities, or agenda. In light of this, the prayer for a $500,000 car would probably not pass the criteria of a prayer "in Jesus name!"

> ⁷If you remain in me and my words remain in you, ask whatever you wish and it will be given to you.
>
> John 15: 7

When the words and values of Jesus are inculcated into the way a person thinks and approaches life, the types of things they ask for in prayer will increasingly be the kinds of things Jesus would ask for. The same could be said about seeking after the wisdom of God or knocking on God's door to reconnect with him. James, the younger brother of Jesus, affirmed something along these lines for those coming to seek God's advice or counsel:

> ⁵If any of you lacks wisdom, you should ask God, who gives generously to all without finding fault, and it will be given to you.
>
> James 1:5

But the words that follow immediately after James' statement give more clarity:

> ⁶But when you ask, you must believe and not doubt, because the one who doubts is like a wave of the sea, blown and tossed by the wind. ⁷Those who doubt should not think they will receive anything from the LORD; they are double-minded, unstable in all they do.
>
> James 1:6–7

The person who seeks God's mind, but does not really believe he will receive God's guidance, gets what he or she really believes! By contrast, the person who believes in God's character of dependability and faithfulness is not frustrated. The person who wants to be in friendship with God (who knocks on his door), but refuses to leave his dirty, sinful shoes outside, ought not to expect the same kind of welcome as the person who turns away from his or her old way of living. God invites everyone to enter his household. Those who knock find the door open to them. However, when they come in, they need to be willing to let go of their old sinful habits. It is not possible to live in darkness and in light at the same time.

The picture of God that Jesus paints is of one who is perfectly faithful and dependable. He invites his followers to come to him with their requests, and he promises to answer their prayers and to fulfill their desires.

His only conditions are that those requests are made with integrity and sincerity and align with his character and purpose. Or as James put it:

> ³When you ask, you do not receive, because you ask with wrong motives, that you may spend what you get on your pleasures.
>
> James 4:3

3. GOD IS OUR FATHER IN HEAVEN.

> ⁹Which of you, if your son asks for bread, will give him a stone? ¹⁰Or if he asks for a fish, will give him a snake? ¹¹If you, then, though you are evil, know how to give good gifts to your children, how much more will your Father in heaven give good gifts to those who ask him!
>
> Matthew 7:9–11

This was actually a radical new concept of God. The Jews of Jesus day, as with Muslims, Hindus, Buddhists, and Animists, had different ways to approach God. He was thought of as stern or austere. Personal and loving, maybe; but somewhat severe as well. Some the Hebrew names for God illustrate this: *Elohim*—strong and mighty one; *Adonai*—judge or ruler; *El-Shaddai*—all-powerful or almighty. Jesus never contradicted these descriptions of God's character. They are all entirely true. He simply added another to their thinking: *Father*.

Earlier on in the Sermon on the Mount, when he taught the crowds how to pray, Jesus suggested that they were not addressing someone far off or unreachable, in whose presence a person had to mind one's language or body posture. Jesus encouraged them to approach God with confidence and the familial intimacy of a child-parent relationship—praying to "our" father.[7] Actually, he went further than that. In his prayers in the garden of Gethsemane, while anticipating his imminent arrest and crucifixion, Jesus directed his prayers to "*Abba*." The apostle Paul picked up the same theme in his letters to the Roman and Galatian churches,[8] encouraging a similar approach to God as "*Abba*." The term was defined as: "a word framed by the lips of infants and speaks of unreasoning trust

---

7. Matthew 6:9
8. Romans 8:15; Galatians 4:6

... the intelligent confidence of a child toward a parent."[9] That is not to suggest one should be flippant with God, or unmindful that he is also all-powerful and has authority as a righteous judge. Proverbs 1:7 rightly says that having a holy fear of God is the beginning of knowledge; God is not to be messed around. However, Jesus encourages his followers to look upon God as one with whom they have a personal relationship. He is "our" Father—a position of intimacy and the provider and the protector of his household.

In the same way that a loving parent would not mock his or her child, or be mean or vindictive, neither is God. This was the reason for Jesus' allusion to a father giving stones instead of bread and snakes given instead of fish. Along the seashore were found limestone stones that were the shape and color of little loaves of bread. The snake analogy was probably a reference to eels, which the Jews knew they were forbidden to eat by the *Law of Moses*.[10] If it was preposterous for a human father to give his child a stone when he asked for a loaf of bread, or a snake (eel) instead of a fish, how much more would the heavenly Father give good things to his children, rather than frustrate them. It is as if Jesus in this analogy was disputing an impression of God that some people held—that of God as some kind of practical joker, or someone unkind and malicious. This is precisely the construct of God many other religions portray—God cannot always be trusted.

For example, there is a famous Greek legend about the goddess Aurora, who fell in love with a mortal youth named Tithonus. Appealing for help from Zeus (king of the gods) Zeus granted her any wish for her lover. She chose that Tithonus might live forever, and it was granted. But Aurora forgot to ask specifically that Tithonus remain forever young. He got to live forever alright, but as each year succeeded, he became older and older and older. The gift became a curse. The Greek view of the gods was that they could not always be trusted.[11]

When the Christ-follower comes to God and *asks* or *seeks* or *knocks*, Jesus said, think of him as a loving father. Approach him as someone who delights in providing for and protecting his children. That is not to say that children of God will always get things their way. A little child who approaches his father and asks if he can play in the sandpit with a

---

9. Vine, *An Expository Dictionary of New Testament Words*, 1
10. Barclay, *The Gospel of Matthew, Volume 1*,.271
11. Barclay, *The Gospel of Matthew, Volume 1*,.271–72

razor-sharp knife will find that the answer is, "No." A loving parent foresees how dangerous such a tool would be in unqualified hands. Likewise, there are times when the heavenly father may refuse us those things he knows will cause harm. Christ-followers do not always get their way. Being told "no" is not necessarily appreciated at the time, but in retrospect loving discipline is often viewed as a great blessing.

This, then, is how Jesus taught his followers to approach our God and Father in heaven. God is always good, and in his mercy and love, he welcomes our approach and gives us what we most need.

SMALL GROUP DISCUSSION QUESTIONS

Matthew 7:7–11

1. How would you describe the perception or understanding of God in your circles of acquaintance (work, neighborhood, family, etc.)?
2. How has your understanding of God altered the more you have gotten to know him?
3. Share experiences you have had of "asking" or "knocking" or "seeking" God that have been responded to?
4. Does God always answer prayers?
5. What does the phrase "in my name" mean when it is applied to prayer?
6. What does the concept of God as Father mean to you personally?
   - How would you respond to someone for whom this metaphor conjures up a bad memory/experience with their earthly father?

16

Pay It Forward

"Pay It Forward" was a Warner Bros. movie released in 2000, starring Helen Hunt, Kevin Spacey, and Jon Bon Jovi. It told the story of Trevor McKinney, a twelve-year-old Middle School boy. Trevor was inspired by an assignment in his social studies class to do something that could change the course of the world—in a positive way.[1] Trevor's project was simple. He would do something good or kind for three people, something they could not do for themselves. In return, the recipients had to do something similar for three other people in their respective circles of acquaintance. They, in turn, would do the same thing for three more people, and so on. Rather than repaying the person who showed kindness, the recipient would "pay it forward" in the sense of doing a kind deed for someone else. As the plot of the movie develops, the central character becomes discouraged that his original plan was not working. In reality, a whole movement was spawned that spread across several states.

As with any Hollywood movie, there are a range of conjoining themes and back-stories. But the title and the central idea of doing something kind for someone else, without expectation of reward in return, is remarkably similar to a life principle that Jesus taught.

We live today in the age of "executive summaries." Rather than having to read and digest thick books or lengthy documents, there is often the option of reading an executive summary that gives the gist of the material. Vast subjects are distilled down into the main "big ideas" that are easily grasped. Executive summaries have their limitations and are

---

1. *"Pay it Forward"* (Distributed by Warner Bros, Directed by Mimi Leader, 2000)

not supposed to replace an original document with all its facets and sections. But it saves a lot of time and cuts to the chase on a particular issue.

There were at least two instances in the ministry of Jesus, where he gave what might be called an "executive summary" of what it means to be one of his followers. One was an occasion when a group of religious leaders were deliberately attempting to trap Jesus into saying the wrong thing so that they could charge him with heresy. They asked him to state the greatest commandment within the *Law of Moses, and* Jesus responded: "'Love the LORD your God with all your heart and with all your soul and with all your mind.' This is the first and greatest commandment. And the second is like it: 'Love your neighbor as yourself.' All the Law and the Prophets hang on these two commandments."[2] In other words, all the teaching, and laws, and life values in what we call the Old Testament Scriptures could be summed up into these two commandments. Love God and love your neighbor.

The other occasion where Jesus offered an executive summary was a statement he made in the *Sermon on the Mount*:

> [12]So in everything, do to others what you would have them do to you, for this sums up the Law and the Prophets.
>
> Matthew 7:12

Here is an executive summary that captures the meaning and application of all that has been written about God, and how he would have people live. There is a connection between this verse and the other executive summary statement Jesus made. If clarity is required about what it means to love one's neighbor, this second statement encapsulates it. Do to others what you would want or hope that they would do for you.

The sentiments of this verse are pretty famous, even amongst those who do not know much about Jesus or the Bible. It often goes by the term *Golden Rule*. It has been called the capstone or summit of the entire *Sermon on the Mount* discourse. If a person grasps nothing else from the example and teaching of Jesus apart from this verse, they have probably got the essence of how people should love and treat one another.

There are lots of implications to consider regarding this statement from Jesus. Once again, it points to the fact that Christian faith is significantly more than merely a philosophy or belief system. Being a Christ-follower is more involved than just believing the right things about God.

---

2. Matthew 22:37–40

The word "belief" is sometimes used as a synonym for the term "faith," As if to have faith is to have a belief in the existence of God and all that he represents. However, Jesus' definition of faith went deeper than merely believing the right things. It implied action or a change in behavior as a response to that belief. (Indeed, the devil believes in the existence and attributes of God, but that belief does not save him . . . !)

Christian faith challenges and changes the way a person behaves. It affects the way they look at life and the way they interact and relate with others. The Golden Rule is the quintessential statement on Christian behavior. It has been called the "Everest of ethical teaching."[3] If everyone in the world were to start doing for others, as they would want others to do for them, the nature of the world would be radically altered. Wars, violence, offensive behavior, theft, and dishonesty would disappear. What better description might there be of a utopian society than one where everyone did unto others, as they would like others to do unto them?

When it comes to recorded ethical teaching throughout history, the Golden Rule stands out as unique to Jesus. There are several ethical statements in ancient philosophical writings that hint at something similar, but they all tend to be expressed in a negative sense. For instance, the Chinese philosopher, Confucius (who predates Jesus by 500 years), is credited with the statement: "Do not to others what you would not wish done to yourself."[4] Someone once asked Confucius: "Is there one word which may serve as a practice for all one's life?" To which Confucius replied: "Is not reciprocity that word?"[5] Ancient Greek, and even early Buddhist, literature encouraged people to not, or to refrain from, doing the kinds of things that they would not want others to do to them.

A few decades before the time of Jesus, a heathen Gentile approached the two leading scholars in the Jewish world of the day, Rabbi Shammai and Rabbi Hillel, with a challenge. The man was prepared to convert to Judaism provided they could teach the whole of the Jewish *Law* while he was standing on one leg. In other words, give an executive summary. Rabbi Shammai was said to have driven the man away with a piece of wood he had in his hand. Rabbi Hillel offered a more ingenious response. He said: "What is hateful to yourself, do not do to anyone else. This is the whole of the Law; all the rest is only commentary."

---

3. Barclay, *The Gospel of Matthew, Volume 1*, 273

4. Stott, *The Message of the Sermon on the Mount*, 190

5. Barclay, *The Gospel of Matthew, Volume 1*, 274

It is quite probable that this little interchange between Rabbi Hillel and the heathen became part of religious folklore by the time of Jesus' ministry. Jesus statement does sound similar. Except that he frames the idea in a positive light. Don't only "not do" things that you would not like others to do to you. That is passive. It does not require a lot of energy or fortitude to "not do" something. That might be like saying that a person has done his or her neighbor a kindness by not stealing from them. To "not do" something is not the same as "doing" something. What Jesus suggested is proactive. He was talking about actually doing the kind of things a person would like done for them. It was a call to affirmative action, rather than a law of restraint.

The Golden Rule has been called "the positive law of reciprocity." The idea of negative reciprocation is well understood—the law of tit-for-tat. If someone does bad things to another, they have a right to see that equally bad things are done in return. On the other hand, if someone does a good or kind thing to another, they might be repaid with kindness.

International immigration policies are often fashioned after this principle. Immigration requirements for citizens of a foreign country entering another are influenced by the warmth of diplomatic relationships between the two countries. When living in Bangladesh in the late 1980s, for some reason (that hardly anyone understood) those entering the country on a New Zealand passport were not required to obtain a visa. Citizens of most other countries required a special visa, but New Zealanders were exempt (at least in those days; it has changed in recent years). This selective policy apparently stemmed from a position the New Zealand government took when the nation of Bangladesh was first constituted. In 1971, after a bloody civil war that separated Bangladesh from Pakistan, the New Zealand government was one of the first countries to recognize Bangladesh as a sovereign state. In response to treating a fledgling nation with respect and dignity, a (probably) nameless immigration policy writer placed New Zealand citizens on an immigration list of nationalities that did not require a visa!

Maybe another example of this aspect of the Golden Rule is the saying: "What goes around comes around!"

Of course, then there are other suggested permutations to the Golden Rule in the public domain. There are those who encourage a kind of pre-emptive strike policy: "Do others before they do you!" I knew of a prison chaplain, a fine Christian leader, whose serious advice to new prisoners entering a period of incarceration, was that they be the first person to throw a punch at a fellow inmate who was being intimidating. Rather than being passive, better to get in first and set the relational pecking order. Similar principles are applied in the competitive world of business. There is also the *Platinum Rule*, which emphasizes ingratiating oneself to another. "Do unto others as they would have you do unto them, not as you would have them do unto you." Or for the more ruthless and arrogant: "He who has the gold makes the rules!"

What Jesus suggested was something more profound than either tit-for-tat or standing up for oneself. He put forward an idea that could literally change the world, and the impression people have of his followers. It is another example of the principle the apostle Paul wrote about to the Galatian Christians when he said: "people reap what they sow."[6] The way one person treats another provides a template for how others will treat or respond toward them. Sow in kindness, if that is how one would like to be treated and watch how that kindness is often reciprocated.

The meaning of the Golden Rule is not a difficult or complicated concept to grasp. The more significant challenge may be in identifying the kinds of situations in life where it might be put into practice. Here are four practical life situations where the principle of "doing unto others, as we would have them do unto us" might find an application. Perhaps implementing some or all of these could become a strategic experiment to find out what happens as a result.

1. OUR PLACE OF WORK

Imagine the impact of applying the Golden Rule ethic to the attitude and diligence with which people work for their employer. What impact might result from being the kind of employee a person would love to have working for them if they were the boss? When Paul wrote his letter to the Colossian Christians, he made an interesting comment along these lines. He suggested adopting a posture toward those who supervise as if their supervisor was Jesus himself:

> [23]Whatever you do, work at it with all your heart, as working for the LORD, not for human masters, [24]since you know that you will receive an inheritance from the LORD as a reward. It is the LORD Christ you are serving.
>
> Colossians 3:23–24

---

6. Galatians 6:7

Maybe this speaks to those who feel undervalued or treated poorly, perhaps even a little exploited? What might happen if they imagined the boss they serve is Jesus? Would that lead to a change in attitude? Would there be a different work ethic, or perhaps different punctuality and focus? More importantly, might it be possible to change the manner with which they are treated (or mistreated) if they started treating their supervisor with the level of respect they would like to receive? Or imagine the kind of influence or impression Christ-followers might have on their employees if they treated them as they would like to be treated—if the roles were reversed?

2. OUR BUSINESS TRANSACTIONS

The Golden Rule applies to financial commitments in the marketplace, or perhaps relationships with a neighbor over property issues. What might be the result from dealing with scrupulous honesty toward those from whom one expects honesty in return? In the book of Proverbs, there are several references to honest scales and weights. For instance:

> [11] Honest scales and balances belong to the LORD; all the weights in the bag are of his making.
>
> Proverbs 16:11

> [23] The LORD detests differing weights, and dishonest scales do not please him.
>
> Proverbs 20:23

Verses like these were often a puzzle to me until we lived in Bangladesh. In the local bazaar (market) food and produce such as rice or flour or vegetables were sold by weight. They did not have the electronic scales common in western supermarkets, so the means of establishing the weight of produce was a crude handheld balance scale. The commodity being purchased was placed on one side; on the other a collection of lead weights. The shopkeeper would keep adding weights until the scales evened out or balanced. The shopkeeper tallied up the measure of the lead weights and established the value of the item being purchased. However, dishonest shopkeepers would use lead weights labeled to be a certain weight which were actually a bit lighter. In this way they could charge for produce that equaled 10lbs when in reality, it only weighed 8lbs.

Jesus' point? If a person wants or expects other people to be fair and honest with them, they should be fair and honest with other people. Do not rip people off; do not defraud or deceive. Do not use dishonest means to gain an advantage over other people. What goes around, comes around!

3. RANDOM ACTS OF KINDNESS TO STRANGERS

What if Christ-followers were to pay-it-forward by deliberately doing kind things for people they might not know? Maybe acts as simple as holding a door open for a person entering a building, or allowing a car to change lanes on a busy stretch of road? What does it cost to pass on a smile, rather than a scowl, to the person who looks downcast or flustered? Or to wish them a blessing for the rest of their day?

A friend was standing in line at a supermarket. The woman in front was juggling two tired young children, and the checkout operator had just processed her full cart of groceries. When she went to pay, the harried young mother discovered, to her dismay, that she had left her purse at home and had no means of paying. She was obviously flustered and embarrassed. Our friend stepped forward, handed the checkout operator her credit card, and paid for the young mother's groceries. She could imagine the stress this stranger was under, and although the person she helped vowed to repay the kindness, our friend insisted that she not bother. She said later that in the big scheme of things, what was a cart full of groceries worth if it helped someone in a difficult circumstance?

My wife found herself doing something similar in a shop that sold second-hand clothes. She was waiting to be attended to by a shop assistant and noticed two homeless men inquiring about sleeping bags for sale. The shop assistant tried to put off the homeless men and serve my wife as a preferred customer, but Liz insisted she serve these men first. When the women returned from the storeroom with two outstanding sleeping bags, Liz stepped forward and paid for them herself. The response of the two homeless men was interesting. They were extremely grateful, but they explicitly stated that they recognized the action my wife took was a supremely Christian act on her part.

What kind of social revolution of love might be spawned if Christ-followers were to invite the Holy Spirit to open their eyes, and prompt them to do random acts of kindness to strangers that they encounter in the course of everyday life—doing for others as they would like to have others do for them?

4. OUR RESPONSE TOWARD OUR ENEMIES

While it is understood that Christians are not supposed to acquire enemies, the history of the Christian church has demonstrated that it inevitably happens. The Bible says that there is an enemy who seeks to undermine and destroy, and for no real or rational reason followers of Jesus have been the recipients of vile cruelty and hostile persecution. In many parts of the world, the nature of opposition and persecution is relatively mild and more subtle. But in other parts of the world, it is overt and oppressive. This was certainly evident in the earliest generations of the Christian movement. In response to such persecution the apostle Peter offered some interesting advice:

> [9]Do not repay evil with evil or insult with insult. On the contrary, repay evil with blessing, because to this you were called so that you may inherit a blessing . . . [17]For it is better, if it is God's will, to suffer for doing good than for doing evil.
>
> 1 Peter 3:9; 17

Peter offered a strategy for coping with insults and hatred and opposition. Do not retaliate with like; instead respond with blessing and kindness. No doubt, Peter learned this principle directly from Jesus who encouraged his followers to:

> [44] . . . love your enemies and pray for those who persecute you.
>
> Matthew 5:44

Then there is the advice that the apostle Paul gave to the Christians in Rome, who would shortly see himself, and several of the original apostles, cruelly persecuted and executed for their faith:

> [17]Do not repay anyone evil for evil. Be careful to do what is right in the eyes of everyone. [18]If it is possible, as far as it depends on you, live at peace with everyone. [19]Do not take revenge, my dear friends, but leave room for God's wrath, for it is written: 'It is mine to avenge; I will repay,' says the LORD. [20]On the contrary: 'If your enemy is hungry, feed him; if he is thirsty, give

him something to drink. In doing this, you will heap burning coals on his head.' ²¹Do not be overcome by evil, but overcome evil with good.

Romans 12:17–21

There is no question that this advice from Scripture is counterintuitive. It does not seem natural or justified to show love and kindness toward those who give you a hard time. But what if it is the way of the upside-down kingdom of God? Throughout the history of Christianity, it has had some amazing success.

In its first three hundred years, the Christian church grew from a fledgling community of one hundred and twenty believers in an Upper Room in Jerusalem, a forgotten and backward part of the Roman Empire, into a massive movement numbering around thirty-three million people. Over half the Roman Empire claimed to be Christian by the middle of the fourth century. Yet, during that same period, Christians were repeatedly hated and persecuted in vile and cruel waves of contempt and violence. They were accused of heinous crimes, ripped to shreds by wild beasts, crucified in the thousands, beheaded and imprisoned. Yet, despite the extreme persecution, the movement kept on growing.

There are many reasons suggested as to why the Christian movement spread, despite its' fierce opposition. One of the most notable was the persistence of Christians showing love and kindness to strangers and persecutors alike, even in the midst of their suffering. For instance, severe plagues spread across the Empire and wiped out millions of people (some estimates suggest as many as fifteen percent of the Roman Empire were killed). Those with deadly diseases were often summarily abandoned by their families who fled, rather than be contaminated. There were stories of Christians who cared for the sick and buried the dead. In the barbaric age of infanticide, where unwanted babies were thrown out onto the streets to die, there were stories of Christ-followers who rescued and raised abandoned children. Girls and women in Christian households were educated and treated with respect. Over time followers of Jesus developed an inescapable reputation for showing love, and doing kind things, toward others—even those they did not know or have a connection with. The ethic of love by which they lived was impossible to hide, and little by little the tide of popular opinion regarding their faith began to change. Some have even suggested that the supposed conversion of Emperor Constantine was more likely a political recognition that since so many of his subjects had become Christians; he may as well join them, rather than oppose them.

The way of the kingdom of God is to show loving-kindness and to treat others, even those who oppose us, in the manner with which we would like to be treated.

At the risk of being alarmist, or a predictor of doom, perhaps the transition occurring in the age in which we live is worth considering. Western nations around the world may well have been founded on Christian principles, but the tide of popular opinion is turning against followers of Jesus—especially those who take the Bible seriously. For a variety of reasons, the Christian church has lost its favored place in western culture, and in the years to come may well find itself openly persecuted and censured. May this yet be the church's finest hour as Christ-followers pattern themselves on the example of those who have gone before and put the words of Jesus into practice:

> [12]"Here is a simple, rule-of-thumb guide for behavior: Ask yourself what you want people to do for you, then grab the initiative and do it for them. Add up God's Law and Prophets and this is what you get.
>
> Matthew 7:12 (The Message)[7]

---

7. Peterson, *The Message*

SMALL GROUP DISCUSSION QUESTIONS

Matthew 7:12

1. What is the kindest thing someone has ever done to/for you?
2. Matthew 22:37–40 and Matthew 7:12 are a bit like "executive summary" statements on the whole of the Old Testament (the *Law and the Prophets*). What do you think Jesus had in mind when he made these statements?
3. What are some practical ways that you might have an opportunity to put the Golden Rule into practice in your context?
4. Is there ever a place for not doing unto others as we would hope or expect they would do unto us?
5. Read what Paul wrote in Romans 12:17–21. How does this passage challenge your thinking or behavior?

17

Choice

A husband and wife, before their marriage, decided that he would make all the major decisions and she would make the minor ones. After 20 years of marriage, he was asked how this arrangement had worked. "Great!" he said. "In all these years I have never had to make a major decision!"

Choices, or decisions, are a feature of everyday life, for every person. In every direction that a person turns, some choices must be faced. There are choices to be made over which route to take when traveling. When buying groceries or clothes, there are choices between shops, and innumerable choices as to which brand to buy. Choices are made at work over the degree to which employees obey instructions, fulfill their responsibilities, and are rewarded accordingly—or to which they disregard authority and suffer the consequences. Today, you chose to begin reading this chapter, and no doubt at its end, you will evaluate whether or not you made a good choice!

Some choices are relatively inconsequential; others have serious implications and significant consequences. Not only do people make choices for themselves, but they also love to critique the choices and decisions others make. Leaders in politics or national leadership are particularly prone to criticism. From the safety of the sidelines or a favorite armchair, people seem to know, with crystal clarity, what political leaders ought to decide when faced with a range of options. They may not have the slightest inclination of what it is like to shoulder the weight of such responsibility, but they are quick to identify a wrong or unwise choice.

Take, as an example, the awful choice British Prime Minister, Winston Churchill, was forced to make during WWII. The British secret service had broken the Nazi code and informed Churchill of German Luftwaffe plans to bomb the city of Coventry—a major producer of munitions. He was faced with two alternatives. He could give the order to evacuate the citizens of Coventry and save hundreds of lives. However, this would be at the expense of revealing to the enemy that their secret code was broken, so that future intelligence would not be forthcoming. Or he could take no action, potentially resulting in hundreds of people losing their lives in bombing raids. Such a decision would likely keep decoded information flowing, and possibly save many more lives in the future. Churchill had to make a choice. Historians debate some of the detail around this, but effectively the decision was made not to evacuate the city. Bombing raids on 14th November 1940, resulted in the death of more than five hundred people and the destruction of a large proportion of the city.[1]

When making decisions or deciding between available options, the personality and temperament of a person come into play. According to personality assessment tools, like the Myers Briggs Temperament Indicator (MBTI),[2] different personality types achieve closure in decision-making in different ways. Some people are very decisive and able to reach a decision quickly. Other personality types prefer to keep as many options open as possible, for as long as possible, rather than settling on a choice too quickly. Neither personality type is better nor more correct than the other. People are simply wired differently and process in a variety of ways. However, it is not possible to avoid making decisions or choices in life.

Jesus had something important to say about this in his famous talk on a Galilean hillside. He talked specifically about how the choices people make accord with the values they live by, and more importantly, he talked about the consequences of these choices.

> [13]"Enter through the narrow gate. For wide is the gate and broad is the road that leads to destruction, and many enter through it.
> [14] But small is the gate and narrow the road that leads to life, and only a few find it."
>
> Matthew 7:13–14

---

1. Snodgrass, *Between Two Truths—Living with Biblical Tensions*, 179.
2. https://www.myersbriggs.org

When God created the human race, it was with a particular trait called *free will*. People are not pre-programmed to behave in a certain way, as a computer or robot might be. This was possibly a risky decision on God's part since the exercise of that free will has not always been good or wise. Nevertheless, people have the freedom to choose what they will do and what they will become. This free will extends even to the point of choosing whether to love God and obey him or to reject him altogether. While the Bible suggests God created human beings with an innate need or capacity to have fellowship with him, and that he longs to receive our love and our worship, this can only ever occur as an act of free will. God has not programmed humankind in such a way that this choice is inevitable.

Throughout both the Old Testament and the New Testament, the people of God were repeatedly confronted with choices as to whether or not they would follow and obey him. If they did, they would enjoy the benefits of that decision. But if they chose to ignore him, and they were seemingly free to do so, they would also reap or earn the consequences of those choices. Toward the end of Moses' life, he summoned the whole family of Israel together and challenged them to choose wisely:

> [19]This day I call heaven and earth as witnesses against you that I have set before you life and death, blessings and curses. Now choose life, so that you and your children may live
>
> Deuteronomy 30:19

Joshua did something similar toward the end of his life:

> [15]Choose for yourselves this day whom you will serve, whether the gods your forefathers served beyond the river, or the gods of the Amorites, in whose land you are living. But as for me and my household, we will serve the LORD!
>
> Joshua 24: 15

Likewise, the prophet Jeremiah:

> [8]This is what the LORD says: See I am setting before you the way of life and the way of death.
>
> Jeremiah 21: 8

In each of these challenges, the decisions the people made would lead to a particular end or conclusion. Jesus offers another example of such a choice. Two alternatives are set before us, in the form of two gates. The imperative suggests that one, or the other, must be passed through. One gate is very big and wide—something a person can pass through with ease. The other gate is narrow and not so easy to get through. On the other side of these two gates are two roads. One is a very broad road—smooth and easy to travel on. Were he making this analogy today, he might have described something like a multilane freeway, with no traffic. The other gate leads to a narrow road that is not so easy to travel along. There are many obstacles and challenges along the way—perhaps like an unsealed, windy, country road. At the end of these two roads, according to Jesus' analogy, is a destination. Neither road continues indefinitely. They both reach a conclusion. At the end of the broad or easy road is what Jesus calls *destruction*. At the end of the narrow or difficult road is what Jesus calls *life*.

The point of Jesus' analogy was all about values, which influence the kind of life a person chooses to live. Such choices lead to unavoidable consequences. It might be described as the "law of cause and effect." Decisions made today affect what will happen, or be experienced, tomorrow.

There is an approach to life that is totally selfish and carefree; that does what it wants, when it wants, and how it wants. It is a road without boundaries or restrictions—you can do whatever you like. It is an easy road to travel. However, the destination it leads to, Jesus said, is destruction or ruin. The people traveling the broad road are oblivious to what is around the next corner, and to its end. They are enjoying the trip, but they do not know, nor seem to care, where it is heading.

At the conclusion of the other road, Jesus said, is life—as distinct from death and destruction. Two Greek words are translated as life in our English Bibles.

One is *bios*, describing life in a chronological sense. It refers to the duration of days, time spent being alive and breathing, as opposed to being dead. The other is *zōē*, which refers to the quality of life—life that is full, abundant and purposeful; life as God has it and which he offers to us.[3] In a chronological sense, *zōē* describes life that never ends, along with life that is full of purpose and significance. It is this word *zōē* that Jesus used to describe the life that is the destination of the narrow road.

When Jesus drew his pictorial analogy of gates and roads, he was really setting before people the choice of two destinations. Since we are

---

3. Vine, *An Expository Dictionary of New Testament Words*, 666.

beings created by God, with a free will, decisions are inevitably made about where our life leads. People choose the destination they want—life or destruction. Though to be sure, there are probably few people who would consciously choose destruction for themselves. Everyone wants to live a happy, contented, and purposeful life—no one deliberately chooses to be unhappy, miserable, or unfulfilled. The point Jesus was making was that there is a need to make wise choices in order to reach the desired end. If life in all its fulness and potential is the destination people desire, they must select the correct road or route that will take them there. However, Jesus adds that this road to life is not necessarily easy or popular.

Jesus once described his fundamental purpose in sharp contrast to the objective of a thief:

> [10]The thief comes only to steal and kill and destroy; I have come that they may have life, and have it to the full.
>
> John 10:10

God's desire or ambition for the human race is that we enjoy life to its absolute fullest. For this reason, Jesus came. But God does not force his will upon people. If one wishes to experience the quality of life God offers, one must choose to travel the route that he or she has determined will get them there. All roads may well have led to Rome in the ancient world, but this principle does not apply to how a person may connect with God. All religions are not the same, nor do they lead to the same destination, despite what others may say.

Looking more closely at what Jesus said, there are several significant implications to his analogy:

1. THE POINT OF ENTRY IS NARROW

Access to the abundant or everlasting life that God offers is precisely defined. According to other statements Jesus made, there is only one way, and that is through the forging of a faith relationship with him. Using the analogy of a sheep pen, as descriptive of what it means to be part of God's flock, Jesus said:

> [7]I tell you the truth, I am the gate for the sheep.
>
> John 10:7

On another occasion, he said:

> ⁶I am the way and the truth and the life. No one comes to the Father except through me.
>
> John 14:6

Presumably, this was an important principle Jesus taught his closest disciples. Only a short time after Jesus' resurrection and ascension, the apostle Peter was declaring this unique and exclusive route to life:

> ¹²Salvation is found in no one else, for there is no other name under heaven given to mankind by which we must be saved.
>
> Acts 4:12

When Jesus used the analogy of the narrow gate, he possibly had in mind the two types of gates or entrance points into walled cities in his day. There was typically a main gate that was large and wide where many could walk through side-by-side or even on horseback. After dark, that wide city gate was usually closed and guarded so that occupants of the city would be kept safe. However, another way in was needed for travelers and merchants who arrived in the evening. Often, in a separate part of the city wall, a narrow gate was provided for late travelers to enter through. There were certain features about the narrow gate that Jesus may have had in mind.

The narrow gate was inevitably designed so that people could only pass through one at a time—unlike the wider, main gate to the city, which could be entered four or five abreast. With the wide gate, it was possible to carry someone else through, but entry via the narrow gate was a person-by-person, one-at-a-time experience. Perhaps Jesus was imparting the truth that the life and salvation that God offers humanity must be personally and individually accepted. God has no grandchildren; only children. Christianity does not necessarily transfer to parents, spouses or others who are close to us. The journey toward the life God offers must begin with an individual and personal choice to pass through the narrow gate.

To access the city through this gate, a traveler often had to dismount and enter on foot. Perhaps Jesus' reference also conveyed the necessity of a man or woman hopping down off their "high horse" in order to receive the life God offers. An individual cannot elevate him or herself and expect to enter the life God offers. Pride and conceit do not exist in the city of God.

In many cities, the narrow gate was also constructed so that someone could not walk through while standing up. A person needed to bow their head, or in some cases get down on their hands and knees. Maybe Jesus used this imagery to convey the need for submission on the part of a person who wants the life God offers. Those who are recipients of this abundant life do not look God in the eye, equal to equal, and demand their rights. They come to him on their knees, submitting to his LORDship and leadership.

2. THE ROAD TO LIFE IS CHALLENGING

This was not the only time that Jesus warned his followers that life would be difficult. He was incredibly up-front about that. He said things like: "Everyone will hate you because of me . . ."[4] or "I have chosen you out of the world . . . that's why the world hates you . . . If they persecuted me they will persecute you also."[5]

Following Jesus is not an easy road to travel, especially when compared to the broad road that leads to destruction. When driving on a broad or wide road, there is a wider margin for error—one need not steer so carefully. On a narrow road, a driver has to be more alert—there is less room to drive as one pleases.

Jesus' analogy of a narrow road points to a life of discipline, a life that trains and shapes a person's character. The word "discipline" has acquired an unfortunate connotation in contemporary culture. It tends to convey the idea of punishment or restraint, but that is not the origin of this word. It actually refers to training and learning. A marathon runner does not simply wake up one morning, decide to run a marathon, and turn up at the starting line of the race. To complete that distance, he or she submits their body and mind to the rigors of a disciplined training program. They watch their diet and set strict routines that will help build strength and stamina. They go on training runs and set distance and timing goals for themselves. They visualize their goal and are focused on its achievement. The road to life, Jesus said, consists of living under God's discipline. It means following the course in life that *he* wants or chooses, rather than merely following their own desires.

---

4. Matthew 16:22
5. John 15:19–20

One of the contemporary criticisms of Christian faith is a perception of rules and restrictive values that allegedly inhibit liberty and freedom. Boundary fences supposedly stifle freedom and creativity. Tony Campolo tells the story of a group of liberal educators who tried an experiment with kindergarten children and their playground. They took away all the boundary fences around the property because, they believed, these created harmful restrictions for children as they played. By removing them, they hoped that children would feel the freedom of having no barriers and develop their own values and limits in their play. An interesting thing happened. The children tended to huddle in the center of the playground and showed signs of deep insecurity as they played. Eventually the educators put the boundary fences back. Again, something really interesting happened. The children resumed playing all over the playground, even right up to the edges of the property that were now bounded by fences.[6] The experiment proved the opposite of what was expected.

Living without boundaries and defined values makes about as much sense as removing side railings from a high bridge because they inhibit the view, or because they insult responsible adults who know how to drive.

The narrow road to life points to the fact that a Christ-follower has given up his or her rights to self-determination. They have chosen to no longer be free to do or live just as they please. At any time they want, they can take those rights back, in the same way that car drivers are technically "free" to drive their car on whatever side of the road they fancy. If either party wants to get to their ultimate destination however, they must stay on the right path. That means living under the discipline and instruction that God has laid down for his followers. Seeking this discipline and instruction from God is the reason Christians place such importance on the teaching of the Bible. If the road to abundant life is narrow and hard to follow, then the Bible provides a spiritual road map to show us the way.

3. ONLY A FEW FIND IT.

The road to life in Jesus' analogy was not widely regarded as the most popular route to happiness. The broad road, where a person can live as they please and do as they want, is much more popular. Jesus said that those aiming to arrive at the destination of abundant life must be

---

6. Winslade, *Boundaries—Rediscovering the Ten Commandments for the Twenty-First Century*, 7

prepared to be in the minority. It implies forgoing the safety of numbers. Those who follow the path to life need to be prepared to stand against the tide of popular or majority opinion. They are like a salmon that swims against the stream. The path or ideology that Christians live by will at times run counter to the broad or easy road that leads to destruction.

At the beginning of his first pastoral letter, the apostle Peter offered an interesting challenge:

> [15]But just as he who called you is holy, so be holy in all you do;
> [16]for it is written: "Be holy, because I am holy.
>
> 1 Peter 1:15–16

The word or concept of being holy is often misunderstood. Some think it implies spiritual piety or being extra-specially god-like in one's character. The original Greek word (*hagios*) fundamentally implies being "separated" from the rest.[7] Words like "different" or "distinctive" or "set apart" may be more relatable. In the same way that God is different, or distinctive, or set apart, those who belong to his family are also to be different or distinctive or set apart from the culture they live amongst. People who are "different" in culture are often looked upon with suspicion and disdain.

In Romans 12, the apostle Paul encourages Christ-followers to stand out as distinctive deliberately. We are non-conformists:

> [2]Do not conform any longer to the patterns of this world, but be transformed by the renewing of your mind . . .
>
> Romans 12:2

The road to life is not a popular or easy route, but the end result makes it worth the effort. Nothing of value in life comes without sweat or discomfort of some sort. And Jesus suggested that the larger proportion of people in our world will not follow or find this narrow road. Jesus' analogy is a challenge to the theological position known as "universalism," which suggests that in the end, God will let everyone into heaven on account of his kindness. The idea that a loving God might banish people to hell seems incomprehensible and untenable. Yet, Jesus said that those who will find the path to eternal life will be comparatively few. The majority will not make it.

---

7. Vine, *An Expository Dictionary of New Testament Words*, 556.

Is it really God who chooses to condemn and consign people to judgment and destruction? Or is that a choice each person makes for him or herself? Jesus seems pretty clear: God offers all the people of this world the gift of eternal life—abundant both in quality and longevity. He unequivocally invites people into restored friendship with God and all the blessing and benefits that go along with that. Individuals make the fundamental choice as to which gate they enter and which road they travel.

William Arthur Dunkerley was an English journalist, novelist, and poet. He published his poetry under the name: John Oxenham. On the issue of choice, he wrote the following:

> To every man there openeth
> A way, and ways, and a way.
> And some men climb the high way,
> And some men grope below,
> And in between on the misty flats
> The rest drift to and fro.
> And to every man there openeth
> A high way and a low;
> And every man decideth
> Which way his soul shall go.

SMALL GROUP DISCUSSION QUESTIONS

Matthew 7:13–14

1. When you have to make a significant decision or choice in life, how do you go about finding the will of God?

2. Free choice is spoken of as a gift God has given to everyone through creation. How do you respond to that?

3. Having chosen the "gate" or "road" that leads to "life" what are some of the difficulties or obstacles you have found in your way?

4. What might be an example of "broad road" living that tempts you from time to time?

5. The "narrow road" is about disciplines. Who actually has more fun—those who live by disciplines (boundaries) or those who do not?

6. Who do you know within your circle of acquaintances who is currently choosing the wide/easy road, for whom you can pray as a group that they will choose more wisely?

18

Telling the True from the False

"The large central building was ringed by bright colors. It looked like a parking lot filled with cars. When the plane dipped lower, the cars turned out to be bodies—hundreds of bodies—wearing red dresses, blue T-shirts, green blouses, pink slacks, children's polka-dotted jumpers. Couples with their arms around each other, children holding parents. Nothing moved. Washing hung on clotheslines. The fields were freshly plowed. Banana trees and grapevines were flourishing. But nothing moved..."[1]

So reported Donald Neff, a TIME magazine correspondent and one of the first reporters to fly into the obscure hamlet of Jonestown in the jungles of Guyana. This awful tragedy occurred on 18th November 1978. Nine hundred and eighteen people died in an act of mass suicide. They were followers of the charismatic religious leader, Rev. Jim Jones. Most of them were American citizens and part of a religious movement known as The People's Temple. The People's Temple began as a reasonably orthodox church; initially in Indianapolis, then in San Francisco, and again in the city of Ukiah in Mendocino Country (northern California). By all accounts, they did good work amongst poor communities and with drug addicts.

The community in Guyana had practiced their ritualistic mass suicide by having everyone drink a special drink on command prior to that fateful day in November 1978, when a Congressman had flown to Jonestown, with a news crew, to investigate mounting claims from

1. TIME—"Nightmare in Jonestown," 4th November 1978, 14

former defectors. After landing they were shot and killed on the small airstrip near the community. At this point, Jim Jones gave an order over the loudspeaker informing the community that it was time again for them to drink. Large buckets of purple Kool-Aid, laced with a concoction of potassium cyanide and potassium chloride, were distributed amongst the people and served out in cups. Parents and nurses used syringes to squirt fatal doses onto the tongues of babies.

How to describe Jim Jones' theology has been a matter of debate over the years. Some say he started out as an orthodox Christian. Others suggest he was really an atheist and a socialist, dressed in religious garb, but devoid of any deep personal faith. He certainly knew how to move a crowd. He was a friend to numerous influential people, including governors, big-city mayors, and even the wife of the then US President. He was a powerful and convincing preacher, with a reputation for performing miraculous healings. He convinced people that he was an anointed mouthpiece of God. However, as media investigations began to focus in on him and his movement, he became increasingly paranoid. In 1973, he was able to convince over nine hundred people to move with him to a new colony he had created in the bushland of Guyana.

Jim Jones is someone history defines by the term "false prophet." He manipulated orthodox religion and duped hundreds of people into a sad and premature death. He was certainly not the first deceptive charismatic leader to hang around the fringes of the Christian faith, and he probably will not be the last.

How does this kind of tragedy happen, and how can it be stopped? Why do seemingly intelligent, rational, well-educated people allow themselves to be duped by someone claiming to be, or to speak on behalf of God? Are people like Jim Jones, David Koresh (the leader of the Branch Davidians who died in a blaze of fire in Waco, Texas in 1993), or cult leaders like Sun Myung Moon (of the Moonies) deliberately and intentionally evil? Or were they deeply sincere in what they believed, and just sincerely deluded? Why are people with rational minds deceived by the power of their words so they are guided by these false prophets and act in obedience to their instruction?

We know from church history that tragic instances like this are not confined to the twentieth and twenty-first century. These kinds of scenarios have occurred many times over hundreds of years. Jesus gave essential and timeless advice about the dangers of such people in his *Sermon on the Mount,* words that the Christian community ignores at its peril:

> ¹⁵"Watch out for false prophets. They come to you in sheep's clothing, but inwardly they are ferocious wolves. ¹⁶By their fruit you will recognize them. Do people pick grapes from thorn bushes, or figs from thistles? ¹⁷Likewise, every good tree bears good fruit, but a bad tree bears bad fruit. ¹⁸A good tree cannot bear bad fruit, and a bad tree cannot bear good fruit. ¹⁹Every tree that does not bear good fruit is cut down and thrown into the fire. ²⁰Thus, by their fruit you will recognize them.
>
> Matthew 7:15–20

Why would Jesus give such a strong warning to his followers? The obvious implication is that deception and counterfeit versions of the truth are an ever-present potential threat amongst people who follow God. Over the centuries, attempts have been made to silence or impede the advance of Christianity by overt and physical persecution. Believers have been tortured and martyred for their faith; in the hope it will act as a deterrent. But such tactics seldom work. In fact, quite the opposite. Overt and hostile persecution is like throwing a bucket of water onto a fire of burning oil. The fire spreads, rather than extinguishes. However, covert opposition to what God is doing in the world is not always easily recognized. The devil, who opposes the things of God, is cunning, devious, subtle and subversive. A clever and effective strategy, frequently used by the evil one, has been *infiltration*. Rather than oppressing believers from the outside, a more insidious tactic has been employed—leading people astray from *inside* the church.

Jesus specifically warned his followers that there would be false teachers, false prophets, and corrupt leaders who would rise and lead unsuspecting believers into deception. They would not necessarily be inherently bad, evil or insincere people, some are merely misguided, inaccurate, and sincere in their erroneous beliefs.

In light of this, Jesus' advice is simple. It can be summed up in four words: *Do not be gullible!* Do not allow yourself to be taken in. A person may claim to speak or minister in the name of God, but this does not necessarily mean that he or she is genuinely doing so.

In understanding Jesus advice, the word "prophecy" refers to "speaking forth of the mind and counsel of God."[2] Similarly, the term "prophet" refers to the messenger or the "one who speaks forth or

---

2. Vine, *An Expository Dictionary of New Testament Words*, 893

proclaims a divine message."[3] There are many forms that prophecy can take. In the Old Testament era, prophets were recognized as people in a special relationship with God, who would "hear" or discern specific words of instruction from God for his people. Under the occasional and specific anointing of the Holy Spirit, a prophet would discern a statement or piece of advice and pass it on. It might have been a word given to an individual, or a national leader (like a king). On other occasions, it was a word to a society in general who were doing something about which God wanted them to address.

In the New Testament era, since Pentecost (when the Holy Spirit began to imbue every Christian, rather than just a select or special few), the definition of prophecy has taken several forms. It may be a specific word of instruction or encouragement that one person receives and passes on to another. It may be a divinely uttered statement in a gathered community for worship. It can also be in the form of teaching or impartation of words from God, perhaps through preaching at a church service or during a Bible study. In each instance, the prophet acts as a mouthpiece or mode of delivery for God's message. Prophecy is specifically listed as a "gift" of the Holy Spirit, made available for the edification of the church, to be encouraged and welcomed.[4] Of course God does not only speak through prophets, but there are special moments or occasions where God uses people with that gift to give voice to his word.

When Jesus used the term "false prophet," the Greek word is *pseudoprophet*. "Pseudo" referred to a liar or someone with deceiving lips. Jesus was referring to people who claim to be presenting a word or piece of instruction from God that is incorrect or mistaken. The false prophet may do so knowingly, and with malicious intent to deceive, or they may simply be misguided or mistaken. In other words, the false prophet may not be deliberately attempting to undermine or divert God's people. As noted, he or she may be deeply sincere in what they say or believe, but they are mistaken or inaccurate.

All of this is to say, purported prophets and prophecies are not automatically to be regarded as infallible. The prophet is human and has clay-feet just like everyone else. They can be right on some occasions, and wrong on others.

---

3. Vine, *An Expository Dictionary of New Testament Words*, 894
4. 1 Corinthians 12:28–29; 14:1–33

The warning about false prophets and false prophecies was something well understood in the Jewish culture of Jesus' day. Several notable prophets in Israel's past, like Jeremiah, Ezekiel, and Zephaniah, among others, had spoken about it at length.[5] It was also a theme at least three New Testament authors picked up on in their later writings. From the tone in which they wrote it was not an insignificant issue for the first generations of the church:

> [1]But there were also false prophets among the people, just as there will be false teachers among you. They will secretly introduce destructive heresies, even denying the sovereign LORD who bought them—bringing swift destruction on themselves. [2]Many will follow their depraved conduct and will bring the way of truth into disrepute.
>
> 2 Peter 2:1–2

> [1]Dear friends, do not believe every spirit, but test the spirits to see whether they are from God, because many false prophets have gone out into the world.
>
> 1 John 4:1

> [17]I urge you, brothers and sisters, to watch out for those who cause divisions and put obstacles in your way that are contrary to the teaching you have learned. Keep away from them.
>
> Romans 16:17

> [8]See to it that no one takes you captive through hollow and deceptive philosophy, which depends on human tradition and the elemental spiritual forces of this world rather than on Christ.
>
> Colossians 2:8

The common theme is evident. Just because a person claims to be speaking on God's behalf does not automatically mean they and their words should be accepted as such. Do not be gullible. Many people have been taken in by refusing to exercise appropriate discernment, and the result has been disastrous.

This leads to the obvious question: How does one tell the difference? How is it possible to know, or discern, between a genuine representation

---

5. Jeremiah 6:14; 8:11; Ezekiel 22:27; Zephaniah 3:3

of God's voice or direction, and that which is counterfeit? From the teaching of Jesus, and the broader counsel of Scripture, several steps can be taken.

1. INVESTIGATE OR CHECK THE VALIDITY OF WHAT IS BEING COMMUNICATED

This is clearly the point of Jesus' warning, along with the counsel of New Testament authors like Peter, John, and Paul. Do not merely accept or swallow that which is heard or seen. Check it out. A certain amount of skepticism or caution is a godly virtue in this respect. Indeed, genuine prophets will encourage people to weigh carefully what they say, to check that it truly is a word from God, rather than blithely accepting it on their say-so. The genuine prophet couches his or her words with humility, not dogmatism. Maybe instead of a bold and (seemingly) incontrovertible phrase such as: "Thus says the LORD. . .!" the humble prophet (who is mindful of his or her humanity) says: "I believe the LORD may be saying . . ." There is always to be an implicit invitation for the recipient to check it out for him or herself. The dogmatic pronouncement can be intimidating and leave little room for question.

Some people have allowed themselves to be distracted or deceived by assuming that because a previous prophetic word proved to be accurate, every time that same prophet presents a word in the future, it will automatically be accredited as accurate. There is a particularly pernicious heresy amongst some Christian circles that teaches a prophet is accurate 100% of the time or they are wrong 100% of the time. Such teaching is simply false. Prophets are sinners, saved by grace (just like the rest of us), and far from infallible. It is possible that they may be accurate on some occasions, and mistaken on others, albeit it with best intentions.

Without exception, Christ-followers are encouraged to weigh carefully what someone presents as a word from the LORD. A prophet who does not display a humble approach, or who states arrogantly what others must do and believe, is not speaking with God's authority. He or she may not be a bad or an evil person *per se*, but there is something worth questioning about the advice being given.

2. TEST THE MESSAGE AGAINST THE COUNSEL OF SCRIPTURE

This has always been the litmus test on genuine prophetic revelation. God does not contradict himself. Is the instruction or revelation a prophet is giving consistent with what the Bible teaches about God, his character, expectations and relationship with his people? How does the prophet's revelation compare with the life and teaching of Jesus, our supreme role model? If there is a discrepancy between the presented prophetic word, and that which the Bible teaches, it is safe to assume it is not a genuine word.

This was a significant issue for the church in the second and third centuries. There were some weird and wonderful (mainly weird!) revelations and writings that began to circulate amongst Christian communities. Some of them seemed to have a ring of orthodoxy at some level. But on significant points of doctrine, there was a clear departure from what had been recorded by eyewitnesses to the teaching and ministry of Jesus.

In recent years, fictional books like Dan Brown's "The Da Vinci Code" have alluded to a range of other "gospels" written about Jesus. These writings were supposedly, and mischievously, excluded from the canon of the New Testament by a conspiracy amongst the early church fathers. The implicit innuendo being: "How can we be sure that what we have in the New Testament is all that should be there? The restriction of gospel writings to those that made it into our New Testament is a bigger subject than can be discussed here. Suffice it to say that several spurious manuscripts (from the second century) were rejected. They were clearly inconsistent with first-hand accounts of the teaching of Jesus, and other verified portions of God's word. The early church fathers applied Jesus' teaching about testing prophesy for accuracy and authenticity.

In the earliest days of the nation of Israel, Moses gave some timeless advice about testing prophecy:

> [1]If a prophet, or one who foretells by dreams, appears among you and announces to you a sign or wonder, [2]and if the sign or wonder spoken of takes place, and the prophet says, 'Let us follow other gods' (gods you have not known) 'and let us worship them,' [3]you must not listen to the words of that prophet or dreamer. The LORD your God is testing you to find out whether you love him with all your heart and with all your soul. [4]It is the

LORD your God you must follow and him you must revere. Keep his commands and obey him; serve him and hold fast to him.

Deuteronomy 13:1–4

For Christ-followers today, the Scriptures are a clear and substantive revelation for how one understands and relates with God. If someone prophesies or presents a revelation claiming to be from God, that conflicts with Scripture, they (and their words) are to be judged in error. Actually, the very next verse in Deuteronomy 13 suggests that in Moses' day, the willful contradicting of God's revelation was to be treated as a capital offense![6]

3. CONSIDER THE FRUIT OF THE PROPHET'S LIFE AND MINISTRY

Jesus used strong words to describe false prophets. He referred to them as "ferocious wolves." Switching metaphors, he gave two horticultural analogies about how they can be recognized:

> [16]By their fruit you will recognize them. Do people pick grapes from thornbushes, or figs from thistles?
>
> Matthew 7:16

There is a type of thorn bush called "buckthorn" which had little black berries that resembled grapes. There was also a certain thistle with a flower that at a distance looked like a fig.[7] Those in Jesus' day would have been very familiar with both, so Jesus used them to make his point: Do not be taken in by superficial or first impressions. Look closely and carefully. There may be a superficial resemblance between the true and the false but be cautious. A person may seemingly operate in the power of the Spirit and may claim all sorts of results and consequences from his or her ministry. However, what is the actual fruit that comes from their ministry? In some instances, what at first glance appears to be godliness and spirituality, on closer examination may prove to be something else. That which looked like grapes or figs may turn out to be sharp and hurtful.

---

6. Deuteronomy 13:5
7. Barclay, *The Gospel of Matthew, Volume 1*, 283–84.

Once again, Moses offered a means of testing the reality of a supposed prophetic word—does it come true?

> [21]You may say to yourselves, "How can we know when a message has not been spoken by the LORD?' [22]If what a prophet proclaims in the name of the LORD does not take place or come true, that is a message the LORD has not spoken. That prophet has spoken presumptuously. Do not be afraid of him."
>
> Deuteronomy 18:21–22

Fruit never lies. A person can call an orange tree an apple tree as much as they like, they can even put a sign on the tree stating it is an apple tree. But when the harvest comes, and fruit begins to develop, the truth is known. Jesus said:

> [17]Likewise, every good tree bears good fruit, but a bad tree bears bad fruit. [18]A good tree cannot bear bad fruit, and a bad tree cannot bear good fruit.
>
> Matthew 7:17–18

When Jesus said this, the implication was more than just a reference to fruit coming from the prophet's words or his or her ministry. Fruit as a metaphor in the Bible that illustrates character, lifestyle, and behavior. A man visited a church in another town and heard one of the most brilliant sermons he had ever listened to. After the service, he commented to several people how incredibly fortunate they were to have this minister in their church. He wondered why those with whom he spoke looked blank and studied their shoes in awkward silence. Finally, one of them said to the visitor, "Yeah, he preaches a good word, but you should see the way he treats his wife and kids."

When Paul wrote to two young pastors that he was mentoring, Timothy and Titus, he specifically listed qualifications to look for in those appointed to leadership positions in the church.[8] Interestingly, he mentioned virtually nothing about leadership experience or spiritual gifting. The qualifications required were not about ability, capacity or function. They were almost all about character. Paul mentioned character traits like faithfulness, showing hospitality, self-control, sobriety, healthy home-life, a good reputation with people outside of the church . . . In other words, the character of the prophet either accredits or discredits the integrity of

---

8. 1 Timothy 3:1–10; Titus 1:5–9

his or her message. Do their life and character reflect that of the one on whose behalf they speak? Are they in a place of spiritual accountability, in as much as they seek to make others accountable? Is he or she teachable and participating within the fellowship of Christ's body, rather than being aloof and mystically itinerant? Do the words shared have the effect of building people up and encouraging them in their spiritual walk, or are they almost always negative and destructive?

At the end of the first century, the early Christian church developed a code of ethics for those who spoke in churches and were itinerant. It was called the *Didache*. Among other things, it laid down a range of character qualities by which prophets and itinerant ministries could be measured. On the one hand, such ministries were to be honored and welcomed in the church. On the other hand, if the ministers stayed too long in one place, if they asked for money and special treatment, or if they abused the hospitality they received, they were not to be regarded as genuine.

To be sure, authentic prophecy does not necessarily require a perfect prophet. Based upon events described in Numbers 22, if God can communicate through Balaam's donkey, he can communicate through an imperfect prophet. The issue is not about always having to be right, as much as an attitude of humility that admits human frailty and welcomes personal accountability within the body of Christ. In the end, character is the important authenticating key.

Likewise, warnings about the potential for false prophesy does not give a license for people to become "heresy hunters," nor to foster a culture of suspicion or conspiracy theories about those who speak for God. That would be an equal and opposite error to those who are gullible and believe every claimed prophetic word. Christ-followers remain open to God speaking through whomever he chooses, even from those who might be considered the least amongst us.

A closing thought to ponder. Two types of people will ultimately be judged concerning false prophecy. Firstly, and obviously, there are false prophets. God opposes those who lead his children astray. Jesus even suggested that such people have a large millstone hung around their neck and be drowned in the depths of the sea.[9] So, the likes of Jim Jones and other willful false prophets will not escape God's displeasure. But maybe they are not at fault alone. Might some blame fall on those who mindlessly and willfully swallowed the deception of a false prophet, for their

---

9. Matthew 18:6

refusal to follow God's advice about testing the "word" given? Did they weigh it carefully according to the objective wisdom God has given us in the Bible, and the collective discernment of the Body of Christ? In the end, there may be some people who are deceived because they allowed themselves to be deceived!

SMALL GROUP DISCUSSION QUESTIONS

Matthew 7:15–20

1. What is your experience of prophetic revelation—either having someone pass on a "word from the LORD" or sensing/hearing God speak to you directly?

2. How would you sum up the main points of this passage?

3. False prophecy was a significant issue in the early church. What do the statements in the following verses say to you: 2 Peter 2:1–2; 1 John 4:1; Romans 16:17; Colossians 2:8?

4. How do we investigate whether or not a presented "word from the LORD" is genuine or accurate?

5. What do we do if a presented "word from the LORD" is regarded as inaccurate or incorrect?

6. Jesus placed a lot of significance on the "fruit" of a prophet's life or ministry. What does this mean? What does it not mean?

7. People who deliberately lead others astray by false prophecy are obviously culpable. But what about those who accept or allow themselves to be deceived? What responsibility do they have?

19

Religion or Relationship

Theodore Roosevelt, the USA's twenty-sixth President, occupied the White House from 1901, following the assassination of William McKinley, through 1909. His face is etched into Mount Rushmore, North Dakota, as one of the four most significant presidents in the history of the United States. As for all famous people, anecdotes of his life were recorded for posterity—some flattering, others not so much.

One spoke to the scrupulous honesty and integrity by which Teddy Roosevelt was said to live. In between a stint in the New York State legislature, and his appointment as Vice-President, Roosevelt retreated to rural life in North Dakota, as a rancher. On one occasion, the men working for him rounded up some wild cattle. One of his cowpunchers lassoed a maverick steer, lit a fire, and prepared the branding irons that would mark the beast as belonging to Roosevelt. However, when this occurred they were on part of the ranch claimed by Gregor Lang, one of Roosevelt's neighbors. According to the cattleman's rule, the steer belonged to Mr. Lang. As his cowboy prepared to apply the brand, Roosevelt called out: "Wait, it should be Lang's brand, not mine."

"That's all right, boss," said the cowboy.

"But you're putting on my brand," Roosevelt said.

"That's right," said the man, inferring that no one would be the wiser. Roosevelt then shouted at his employee: "Drop that iron! Get back to the ranch and get out. I don't need you anymore. A man who will steal for me will also steal from me."[1]

1. Today in the Word, March 28, 1993.

Roosevelt was also a politician and knew how to play to the crowd. On another occasion, during one of his political campaigns, a delegation called on Mr. Roosevelt at his home in Oyster Bay, Long Island. The President met them with his coat off, and his sleeves rolled up. "Ah, gentlemen," he said, "come down to the barn, and we will talk while I do some work." At the barn, Roosevelt picked up a pitchfork wanting to give the impression that he was an honest, hardworking man. But he couldn't see any hay, so he called out to one of his men in the loft above, "John, where's all the hay?"

"Sorry, sir," John called down from the hayloft, not realizing Mr. Roosevelt's guests were standing within earshot. "I ain't had time to toss it back down again after you pitched it up while the Iowa folks were here."[2]

Sometimes the image of themselves that people like to portray for others is not always genuine or consistent. Sometimes they get away with it, other times they get caught out! On one occasion, the actor, Robert Redford, was walking through a hotel lobby. A woman saw him and followed him to the elevator. "Are you the real Robert Redford?" she asked him with great excitement. As the doors of the elevator closed, he replied, "Only when I am alone!"

In the penultimate section of Jesus' Sermon on the Mount, he addresses the subject of genuineness or authenticity in a person's faith relationship with God. What he said reflects his words in the verses immediately prior (discussed in Chapter 18), where he pulled the rug from beneath the feet of those who were false or pseudo-prophets. Jesus now turns the spotlight onto those who might be deemed false or pseudo-disciples:

> [21]"Not everyone who says to me, 'LORD, LORD,' will enter the kingdom of heaven, but only the one who does the will of my Father who is in heaven. [22]Many will say to me on that day, 'LORD, LORD, did we not prophesy in your name and in your name drive out demons and in your name perform many miracles?' [23]Then I will tell them plainly, 'I never knew you. Away from me, you evildoers!'"
>
> Matthew 7:21–23

These verses have been labeled the scariest in all of Jesus' teaching! They effectively knock you off balance. If, after reading them, you feel a desire to go somewhere quiet and spend an hour in prayer, checking

---

2. "Bits & Pieces," November 12, 1992, 19–20

that you are on the right side of the salvation ledger, you are in good company! "Am I as secure and certain about my relationship with God as I believed I was?"

Perhaps the first thing to be noted from these verses is that a day of reckoning will be faced in the future. There will be an "... On that day" event, at the end of the age, where formal review and entry to heaven will be granted or denied. God will judge the living and the dead. Just when and how this occurs is (perhaps deliberately) shrouded in mystery, but the Bible, on numerous occasions, refers to a time when every person will stand before God and give account of themselves. On the other side of that judgment process, those counted as righteous will be ushered into the kingdom of heaven—where the reign and will of God are unopposed.

A second point to note is that according to Jesus there will be some surprises as to who is allowed in and who is not. Apparently, there will be some who thought they had met the criteria for entry, only to be disappointed. From time to time, there are news reports of people purchasing tickets to a sporting fixture or a concert over the internet, only to discover they have been caught in a scam. When the tickets are downloaded or arrive in the mail, they look genuine enough. However, come game day, the scanners at the gates do not recognize them as valid. According to Jesus, it sounds like something similar is going to happen on judgment day for some people who thought they had valid entry tickets into God's eternal-life-stadium!

A third point we learn from these words of Jesus is the identity of these disappointed people. According to Jesus, they are not your regular pagans or atheists who do not believe in God. No one would expect such people, who reject God altogether, to make it into heaven. Jesus also does not seem to be referring to flaky, nominal, or Christmas-and-Easter-only church attenders. Nor does he seem to address Bible-thumping-hypocritical-legalistic types, those he often criticized for putting heavy religious burdens on people and missing the point of genuine faith. No, Jesus includes people who are on the charismatic prayer and prophecy team! People who have heard and delivered prophetic words, cast demons out of people, and performed miracles. Those who are refused entry include people who seemingly have experienced the power of God working through them, and who have ministered in the name and authority of Jesus!

Consequently, the question has quite legitimately been posed: just whom was Jesus addressing when he spoke these words? Who did he have in mind? Can anyone feel secure in their expectation of eternal inheritance if those who minister in his name are not guaranteed entry?

Some have wondered if Jesus was employing the literary device of hyperbole to make his point. To move people from "A" to "B," he suggests that they aim for a more distant point "C" in order to overcome inertia and avoid falling short of the goal.

Others suggest that maybe Jesus was addressing the phony prophets and faith healers who would emerge in subsequent generations of the church, and lead people astray. For instance, in Acts 8, there is the account of a popular sorcerer in Samaria called Simon, who amazed people with displays of power. When he saw the dramatic manifestations that occurred when Peter and John were praying over believers in order that they would be filled with the Holy Spirit, he wanted to buy the ability to achieve the same effect. Or in Acts 19, there is a group of young men trying to free people afflicted by demons by repeating a simple formula, who experienced a very different result. The demon responded:

> [15] . . . "Jesus I know, and Paul I know about, but who are you?"
> [16] Then the man who had the evil spirit jumped on them and overpowered them all. He gave them such a beating that they ran out of the house naked and bleeding.
>
> Acts 19:15-16

Still others wonder if Jesus was referring to those who confuse religious activity with a genuine relationship with God—assuming that if they perform the requisite religious rituals, entry into heaven will be guaranteed. Certainly the prevailing view of the day was that if you were born a Jew, and if you ate the right food, cleaned yourself in the required ceremonial way, gave an appropriate offering, prayed the right prayers, and kept all the other pedantic religious rules . . . salvation or entry into God's kingdom was guaranteed. There were several poignant moments in the ministry of Jesus where he certainly "pricked that bubble." The religious leaders of his day had significantly missed the point of the *Law of Moses*, turning it into a heavy oppressive burden. Living God's way had been transformed into a schedule of obligations and restrictions that was unbearably onerous and impossible to fulfil.

The specific audience Jesus addressed this message towards is unclear. However, there are at least two timeless principles that can be drawn from these confronting words:

1. RELIGION IS NOT THE SAME THING AS RELATIONSHIP

Jesus describes people engaged in a range of religious activities, but they seem to be unrecognized by him. Religious activity does not necessarily gain God's attention. It is quite possible to fool ourselves into thinking we are right with God because we perform certain religious rituals, only to discover that we have missed the point altogether. Or to express this another way: God is less interested or impressed by what we do for him than he is in forging a personal relationship with us, where we talk with him, seek his advice, and enjoy his company. Rather than merely knowing about God, we get to know him.

Throughout human history, and all around the world, there have been any number of religions and religious practices that have conditioned people to think that if they perform certain rituals, everything will be fine. For the Muslims, it might be facing Mecca to pray five times a day. For the Hindus and Buddhists, it might be burning incense, spinning prayer wheels, or making animal sacrifices at the temple. For nominal Christians, it might be showing up at church from time to time, participating in communion several times a year, making a formal confession, or donating money to the church or to charity. They believe if they do these kinds of activities, God will be satisfied. Some devout Christians may have the idea that if they have a daily quiet time, attend a prayer meeting or get involved in serving at their local church, all will be well in the end.[3]

According to Jesus, God is less interested in these rituals that we perform than he is in knowing us, or more importantly, us knowing him.

When Jesus taught his disciples how to pray, he introduced a radical idea for the people of his day. Rather than following a formula, he suggested that when we pray, we talk in familial terms with our Father in heaven.[4] We do not just pray to "the God" or to a far-off deity or inanimate idol. We pray and relate with a loving parent; into whose family we have been adopted.[5]

---

3. A friend once anxiously told me he needed to spend his Saturday morning catching up on five-days of missed daily Bible reading that week, lest he fall out of favor with Jesus!

4. Matthew 6:6;9.

5. On a recent visit to Israel, I saw a delightful picture of this while sitting in a McDonald's restaurant by the Dead Sea. At the table next to us was a Jewish family.

In John 15, Jesus talked about the status we now have with him:

> ¹⁵I no longer call you servants, because a servant does not know his master's business. Instead, I have called you friends, for everything that I learned from my Father I have made known to you.

There is a delightful quote attributed to Martin Luther: "The life of Christianity consists of possessive pronouns. It is one thing to say, 'Christ is a Savior'; it is quite another thing to say, 'He is my Savior and my LORD.' The devil can say the first; the true Christian alone can say the second."[6]

The Christian faith is not about ritual, performance or rule-keeping. It is fundamentally about a relationship with God. Relationship happens when a person spends time together with someone he or she loves. It is where he or she thinks and does those things that they believe the one they love would approve or be encouraged by. When people are in a relationship, the other person's words and values ring in their ears and shape their responses. That's not to suggest that creating traditions or following the routines and disciplines of love are unnecessary. It is good to do ritual-like acts of love and devotion toward someone with whom you are in a relationship. But such actions are not the substance of the relationship. We do them because we want to, not because we have to.

In a good marriage, for instance, the relationship is deeper and more profound than the ceremony that occured once at a given point in time. The married couple cherish each other and tell one another of their mutual love and appreciation. The more time they spend together, the more they can predict what the other might be thinking or what they would do. They "know" each other.

God invites us, not to a ritual or a formula, but to relationship. The whole notion of Christening (i.e., making "Christian") of babies, who—on account of their parents' actions—thereafter are regarded as part of the "household of faith" makes no sense. But then neither does the prevalent notion of believers' baptism as a formal marker of "forever salvation." God is not satisfied, appeased or impressed by the performance of religious practices such as church attendance, eucharist-taking, creed-reciting or tithe-giving religious rituals outside of an ongoing relationship with him.

As the father approached, his little boy called out excitedly, "Abba, Abba!" My mind immediately went to how Jesus modeled the way we approach the One who hears our prayers.

6. Robinson, *Annotations upon Popular Hymns*.

In the end, it will be a person's relationship with God, being known by him, that provides the key to his or her entry into the kingdom of heaven.

2. CHARISMATIC IS NOT NECESSARILY CHRISTIAN

In the preceding verses (Matthew 7:15-20), Jesus warned against being overly impressed by those who claim to speak prophetically on God's behalf. Here he indicates that the same principle applies to us all. Spiritual gifts, or experience of the power of the Holy Spirit, does not in and of itself guarantee salvation. It would seem that people not in a functioning relationship with God may be able to perform acts of faith and charismatic manifestations in His name. At the end of time, when people will stand before God and account for themselves, there will apparently be some surprises.

This might be a word of caution regarding those we might identify as superstars or heroes of the Christian faith. Our culture, fueled by the media, tends to elevate the famous or people with the most significant ministries (for example those who have TV shows or hold events in massive stadiums), as model servants of the LORD. Bigger ministries must mean better; these will be the people who lead the procession into the kingdom of heaven. "Surely, exercise of the charismatic gifts and displays of success guarantee a front-row seat as the kingdom of heaven unfolds?" According to Jesus, that may, or may not, be the case. Jesus suggested that it would be (v.21) ". . . those who do the will of my Father who is in heaven" that are guaranteed entry. What did he mean by that?

Consider another occasion where Jesus talked along very similar lines. In Matthew 25, he told three stories about the end of time and the judgment that would follow. In the third of those stories, Jesus used the imagery of his followers being divided into two categories: sheep and goats. The sheep are ushered into the kingdom of heaven; the goats are not. Once again, there are big surprises as to who gets in and who does not. Those welcomed in appear to be those who went out of their way to feed Jesus when he was hungry; to show him hospitality when he was homeless; to provide him with clothes when he was naked and to care for him when he was sick and imprisoned. These people are invited into God's kingdom. By contrast, those who did not do these things, but appear to regard themselves as very religious and devoted followers of God, are excluded. Both groups asked Jesus when they saw him hungry, homeless, naked, sick or imprisoned. Jesus replied, that whatever they did or didn't do to the least amongst them, they did or didn't do unto him. People gained entry into the kingdom because they showed their love for Jesus through caring and serving people in need.

The implication? Those who genuinely have a relationship with Jesus tend to do the kinds of things Jesus would do. They "... do the will of [our] Father who is in Heaven."

Now, for some people talk along these lines raises a theological problem. Where does the grace and mercy of God fit? "Haven't we been taught that we are saved by faith alone, rather than by doing good works?" When Jesus suggests entry into the kingdom of heaven is reserved for those who "do the will of God," doesn't that contradict the teaching of the apostle Paul—who would later write statements like: "Everyone who calls on the name of the LORD will be saved." (Romans 10:13) Salvation, according to this verse, comes by faith in Jesus and calling upon him to rescue us, rather than through us having to do anything in particular. Or then there is that other statement by Paul:

> ⁸For it is by grace you have been saved, through faith—and this is not from yourselves, it is the gift of God—⁹not by works, so that no one can boast.
>
> Ephesians 2:8–9

How do we reconcile Paul's words with Jesus' criteria for welcoming people into the kingdom of heaven? Theologians have debated questions like this for twenty centuries. Perhaps Jesus and Paul are not actually contradicting each other, as much as describing different sides of the same coin? Clearly, people are saved from the consequences of their sinful state by the grace and mercy of God—by what Christ achieved on the cross and his resurrection. No one earns their entry into heaven by doing a series of good works. Good works do not save; salvation happens through the forging of a personal relationship with God and submitting one's life to the LORDship of Jesus. However, when that indeed happens, good works—like caring for others and doing the kinds of things Jesus would do—are evidence that God's grace has, in fact, saved a person. Good works are not the means of grace; more its outcome.

How, then, does a person "know" they have a relationship with God, such that they can confidently expect that on judgment day God will say to them: "Welcome into my kingdom"? They could take a look at the life they lead, the values they live by, the attitude they have toward others, and the things they do for those in desperate circumstances. Those who know Jesus, and who in turn are known by him, reflect the heartbeat of Jesus. They increasingly think along similar lines; they see and care for people as he does. They are transformed from the inside out, and God's love for others characterizes their lives.

People in genuine relationship with God do not "do" acts of worship or ministry as a means of acquiring favor with God. They do not feel driven to perform token acts of religious observance to merit entry into God's kingdom. They worship and serve and care for the poor because it is the most natural thing to do towards one they love. And come the final day they will hear Jesus' words of welcome: "Come, you who are blessed by my Father; take your inheritance, the kingdom prepared for you since the creation of the world."[7]

In closing, a pastoral word to those who might feel anxious about these confronting words of Jesus and suspect that they may not make the grade. These verses have often given people cause to doubt or feel insecure.

In the first instance, be reassured that it is not too late to turn your life around. The Day of Judgment has not yet arrived. There is an opportunity to do something about your relationship with God and to become known by him. Maybe today is the day to do something about that. Spend time talking with God and invite Jesus to be the LORD of your life—and respond in obedience to the changes he begins to make.

Secondly, many people fear they will be excluded from God's kingdom because of misbehavior or sinful acts they have performed—especially those committed after they became a Christ-follower. They have the mistaken idea that God holds a set of scales on which he weighs all our good behavior against all our bad behavior. If the good outweighs the bad, we make it. If not, we are destined for the other place. That is not what this passage is about. If Jesus were talking about weighing us in a balance, everyone is doomed. It simply is not possible for anyone to do enough religious "good" deeds to merit his kingdom. That's why he offers us a relationship with him as a free gift. It cannot be earned. It costs too much. It is beyond everyone's reach.

No, God offers friendship and relationship as an unmerited gift. The initiative comes from him and the purchase price was met by him, none of this is from us. So, if a person cannot earn salvation by being good,

---

7. Matthew 25:34

neither do they necessarily lose it by being bad. This is not a license to do wrong things, and like any relationship, God can be offended by our doing what we know is hurtful and wrong. Relationships can be neglected and become estranged. However, as in any relationship, we can be restored and forgiven when we humbly ask this of him. These words of Jesus are not aimed at making ordinary human sinners feel insecure. Jesus was talking about those who pretend—who project an image they are one thing when in their heart of hearts, they know they are something else.

According to Jesus, that is a serious delusion!

SMALL GROUP DISCUSSION QUESTIONS

Matthew 7:21–23

1. What experience have you had in life of being (or feeling) excluded?
2. When you first read these verses, how does it make you feel?
3. Who do you think Jesus had in mind when he said these words?
4. If the ability to prophesy, drive out demons and perform miracles was not what Jesus means by "doing the will of the father," what did he have in mind?
5. How would you define your relationship with God (i.e., being known by him)? What nurtures or hinders relationship with God?
6. In Matthew 25:31–46, Jesus told a parable that has a similar theme to this. What are the primary lessons you glean from that parable?
7. How can we be sure/secure in our relationship with God?

20

Building on the Right Foundation

The structural integrity of a building, especially during an earthquake, is a significant factor in architectural design and construction. A building can look alright according to its external appearance, but appearances can be deceiving. Every year there are news reports of multi-story buildings collapsing in different parts of the world, resulting in dreadful loss of life. A fascinating website lists major building failures and collapses, dating all the way back to the first century.[1]

This modern-day parable tells a tale of how such tragedies might occur:

> An architect was commissioned to design a multi-story office block for a large company. The architect, with his engineers, surveyed the land and examined the geotechnical report for the proposed site. The building would be constructed on unstable ground and an earthquake fault line, so it would need to be capable of withstanding a major earthquake. After many months the plans were completed and handed over to the construction company. If followed, the building would withstand a massive earthquake. And this is where the problems began.
>
> The first part of the construction was the digging of the foundations. The plans specified a certain depth, taking into account the extra stability required and the need to reach bedrock. However, the foreman in charge of the excavation and construction of the foundations questioned the architects' and engineers' specifications and concluded they were far too deep. He had

1. https://en.wikipedia.org/wiki/List_of_structural_failures_and_collapses

built dozens of other buildings like this one, and they had only ever had a foundation half the depth stipulated on the plans. He instructed his men to ignore the architect's plan and they dug a foundation half the specified depth. Next came the steel fixing; rods of iron tied or welded together inside the concrete to give it strength. The architect's plans specified a certain thickness and the use of high-tensile steel. This along with narrower than normal spacing was more expensive but necessary to provide the building extra strength. However, the foreman in charge of the steelwork disagreed with the architect's stipulations. Based on past experience, he instructed his men to use thinner, cheaper steel and broader spacings.

And so, the construction of the building went on. Shortcut here, shortcut there. At each stage of the construction process, the various foremen disputed the architect's specifications, considering them to be unnecessary and far too expensive.

Finally, the building was completed and handed over to the company that commissioned it. It looked like what the architect had designed in terms of shape and structure, so the company moved in. It all appeared to be a great success and people congratulated the architect on his design. That is, until one day when there was an earthquake. It was not an unusually large one—about half the size that the building was designed to withstand. Yet the building came down in a crumbling heap. Hundreds of people were crushed and died. Everyone turned on the architect and blamed him. The architect's ability and professional competence were slandered, and his reputation destroyed. The irony was that the collapse of the building was not his fault. The architect's design was perfect. If his instructions had been followed, the building would have withstood an earthquake twice the size. Yet everyone blamed the designer.

In this chapter, we consider the final words in Jesus' Sermon on the Mount. They bear a remarkable resemblance to the principles of design and construction—not so much buildings, as the lives people construct for themselves and their ability to withstand the stresses and strains that come their way.

> [24]"Therefore everyone who hears these words of mine and puts them into practice is like a wise man who built his house on the rock. [25]The rain came down, the streams rose, and the winds blew and beat against that house; yet it did not fall, because it had its foundation on the rock. [26]But everyone who hears these words of mine and does not put them into practice is like

a foolish man who built his house on sand. ²⁷The rain came down, the streams rose, and the winds blew and beat against that house, and it fell with a great crash."

²⁸When Jesus had finished saying these things, the crowds were amazed at his teaching, ²⁹because he taught as one who had authority, and not as their teachers of the law.

Matthew 7:24–29

When it comes to construction-based analogies, Jesus was probably more qualified than most. History may recall him as a brilliant teacher and communicator, but he began life in the family business. Joseph, his father, was a carpenter in the town of Nazareth,[2] and Jesus grew up learning the basic principles of construction and house building from his father. Mark's gospel even refers to Jesus as a carpenter in his own right,[3] perhaps taking on his father's business after his death.

Of course, in those days, there were no such things as building permits, codes of compliance, or geotechnical reporting on soil composition or land movement. There was certainly nothing like city construction inspectors who visit building sites to verify building work has been done correctly. Reading Jesus' words in the twenty-first century, we might be tempted to think this is a silly analogy; who in their right mind would ever build a house in the way of a raging torrent of water? However, in the times and geography of Jesus, this was not an unfamiliar scenario. Houses were constructed quickly, usually of baked mud, and it is not inconceivable that someone might find a really nice, shady place to build a house, only to discover come the rainy season, that it was prone to flooding.

In fact, Jesus was not teaching his followers about house-construction, but about life-construction. Is the type and manner in which a person builds his or her life stable and anchored and durable? Or is it superficially beautiful, only revealing its true nature when something stressful comes along, and it falls to pieces? The point Jesus was making in these verses follows from what he has just said. This passage begins with the word "Therefore," which, as a link word, connects the current section with the one directly before it—upon which it then builds. In this instance, Jesus first spoke of the difference between genuine or real disciples, comparing them with those who are fake or pretenders. Here

---

2. Matthew 13:55
3. Mark 6:3

we find those confronting words: "Not everyone who says to me, 'LORD, LORD' will enter the kingdom of heaven . . ."[4]

Jesus had already told his listeners that when the end of the age comes, there were going to be some surprises as to who was invited into the kingdom of heaven, and who was not. Being religious, he made clear, is not the same thing as having a genuine relationship with God. Now in the current passage, Jesus offers some hints of what it might mean to develop a real relationship with God—a relationship whereby people genuinely know him, as he, in turn, knows them.

Concluding statements at the end of a chapter, book or essay are particularly important. They often sum up the essence of what has gone before. In this instance, there are some valuable life-principles worth noting:

1. STORMS ARE A FACT OF LIFE

Jesus compares two houses that look the same, and experience the stress and pressure of the same storm. The rain comes down, the streams rise, and the wind blows.

In many parts of the world, construction regulations are designed to protect buildings from the threat of one-in-a-hundred-year floods. Right outside the front gate of the house where I currently live, is a metal peg banged into the tar sealed road called a *datum* peg. It provides an official height above which every house in our neighborhood must measure and construct the height of its foundations, in order to mitigate possible future flooding. If Jesus were telling his story today, he might well have likened his teaching to a *datum* peg.

But again, we digress; Jesus' analogy was about life, not about buildings. The fact is, there are numerous metaphorical "storms" in life common to everyone, storms which no one can avoid. Battling the elements and living with stress and difficulty is part and parcel of life. There are storms in the form of health issues, aging, and ultimately death. There are storms of grief over the loss of a loved one. At times there are raging storms in marriages, tornados of friction within families, and anxiety over children and grandchildren. There can be hurricanes of economic worry that buffet us. Then some storms are particularly for those who take God seriously—storms in the form of spiritual warfare and hostility that come from the evil one, whose primary objective is to kill and destroy.

4. Matthew 7:21

Many times, people live hoping for a season in life where all their troubles and storms have passed, and everything is peaceful and tranquil. But that really is just an illusion. At no point has God ever promised that his people would avoid the storms of life that buffet and bully our world. We ought not to be surprised, therefore, by seasons in life that feel like heavy weather. Indeed, some reading these words may be in the midst of some storm at the moment. If so, here is a cheery piece of advice from the pen of James, the younger brother of Jesus:

> [2]Consider it pure joy, my brothers and sisters, whenever you face trials of many kinds, [3]because you know that the testing of your faith produces perseverance. [4]Let perseverance finish its work so that you may be mature and complete, not lacking anything.
>
> James 1:2–4

To be sure, no one particularly likes going through the storms of life, but they simply cannot be avoided. Life is messy and at times, painful. However, James suggests those storms can also have a profound and positive effect, as well. Enduring storms is what helps people to grow and mature.

Jesus wanted people to grasp the fact that storms would come, and that the life that would eventually prevail builds for durability and the capacity to withstand the storms common to everyone. We build for rain, flood and tempest, not just for sunshine. Or, reminiscent of the completely different story of the Three Little Pigs which many will have had read to them in their childhood, we build in the sure knowledge that the wolf is lurking outside, huffing and puffing and trying to blow our house down!

2. DURABILITY IS DIRECTLY PROPORTIONAL TO THE FOUNDATION

This is the basic construction principle in Jesus' analogy. If the foundations are secure, the building will be secure; if the foundations are shaky or shifting, the structure will be unstable and insecure. Hence, builders take meticulous care in laying out the profiles of a new building and digging its foundations. It can look like nothing is happening for weeks while the foundations are being prepared. Yet, everything hinges or rests upon getting those foundations right. Jesus took that basic principle and applied it to life. What is the foundation or bedrock upon which a person's life is anchored? Will this anchor hold fast during the inevitable storms that come from time to time? What is the source of truth upon which their values for living are founded, what is their fundamental understanding of right from wrong?

This has become a somewhat controversial subject in our generation, perhaps more so than for many in the past. It used to be that the undergirding foundation of our society, and therefore the values that individuals lived by, were more clearly understood than they are today. Social norms and values, morals and ethics, were regarded as immutable or fixed across generations. But that is not the age in which we live today. In a post-modern society, the social foundations and accepted beliefs about what is right and what is wrong are repeatedly questioned and challenged. Definitions of truth and facts are no longer definite in this age where there can be "alternative facts." "You can have yours, and I can have mine, and neither is allowed to challenge the other!"

For instance, determining acceptable sexual behavior or sexual identity is flexible these days, rather than fixed. Gender is now more of a choice than an observable reality—the implications of which impact far more than personal identity. Parents expecting a baby marvel at the high-definition ultra-sound images of life in their unborn child, and enthuse over their clear vision of its features and movement; while others, in the cubicle next door, seeing similar images, do not regard the fetus, or "product of conception," as a living being, justifying its forcible removal from the mother's womb. The rights of the mother outweigh the rights of the unborn. If enough people say that mind-altering substances or the terminating the life of an inconvenient, old or infirm person are okay, the law is changed. Those who appeal to absolute moral truth and ethics as the guide for our society are regarded as anachronistic and intolerant of progress.

Imagine a series of boats that previously were tied to solid moorings or anchored to the bottom of the seabed. When winds and currents tried to move them, they remained secure. Today's prevailing worldview is less about anchoring to the seabed, and more about tying all the boats to each other. Western culture, in particular, is a bit like a mass of these boats lashed together, drawing solidarity, courage, and a perspective on normality from each other as the storms come our way. But we are not anchored to anything secure. Together we drift on the tide of popular opinion and new ideas.

Jesus' teaching challenges, or runs counter to, the prevailing worldview in most of the cultures of our world. He suggests that if people really want to survive or prevail through the storms that life throws their way, they need to think carefully about what they are anchored to. How firm is the foundation on which they are building their lives?

In western countries, vast swathes of people have ditched the church and the trappings of religion because they see it as old fashioned and too rigid. Freedom and the ability to float along with the crowd are regarded as a better way to go. They have pulled up their anchor and disconnected themselves from historical foundations. As a consequence, those who still hold to and proclaim what the Bible teaches about morality, are increasingly deemed offensive and labeled as propagators of hate speech. It is simply staggering how far western culture has shifted in the space of a few decades.

Nevertheless, Jesus still challenges people to stop and think about the foundation upon which they are building their lives. Is it solid? Is it durable? Is it time-tested? Will it withstand the storms that are common to, and wash over, us all?

3. IT MAKES SENSE TO FOLLOW THE MANUFACTURER'S INSTRUCTIONS

When it comes to knowing how best something works, surely the person who designed it is the first to ask. The manufacturer's instructions are based upon superior knowledge and experience. The original designer knows how a product or commodity is intended to be used, and its inherent limitations. Ignore the manufacturer's advice at your peril. Jesus warned:

> [24]"Therefore everyone who hears these words of mine and puts them into practice is like a wise man who built his house on the rock . . . [26]But everyone who hears these words of mine and does not put them into practice is like a foolish man who built his house on sand.
>
> Matthew 7:24; 26

What did Jesus have in mind when he said this? To which "words of mine" was he referring? Taking these verses as a summation or concluding statement of what has gone before, look again at all the life principles he addresses. The *Sermon on the Mount* has been called the essence of all Jesus taught about life in God's kingdom for good reason. When a person puts these "words" of Jesus into practice, they build their life on the firmest foundation possible.

Alternatively, Jesus' reference about "listening to" and "doing" his "words" could be seen as a reference to all of his teaching and his life as recorded in the New Testament which provides a role-model for his followers. When people take Jesus of Nazareth seriously, noting all that he did and taught, and when they seek to align their lives with his values, joining with him, and coming into relationship with his heavenly father, they are building a life that is anchored on a durable foundation. The storms will come, the floods will rise, but they are anchored securely to something solid and trustworthy.

Perhaps a third way to understand the "words" and teaching of Jesus might be to take the executive summary he once offered for all the Laws of the LORD. In Matthew 22, Jesus was goaded by a group of religious leaders who were trying to trap him. They asked him which was the greatest commandment that God had given the human race:

> ^{37}Jesus replied: "'Love the LORD your God with all your heart and with all your soul and with all your mind.' ^{38} This is the first and greatest commandment. ^{39}And the second is like it: 'Love your neighbor as yourself.' ^{40}All the Law and the Prophets hang on these two commandments."
>
> Matthew 22:37–40

Here is a foundation on which we can build our lives: love God and love everyone else. Or as St Augustine put it: "Love God and do what you will."[5] When a person truly loves God, they will live in such a way that they do what he wants (or refrain from doing what he does not want). One of the ways we demonstrate genuine love for God is by loving other people.

It is worth noting that Jesus did not say we should just "listen to" or "know" his words. He also said that we need to "obey" them. Hearing or knowing the words of Jesus, without putting them into practice, is worse than being ignorant of Jesus' teaching. Intellect and knowledge are not the same as wisdom. It is possible to know a lot, but not do a lot; wisdom however, is that knowledge put into practice for successful day-to-day living. James once again had a great comment along these lines:

---

5. Augustine of Hippo, *Homilies on the First Epistle of John*, Homily 7.

> ²²Do not merely listen to the word, and so deceive yourselves. Do what it says. ²³Anyone who listens to the word but does not do what it says is like someone who looks at his face in a mirror ²⁴and, after looking at himself, goes away and immediately forgets what he looks like.
>
> James 1:22–24

To put that another way, a person has not truly listened to the words of Jesus until they have entered their being—finding expression in how they live. The words and teaching of Jesus are not just clever rhetoric or well thought out philosophy. They are more than a code of ethics or a list of rules. They are words of eternal life that reconcile sinful men and women to God. They demand a personal response and commitment. To follow the teachings or words of Jesus means that we come into a new relationship with God, whereby we are cleansed and forgiven from our past mistakes and given a brand-new start to life. It is like reconstructing our lives on a solid foundation. A person in a relationship with God has character, strength, power, and the perpetual presence of God continuously within them, enabling them to cope with the storms that rage against them.

There are cynics of the Christian faith who say that trusting God like this is just a crutch. Or as the quote attributed to Karl Marx expressed it: "Religion is the opiate of the masses." Think about this for a second: it may be that such accusations should not be shied away from or argued with. If a person travels through life with a broken leg, it makes good sense to walk with a crutch. To do without is to wobble around in constant pain and risk deformity. We live in a world where storms occur. They are unavoidable. They are common to us all. And, as James suggests, they teach us a lot about character.[6] Being followers of Jesus will never exempt us from the storms in life; the issue is how we negotiate or make our way through them.

This raises the question everyone must answer for him or herself. "Where do I stand today in response to the words of Jesus?" In Matthew's record of Jesus' Sermon on that Galilean hillside, after Jesus had finished speaking, the people in his audience were amazed at his teaching. He spoke as someone with divine authority, in contrast to the corrupt and hypocritical instruction given by the religious leaders of his day. People then were forced to decide what their response to Jesus would be, and so

---

6. James 1:2–4

are we today. On what foundation are you building your life? Is it merely the popular teaching, values and paradigms of the world in which we live? Is it a philosophy of happiness that craves riches, and "things," and power over people? Or is it the counter-culture values and worldview of the Kingdom of God? Are you building on sand, that is easily washed away, or are you building on the secure foundation of Jesus' words, and God's promise that "the one who believes in him will never be put to shame"?[7]

---

7. Romans 9:33

SMALL GROUP DISCUSSION QUESTIONS
Matthew 7:24–29

1. What technological changes have most impacted you in your lifetime—so far?
2. What are some of the significant cultural changes in values (in the past few decades) that affect our country?
   - How do you think these changes have impacted Christians?
3. What are some specific examples from your life where "the words of Jesus" (v.24) have provided a secure foundation for difficult life issues?
4. What challenges you most out of James 1:22–25?
5. At this point in your journey with God, is your most pressing need to "learn more" or "practice what you've already learned"?
6. What will you do differently in the week ahead for considering this passage of scripture?

Bibliography

Anderson, Dudley, *God Tracking Through The Year—Year Two*, (https//:www.Lulu.com).
Augustine of Hippo, *Homilies on the First Epistle of John, Homily 7*
Barclay, William, *The Daily Study Bible, The Gospel of Matthew Vol. 1*, Edinburgh: The Saint Andrews Press, 1975.
Bits & Pieces, March 3, 1994.
Bonhoeffer, Dietrich, *The Cost of Discipleship*, New York: Macmillan, 1966.
Brown, Stephen, *Christianity Today*, (April 5, 1993).
Calvin, John, *Commentary on a harmony of the evangelists, Matthew, Mark and Luke, I*, (1558), Translated by William Pringle, Eerdmans, 1845.
Clarke, Lieut-Colonel Douglas, *Pipeline* (Salvation Army), February 2012, Volume 16, Issue 2.
Coffin, William Sloane, *The Collected Sermons of William Sloane Coffin, The Riverside Years*, Westminister: John Knox Press, 2008
Covey, Stephen R., *The 7 Habits of Highly Effective People*, New York: Free Press, 1989.
Cox, Valerie, *A 3rd Serving of Chicken Soup for the Soul*, Simon & Schuster Digital Sales Inc, 2012.
Foster, Richard, *Celebration of Discipline*, London: Hodder & Stoughton, 1989.
Ironside, Harry, *Illustrations of Bible Truth*, http:www.solidchristianbooks.com.
Jones, Stanley, *Christ at the Round Table*, Nashville: Abingdon,1928.
Kennemer, Kevin, *Focus on the Positive to Reduce Negative Behavior*, https://thepeoplegroup.com/2009/04/focus-on-the-positive-to-reduce-negative-behavior
Klyne, Snodgrass, Klyne, *Between Two Truths—Living with Biblical Tensions*, Zondervan, 1990.
Larson, Craig Brian, *750 Engaging Illustrations for Contemporary Illustrations for Preachers, Teachers and Writers*, Baker Books, 1996.
Luther, Martin, *The Sermon on the Mount (1521)* Translated by Jaroslav Pelikan: Vol. 21 of Luther's Works, Concordia, 1956
MacArthur, John, *The MacArthur New Testament Commentary, Matthew 1–7*, Chicago: Moody Press, 1985.
Martin, Hengel, *Property and Riches in the Early Church*, Philadelphia; Fortress Press, 1974.
May, Bernie, *Learning to Trust*, Multnomah Press, 1985.

Montefiore, CG and Loewe, HMJ, *A Rabbinic Anthology,* Cambridge University Press, 2012.
Neill, Stephen, *A History of Christian Missions,* New York: Penguin, 1964.
Petersen, J. Allen, *The Myth of the Greener Grass,* Tyndale House, 1984
Peterson, Eugene, *The Message,* NavPress, 2002.
Robinson, Charles Seymour, *Annotations Upon Popular Hymns,* Sagwan Press, February 1, 2018.
Sider, Ron. *The Scandal of the Evangelical Conscience,* Baker Books, 2005.
Stott, John, *The Message of the Sermon on the Mount,* Nottingham: Inter-Varsity Press, 1978.
Tasker, RVG, *The Gospel According to St. Matthew,* Grand Rapids: Wm B. Eerdmans, 1978.
Ten Boon, Corrie, *The Hiding Place,* Bantam Books, 1984)
TIME Magazine, Volume 87, No.14, April 8, 1966.
———, *Nightmare in Jonestown,* 4th November, 1978.
Today In The Word, July 1989.
Vine, W.E, *An Expository Dictionary of New Testament Words,* Iowa: Riverside Book and Bible House, 1939.
W. Gunther, Plaut, W. Gunther, *The Torah—A Modern Commentary,* New York: Union of American Hebrew Congregations, 1981.
Wesley, John, *The Journal of the Reverend John Wesley,* London: The Epworth Press, 1938.
Willard, Dalla, *The Divine Conspiracy—Rediscovering our Hidden Life in God,* London: William Collins, 1998)
Winslade, Brian, *Boundaries—Rediscovering the Ten Commandments for the Twenty-First Century,* Eugene: Resource Publications, 2018.

www.ingramcontent.com/pod-product-compliance
Lightning Source LLC
Chambersburg PA
CBHW071431150426
43191CB00008B/1099